Budgetary Politics in American Governments

This comprehensive book describes and analyzes the substance and politics of public budgeting at the national, state, and local levels of government. In doing so, it takes a comparative approach, illustrating the distinctiveness of budgeting at each level, as well as highlighting the features common to all three. A unifying focus is the extent to which budgetary decision makers use the budget as a central vehicle to advance their policy preferences. This fully updated sixth edition provides an extensive and thorough analysis of the causes of the Great Recession, its economic consequences, and the policy responses which pushed the boundaries of conventional monetary and fiscal policy. Also new to this edition is a chapter on the intergovernmental dimensions of public budgeting, along with boxed features highlighting hands-on vignettes of contemporary practical challenges facing budget makers at the different levels of government.

James J. Gosling is Professor of Political Science at the University of Utah.

Budgetary Politics in American Governments

Sixth Edition

James J. Gosling

Routledge
Taylor & Francis Group

NEW YORK AND LONDON

First published 2016
by Routledge
711 Third Avenue, New York, NY 10017

and by Routledge
2 Park Square, Milton Park, Abingdon, Oxon OX14 4RN

Routledge is an imprint of the Taylor & Francis Group, an informa business

© 2016 Taylor & Francis

Library of Congress Cataloging in Publication Data
Gosling, James J.
    Budgetary politics in American governments / by James J. Gosling. –
Sixth edition.
    pages cm
    Includes bibliographical references and index.
    1. Budget–United States. 2. Local budgets–United States.
    3. Municipal budgets–United States. I. Title.
HJ2051.G675 2015
336.73–dc23   2015022674

ISBN: 978-1-138-92343-0 (hbk)
ISBN: 978-1-138-92342-3 (pbk)
ISBN: 978-1-315-67371-4 (ebk)

Typeset in Times New Roman
by Sunrise Setting Ltd, Paignton, UK

Printed and Bound in the United States of America by
Edwards Brothers Malloy on sustainably sourced paper.

Contents

Illustrations

Figures

Tables

Boxes

Preface

For the past thirty-five years, I have taught a course on budgetary politics at the University of Wisconsin-Madison and the University of Utah. The organization of this book reflects the approach I take in the classroom. The course is comparative in its perspective, with discrete sections devoted to the substance and politics of budgeting at the national, state, and local levels. It begins with common building blocks of knowledge to give students a shared conceptual and theoretical foundation. This approach has been particularly useful in a course that draws students with different academic preparation and experience, and enables those who have little training in political science, public administration, or economics to acquire the tools necessary to understand the substance and politics of budgeting in different governmental settings. The ability to generalize and account for significant exceptions lies at the heart of the study of politics. This book aspires to reach that goal.

The book begins by introducing the subject of public budgeting: what it is, the functions it performs, the distinctive features of the budgetary process and the common constraints faced by budget makers, along with the various sources of political conflict over the budget. Attention then turns to theories of budgetary decision making in an effort to help students appreciate how and why budget participants make the choices that they do.

The previous fifth edition added a new chapter, chapter 3, on the organization and structure of public budgets—the nuts and bolts of public budgeting, so to speak. The chapter discusses elements common to all public budgets but also accounts for distinctiveness found at each level of government. It is followed by a chapter on economics and politics, added in the fourth edition, which illustrates how the economy affects budgetary decision making, and how the policy choices of economic decision makers affect the economy.

The focus then moves to the products of budgetary decision making: taxing and spending, put in the context of economic theory. Students learn about the patterns of stability and change in taxation and spending over time—in the aggregate and at each level of government. They also learn about who benefits from budgetary choice and who pays for those benefits.

With this as a foundation, attention turns to an in-depth discussion of the substance and politics of budgeting at the national, state, and local levels. Although one chapter is devoted to each level, the experience of each is related to that of the others.

This new sixth edition adds a new chapter, chapter 9, on fiscal federalism and intergovernmental fiscal relations, covering the intergovernmental dimensions of public budgeting.

Shifting the focus in chapter 10 from budget making to budget execution, the discussion covers the purposes of budget control and the means used to carry it out. Students learn that the budgetary process and its politics do not end with the legislative passage of the budget. Budgets continue to be "made" during the post-appropriations phase of the process through budget transfers, supplements, and controls on spending.

Chapter 1

Public Budgeting in Perspective

Budgeting lies at the heart of public policy making at all levels of government in the United States. Public budgets meet the test of the popular adage, "Put your money where your mouth is; talk is cheap." In more scholarly terms, they illustrate programmed resource commitments that lay bare policy priorities and cut through political rhetoric. Budgets disclose the priorities of key institutional actors in the budget-making process and serve as instruments to measure the relative success of those actors in shaping the final budget version enacted into law.

Unlike the general legislative process, the budgetary process is action-forcing. Governmental policy makers do not decide whether to consider legislation approving a budget; they treat the need for a budget as a given. Most other legislation is much more discretionary in character; participants see a need and propose legislation to meet it. Most often, however, nothing other than their perception of need or opportunity prompts that action. In contrast, budgets expire. When they do, governments no longer have any authority under which to spend public funds. Policy makers have to approve new budgets or continue the existing ones. Typically, they try to use that opportunity to fashion budgets that advance their own policy and fiscal priorities.

Policy makers face fiscal and political constraints when trying to get what they want out of the budgetary process. Tough economic times can create serious revenue constraints when carry-forward balances prove inadequate to offset depressed tax collections. "The money is just not there" is a familiar refrain in times of economic downturn. In such an environment, chief executives often attempt to restrain the spending appetites of agencies by issuing budget instructions that limit agency requests, frequently giving the agencies budget targets within which their requests are expected to fall. A central budget office's instructions may even require agencies to submit alternative budget requests that fall below current funding levels.

Economic conditions affect not only the level of revenue governments receive to finance their many activities, but also the level of spending the budget needs to accommodate. **Recessions**, for example, characteristically increase the number of claims on public assistance programs, pushing up the costs of those programs. Thus at the very time revenues decline, expenditures in recession-sensitive programs are driven up by heightened demand.

Inflationary economic conditions can also increase public spending, requiring salary increases to protect public employees from losses in purchasing power and to meet the rising prices of purchased goods and services. Economic stagnation and high rates of inflation put double pressure on government budget makers; revenues quickly become insufficient to pay for the rapidly rising costs of doing the government's business.

Good economic times encourage increased spending. They generate the revenues necessary to finance the spending priorities of agencies, chief executives, and legislative bodies. Nevertheless, politics constrains policy makers from using the budget to advance their own policies and programmatic priorities and their own political fortunes. Policy makers not only face competition from others over how public funds are to be spent; they also often face pressures to "return" actual or expected revenue surpluses in the form of tax cuts.

Other units of government can also impose fiscal constraints on a government's budgetary choices—constraints that can take the form of reductions in financial assistance or of mandates entailing increased spending. Just as state and local governments have become dependent on federal financial aid (although that dependence has decreased somewhat over the past decade), so have local governments come to rely on state aid as well. State and local governments have built federal aid into their operating budgets to finance ongoing government operations, and the reduction or selective elimination of this aid leaves the recipients with the difficult choice of cutting programs or coming up with revenues from other sources to fill the holes.

One government can also force another government to make expenditures beyond those it otherwise would make (within the limits of federalism). Such requirements, or mandates, can be either programmatic (e.g., they can require that programs meet certain service standards) or procedural (e.g., they can specify that certain records be kept and reports issued), and they can be imposed either by direct order or as a condition of financial aid. At the state level, where local governments are legally dependent on the state for their creation and their continued existence, state mandates placed on local governments most often take the form of direct orders. Federal mandates, on the other hand, tend to be formulated as conditions of federal aid.[1] In either form, they place additional spending pressures on the governments affected.

Judicial decisions and court orders that require governments to expand or improve services, to distribute financial aid in prescribed ways, or to alter employee compensation plans also act to increase public budgets and force additional spending. Although courts have no formal role in the budgetary process (beyond that of the judiciary submitting its own budget requests), they become involved through litigation initiated by plaintiffs who most commonly contend that government programs, either by commission or omission, have denied them equal rights guaranteed by the U.S. Constitution and state constitutions. In deciding in favor of a plaintiff, a court may often order relief. Such relief can require not only monetary settlements but also changes in government programs, both of which—particularly the latter—can be costly. A jurisdiction thus cited has no option but to comply with a court's directive. Funds must be found, and the budget must accommodate the claim.

Federal courts have been the most active in issuing relief orders, and those orders have been largely aimed at the states. Acting to ensure equal protection under the law, as guaranteed by the Fourteenth Amendment, federal courts have ordered states to improve care and treatment standards for the institutionalized mentally ill and developmentally disabled and to pay damages when state or local employees are victims of discrimination or political retaliation. In addition, federal courts have ordered states to improve living conditions in correctional institutions, basing those orders on judgments that—in violation of their Eighth Amendment rights—existing conditions constitute cruel and unusual punishment for prisoners subjected to them.[2]

State courts have prominently intervened in matters related to the public financing of primary and secondary education. Litigants based their challenges on two grounds: equity of funding and adequacy of funding. Litigation in the 1970s and 1980s focused largely on equity of educational finance among school districts in the same state. Legal challenges centered on the large disparities of educational funding generated by wide differences in property values across school districts. In response, courts in several states, starting with California, ruled that the financing methods in place violated equal protection guarantees or state constitutional commitments to provide a quality education to all students. As a common remedy, courts ordered legislatures in the offending states to change aid formulas (and in some cases to increase funding) so that poorer districts receive higher per-student aid relative to wealthier districts, thus helping to close the spending gap between them.

In the late 1980s, litigants in some states shifted the focus of their lawsuits from equity to adequacy, challenging the adequacy of K-12 funding to meet state constitutional guarantees of educational opportunity or of a quality education. Although litigants continued to challenge cross-district inequality in per-student funding, the number of lawsuits dwindled, just as litigation based on funding inadequacy grew. From 1989 through 2007, adequacy-based challenges succeeded in twenty states, whereas equity-based challenges proved successful in eight states. Following the early landmark victories in Kentucky, New York, and Texas, litigants have prevailed in some form in twenty-one of the twenty-eight states in which they have challenged the adequacy of state educational funding.[3]

In response to plaintiffs' victories in adequacy-based litigation, state courts have selectively directed, as remedies, that legislatures augment funding to levels acceptable to the courts or, short of mandating increased funding, that educational policy makers in the states define what constitutes adequate education, identify what it would cost to provide it, and submit the requirements to state legislatures under the watchful eye of the courts.

Reasons for Conflict over Public Budgeting

The budgetary stakes are high, and the competition to set the course of public spending is keen. Public budgeting is very much a political contest in which victors can be distinguished from losers. It is also one in which victories and losses frequently require qualification as positions become compromised and accommodated throughout the budgetary process.

Conflict over public budgeting is high for several reasons. Public budgets (1) allocate a significant share of societal resources, (2) serve as the focal point for policy making in most governmental jurisdictions, (3) illuminate political relationships and highlight conflicts at the heart of politics, and (4) serve as a tool to ensure accountability.

Public Budgeting Allocates a Significant Share of Societal Resources

Total government spending in the United States consumes about 44 percent of the gross domestic product. Breaking it down, federal spending takes 22 percent, state spending 12 percent, and local spending another 10 percent.[4]

Although these comparisons illustrate the relative claims governments make on private resources, the distribution of these claims does not engender significant political conflict in the budget-making process. Nor do taxpayers think a great deal about the collective magnitude of these claims or about the macroeconomic effects of transferring resources from the private to the public sector; instead they look at how these claims, in the form of taxation, affect their own resources. Their reference point is how much they are being asked to pay this year compared to how much they paid last year. The most vigorous political controversy is generated when public budgets, and the taxes required to support them, grow faster than the taxpayers' ability to pay for that growth. Elected policy makers are especially sensitive to the political fallout of tax increases, which can spark voter backlash. Elected chief executives and legislatures therefore usually turn to tax increases only as a last resort to make ends meet in difficult economic times.

Because of **balanced-budget** requirements in most state and local governments, the politics of public budgeting dictate that policy makers first turn to budget reductions and reallocations to balance revenues and expenditures. When these are not feasible or sufficient, few chief executives or legislatures propose tax increases without including significant accompanying budget cuts.

Public Budgeting Serves as the Focal Point for Policy Making

At a minimum, public budgeting sets spending priorities for the year or biennium to come. In setting spending levels, budget makers place relative values on the many purposes of government spending: certain programs are created and funded for the first time, some programs are allowed to grow faster than others, and other programs are reduced or eliminated altogether. In this sense, budget participants decide that at a given time certain policy areas are more important than others and therefore deserve more financial support.

Several states give budget makers the greatest opportunity to use the budget as a policy vehicle by permitting substantive language, in addition to **appropriations**, to be included within **budget bills**. A few states require any substantive language to be tied directly to appropriations, while others include no such restriction. In those latter states, a budget bill can be used to create new statutory law, repeal existing provisions, make changes in others, or place contingencies on the release and use of appropriated funds. The range of state experience is discussed more fully in chapter 7.

In comparison to the states, the U.S. Congress relegates much of the substantive policy that may be included within state budget bills to authorizing legislation outside of the various appropriations bills. Because Congress uses the reconciliation bill as an omnibus budget adjustment bill (discussed in chapter 6) and has increased its practice of "loading up" appropriations bills with riders, restrictions, earmarks, and expressions of congressional intent, this distinction has become weakened.

At the local level, budget legislation tends to be limited to appropriations, a practice consistent with the generally conservative and restrictive parameters states have placed on local budget makers. Yet the composition of local budgets probably serves as an even greater constraint on the ability of local policy makers to use the budget as a vehicle of policy change. Faced with revenue constraints that are usually tight and a budget heavily committed to the costs of employee salaries and fringe benefits, local policy makers have little leeway with which to reallocate resources in pursuit of new policy initiatives, however hard they try. The answer for them has often been to find creative ways to generate new revenues and control the costs of governmental services, a subject pursued in chapter 8.

Among institutional budget participants, chief executives at all levels of government are best positioned to use the budget as a policy-making tool. The budgetary process gives them the opportunity to lay out their vision of how best to use scarce fiscal resources. They set the agenda and establish the priorities to which the legislative branch must react. They also show how the budget package is to be funded. This factor puts them in a strong position, because a legislature that proposes to increase spending must then show how it will be financed. When budgets are required to be balanced and projected surpluses are expected to be nonexistent or negligible, any additional spending a legislature may approve has to be covered by tax or fee increases or by reallocation.

The political process in most government jurisdictions also discourages the legislative branch from using the budget as a policy vehicle. The fragmented nature of the legislative process, with its many bases of power, makes it difficult for a legislature to speak with a single voice as can a president, governor, or mayor. Despite the priorities that top legislative leaders may espouse and urge, the legislative process is geared to reconcile the preferences of a host of different legislators, many of whom hold influential positions in their own right and use those positions to shape the final budget.

In this light, congressional leaders have compared their situation to that of the president. They saw the president presenting a comprehensive spending plan to Congress—one that sets national priorities, identifies policy tradeoffs, and specifies the level of borrowing, if any, needed to finance the spending package. They saw the president's budget as a means of charting both a substantive and a **fiscal policy** direction for the nation. In response, Congress reformed the congressional phase of the federal budgetary process. Central to that reform is the requirement that Congress approve a budget resolution that establishes spending targets and provides a plan for subsequent congressional action on the budget, including committee recommendations and floor action. Those targets setting spending limits both overall and by functional area were intended to allow Congress to offer a comprehensive alternative to the president's budget. The details of congressional budgetary reform and the extent to which it has achieved its objectives are discussed in chapter 6.   Govt TAXING AND SPENDING

Public Budgeting Highlights Conflicts at the Heart of Politics

Because the stakes are high, public budgeting heightens the bases of political conflict; bases that include (1) underlying value differences, (2) differences in instrumental policy preferences, (3) constituency interests, (4) partisanship, (5) role conflicts, and (6) institutional rivalries.

Value Differences

The values policy makers bring to budget making reflect the underlying principles of classic liberal political thought: a belief in individual rights and governmental restraint, with the accompanying conviction that government is a necessary institution for the protection of these rights. Some believe these principles assign a highly limited role to government. For them, government should do only enough to protect life, liberty, and property. They see the private marketplace of supply and demand as the best and most effective allocator of value in society. Others believe that government has an obligation to ensure all individuals an equal opportunity in their pursuit of advancement and personal fulfillment. Still others go a step further and believe that government should take actions necessary to improve the conditions of the disadvantaged and needy. They believe that government should protect what they define as the public interest and correct for market failure.

These different values come into high relief in the budgetary process; a significant element of the budget debate centers on what government should rightfully be doing, how much it should be doing, and at what price it should be doing it. Those subscribing to a minimalist role for government see the need for far less public spending overall, limit their support to selected governmental activities that they view as consistent with government's appropriate role in society, and opt for eliminating or greatly reducing programs that cross the boundaries of normative acceptability. Those favoring a more interventionist role are inclined to support the spending that they view as necessary to advance the public interest.

These are pure types. Policy makers can and do modify their values in different situations. Those who espouse a minimal role for government more readily apply that value when someone else's interests are being minimized. But when "less government" means the elimination of one of their own prized benefits, the principle can become objectionable in its application. Less government may be just fine when it comes to social welfare programs, but government intervention is acceptable in the form of tax breaks, agricultural subsidies, or low-interest loans. Thus, although values do inform choices, they compete with other interests and claims on those choices.

Instrumental Policy Preferences

The policy preferences of budget participants typically reflect their values. For example, those who advocate government intervention as necessary to advance the welfare of the disadvantaged may champion different policy instruments to accomplish that objective. Those who support this government intervention to guarantee equal opportunity are most likely to support such programs as preschool education, need-based student financial aid, and job training—all of which help equip people to compete on a more equal footing. Those who emphasize improving the condition of the disadvantaged are most likely to support efforts to increase the level of public assistance payments, add more low-cost housing, and expand health-care benefits for the needy.

Constituency Interests

The policy preferences of elected officials can conflict with the interests of their constituents. For example, a conservative (classic liberal) member of Congress representing a heavily agricultural district, who typically supports spending restraint and a limited role for government, might vote to include generous agricultural price supports in the budget in response to the economic interests of farmers in his district. Similarly, a state senator who has established a strong record on environmental protection issues but has two breweries in her district might oppose a proposal to require deposits on nonreturnable bottles.

Constituency interests are frequently at cross-purposes; they do not align in uniform, reinforcing ways. Coalitions, nonetheless, can form around common constituency interests. Legislators come together to support actions that benefit their constituents collectively. That process of coalition building has been greatly aided by the availability of computer-based models that simulate the distributional effects of legislative proposals, attracting competing coalitions drawn from representatives of "winning" and "losing" districts—coalitions that can cut across value positions and party lines.

Partisanship

Presidents and members of Congress, governors and state legislators, and some local chief executives and legislative members are elected in partisan elections. Where that occurs, legislative bodies are organized on a partisan basis. Members of the majority party assume all the leadership positions in each chamber, including those of presiding officer as well as all committee and subcommittee chairs.

In a system of partisan politics, the president, governor, or mayor who offers budget recommendations is also a Republican or Democrat who communicates those preferences to a legislative body organizationally controlled by partisans who may be either colleagues or opponents. Legislative bodies with majorities drawn from the same party as the chief executive might be expected to support executive recommendations more readily than they would the recommendations from the standard-bearer of the opposing party.

Partisan relationships, therefore, pose another potential source for political conflict in the budgetary process, and they merit attention in any attempt to describe and account for patterns of influence and choice in public budgeting.

Different Roles of Budgetary Participants

A role can be thought of as the distinctive behavior consistently associated with the position an individual holds in society. The element of consistency is important because consistent behavior leads to clear expectations that that behavior will continue. The role of mother, for example, can be distinguished from the role of daughter on the basis of the pattern of distinctive behavior expected from each in their interactions. Similarly, the role of chief executive officer in a company differs from that of one of the junior accountants. Employees expect the two to act accordingly. If the accountant suddenly circulates a memorandum laying out the company's strategic objectives for the coming year, other employees would probably react with, "Who does he think he is? That's the president's job!"—suggesting that the accountant had clearly violated his role within the organization.

Budget participants are also expected to play roles in the budgetary process. Those roles are identified not only by the participants' positions (budget director, budget analyst, appropriations committee aide) but also, more significantly, by the institutions with which they are associated in the budgetary process.

Institutions develop their own identifiable interests. Thus close observers of the budgetary process come to expect that operating agencies will behave differently from central budget offices or appropriations committees. Agencies are not expected to take initiatives to cut their own budgets; quite the opposite, they are expected to seek increases in their budgetary resources. Their role is to be advocates for their programs. Central budget offices, on the other hand, are expected to keep spending requests and actual expenditures in line with the chief executive's budgetary and fiscal policies. With agencies predictably acting to expand their resources, central budget offices are drawn into playing the role of budget cutters, for they are seldom able to advance the chief executive's budgetary and fiscal policies while at the same time acquiescing to the agencies' acquisitiveness.[5]

The roles of appropriations, fiscal, or finance committees (variously named) appear to entail shaping budgetary alternatives to advance the preferences of their majority-party members (with some inclusion of minority-member interests) in such a way that they broadly represent the "corporate partisan good" of the legislative party as a whole, to the extent that is possible.[6] Thereafter, as the budget bill makes its way through the partisan caucus to the legislative floor for debate and action, disgruntled legislators attempt to see that their pet interests are included by amendment; thus, a legislative body can frequently be expected to increase a committee's ante overall.

Institutional Rivalries

In addition to the roles associated with institutions and the positions within them, members of these institutions develop loyalties to them and come to identify their own welfare with the welfare of their institution. They feel positive when their institution gains advantage, and threatened when their institution is under duress. This phenomenon transcends role and partisanship. Inter-branch rivalries are most apparent, but rivalries can also exist between two chambers of the same legislature, even when they are controlled by the same political party. Each chamber may attempt to "one-up" the other and put its own distinctive stamp on major budgetary policy.

All of these factors can inject conflict into public budgeting and therefore influence the politics of budgetary decision making; yet the substantive nature of the budgetary enterprise can also affect budgetary choice. Budgets can often be highly complex—overwhelming in their size, structure, specialized nomenclature, programmatic diversity, and technical subject matter. Faced with such complexity and information overload, budget makers look for ways to simplify decision making. One means of doing this is to treat the base-level budget as a given and focus only on requested or recommended increments to that base. As will be discussed in detail in chapter 2, however, budget participants make choices at two distinct levels: the macro level and the micro level. Macro decisions concern the overarching issues of budgeting: how much a government should tax, spend, and borrow; how fast spending should grow; and what relative budget shares the major functional areas of the budget should receive. Micro-decisions deal with which distinct budget items to include in the budget and how much funding to request, recommend, and approve for each of the various programs and their subprograms.

Not all of the budget is equally subject to choice. Some spending items are less controllable than others. Funds must be made available to honor a government's contractual obligations, to pay holders of governmental securities, and to pay for financial assistance or services to those who meet statutorily established eligibility standards and thereby have a legal right to receive them. Much more about the relative controllability of spending is covered in the chapters dealing with budgeting at the federal, state, and local levels.

The process of budgetary decision making is truly iterative. Budget makers' ideas about what constitutes appropriate spending levels can influence their choices on individual decision items. At the same time, the relative strength of their feelings about the need for approval of many of those individual budget items can prompt them to support higher aggregate spending levels. Yet, as discussed earlier, those decisions are also a function of each decision maker's values, instrumental policy preferences, constituency interests, partisan loyalty, and institutional role.

Public Budgeting Serves as a Tool to Ensure Accountability

Budgets serve as yardsticks with which to measure accountability. Public budgets are action plans, containing **authorizations** for government agencies to spend public funds for approved purposes. They represent commitments. Not only elected representatives but also interest groups, the media, and individual citizens can subsequently compare the budget as implemented with the approved budgetary plan. Also consistent with the principle of accountability is the idea that implementation must be controlled to ensure that spending does not exceed authorized levels, that funds are used for approved purposes, and that spending is consistent with legislative intent. If governmental agencies could circumvent the established priorities and limits (if there were no effective controls on budget execution), the entire process of budget making would become meaningless.

Control over budget execution ultimately resides with the legislature, but most legislatures delegate some of their authority to the executive branch. Legislatures commonly give chief executives the statutory authority to ensure that spending by agencies of the executive branch follows the budgetary plan. Executive budget offices, acting as the chief executive's agents, usually allot appropriations authority to agencies for spending. **Allotments** may cover an entire fiscal year or, more often, can be divided down into quarters or even months. They serve as the primary executive instrument to control spending.

They also can be used to prevent funds from being spent; even if funds are appropriated, if they are not allotted, they cannot be spent. This is effectively the authority to impound, and it gives chief executives a powerful tool with which to restrict spending during periods of severe economic downturn. It also gives them a strong political tool with which to limit spending for items they oppose. However, legislative bodies at all levels of government have responded by placing limits on the extent to which chief executives can refuse to allow appropriated funds to be spent.

Budgets also can be adjusted during the course of the fiscal year. Changes in the economy, actions by higher levels of government, and unplanned levels of demand for governmental services may require that a budget be modified after its initial passage. Although legislatures ultimately possess the authority to approve midyear adjustments, they usually delegate some of this authority to the executive branch. In exercising such delegated authority, central budget offices often make judgments about legislative intent—judgments that can engender political conflict with the legislative branch. The political nature of budget execution and control is discussed more fully in chapter 10.

Notes

1 Max Neiman and Catherine Lovell, "Federal and State Mandating," Administration and Society 14 (November 1982): 356–7.
2 Penelope Lemo, "Taking Your Prison Back from the Feds," Governing 6, no. 4 (January 1993): 22–3; Donald Axelrod, A Budget Quartet (New York: St. Martin's Press, 1989), 48–63.
3 Data on litigation outcomes provided by the National Access Network, www.schoolfunding.info/litigation; Mark A. Rebell, "Educational Adequacy, Democracy, and the Courts," paper prepared for the National Research Council's Conference on Achieving High Educational Standards for All, November 2002.
4 Bureau of the Census, U.S. Department of Commerce, 2012 Census of Governments: Finance – Surveys of State and Local Governments, December 16, 2014; Office of Management and Budget, Budget of the United States Government, FY 2015, Historical Tables, Table 1.1.
5 Aaron Wildavsky, The Politics of the Budgetary Process (Boston: Little, Brown, 1964); Ira Sharkansky, "Agency Requests, Gubernatorial Support, and Budget Success in State Legislatures," American Political Science Review 62 (December 1968): 1220–31; Hugh Heclo, "Executive Budget Making," in Federal Budget Policy in the 1980s, ed. Gregory B. Mills and John L. Palmer (Washington, D.C.: Urban Institute Press, 1985), 255–91; James J. Gosling, "Patterns of Influence and Choice in the Wisconsin Budgetary Process," Legislative Studies Quarterly 10 (November 1985): 457–82; James J. Gosling, "The State Budget Office and Policy Making," Public Budgeting and Finance 7 (spring 1987): 51–68.
6 Gosling, "Patterns of Influence," 470.

Chapter 2

Budgetary Decision Making

Making choices about public budgets is a formidable task. Budgets can be highly complex—almost overwhelming in their size, structure, specialized nomenclature, programmatic diversity, technical demands, and tight decision-making time lines. Yet because budgeting lies at the very heart of politics, determining who benefits from government programs and who pays the bills, budget makers also face the constraints common to political choice: they must make decisions in an environment of competing normative values, divergent policy priorities, and the strain of balancing self-interest and the public interest. This chapter discusses how budget participants deal with these constraints in making budgetary choices.

Facing the Constraints of Budgetary Choice

Budgetary choices are made in an environment characterized by greatly compressed time lines, information overload, complex technical issues, competing values (leading to different definitions of the problems requiring government action), and alternative ways of addressing those problems. All these factors contribute to budget makers' efforts to simplify budgetary choice.

In his classic study *Administrative Behavior*, Herbert Simon observes that decision makers simplify choice by making decisions within a closed system of "givens." Cues inconsistent with those givens are screened out as prospective influences on decision making. Thus the search for solutions to problems is undertaken only within the confines of a restricted set of options that is in harmony with the givens. Decision makers need not compare the means and ends of an indefinite number of alternatives in making choices; they "satisfice" instead, by restricting their search to options consistent with the established givens, selecting the first alternative that appears to meet their objectives.

In categorizing decision making as an activity characterized by satisficing, Simon takes issue with the classic model of rational decision making. According to that model, rational decisions require that decision makers

1   identify their objectives and rank them in order of priority;
2   identify all alternatives that might realize those objectives;

3   select criteria by which to evaluate each alternative;
4   choose the alternative that best satisfies the criteria and attains the
     objectives.[1]

For advocates of rational decision making, this model was advanced as the
way rational decisions should be made; doing less would be something other
than rational choice. Simon, the empiricist, argues that decisions are in fact not
made that way, and suggests that his model more closely represents the way
complex choices are made in practice.

Charles Lindblom, building on the work of Simon, also takes issue with the
rational-choice model. In Lindblom's view, decision makers do not approach
problems in the comprehensive fashion dictated by the rational model; instead,
they focus on piecemeal, adjustive choice. They focus on the increments of
change by examining only limited alternatives that involve small changes from
existing policies and by adjusting their choices on those increments to the
choices of prior actors.[2] In this way, reminiscent of Simon, they engage in a
form of "satisficing."

For Lindblom, incremental adjustment sidesteps problems posed by disagree-
ment on values and objectives. Decision makers do not begin by clarifying
their values and then ranking their objectives, consistent with those values,
in prioritized order. To the contrary, the values underlying the objectives of
preexisting choices remain essentially intact; only adjustments on the margin
become the subject of inquiry. The inheritance of prior choice remains largely
undisturbed. In focusing on increments of change rather than objectives, individuals can often either agree on actions to be taken (even if they hold conflicting
values) or permit their values to become clarified or changed in application.

With mutual adjustment, decision makers choose the ends and means simultaneously, something the rational model does not allow. The prior or expected
choices of others provide signals about the likely political success of different means; and in the politics of accommodation, these cues may often prompt
modifications in the sought-after ends themselves. Procedurally, the flexibility
inherent in adjustive choice allows complex problems to be broken down into
their simpler components, so that subgroups can deal with each, ultimately
putting together a solution through mutual adjustment.

As choices on the margin are adjusted to choices of other decision makers,
values neglected by some decision makers may be represented by others.
For Lindblom, public policies achieved through adjustive, piecemeal choice
generally embody a broader community of values than is possible under the
top-down rational model. To Lindblom, that is the way decisions should be
made in a democratic society. Given mankind's limited intellect, the incrementalism of adjustive choice is not only a way in which decision makers cope with
complexity; it also reflects a certain "intelligence of democracy."[3]

Aaron Wildavsky, commonly recognized as the father of budgetary incrementalism, was greatly influenced in his early work by the theories of both

Simon and Lindblom. On the basis of his early research on the politics of the federal budgetary process, Wildavsky concluded that budget makers treat the budgetary base as a given of sorts, freeing their attention to the budgetary increments of change requests and recommendations that depart from the base. For Wildavsky, budget makers do not make such choices in isolation; they do so in relation to the anticipated decisions of other institutional participants. Like Lindblom, Wildavsky observes that participants adjust their budgetary choices to what they expect other participants will do. The institutional roles of participants in the budgetary process serve as the basis for that anticipated choice.

It is clear to Wildavsky that in adjusting their choices to the expected behavior of other institutional actors, budget makers think in terms of percentages as they consider incremental departures from the base. Thus central budget officers focus on the percentage increases requested by the agencies. In turn, legislative budget participants look at the percentage increases over the base recommended by the chief executive. In focusing on the percentage increments from the base and on reciprocal expectations of budgetary behavior, budget makers greatly simplify their decisions. They avoid the overwhelming problem of comparing the values of all existing programs with all possible alternatives for each, as the rational decision-making model dictates. For Wildavsky, then, budgeting is experiential, simplified, satisficing, and incremental.[4]

Budgeting is incremental, not comprehensive. The beginning wisdom about an agency budget is that it is almost never actively reviewed as a whole every year in the sense of reconsidering the value of all existing programs as compared to all possible alternatives. Instead, it is based on the previous year's budget, with special attention given to a narrow range of increases or decreases. Hence those who make the budget are concerned with relatively small increments to an existing base. Their attention is focused on a small number of items over which the budgetary battle is fought.[5]

Just as Lindblom sees a certain "intelligence" in mutual adjustive choice, Wildavsky believes that incremental budgeting has a rationality of its own. It uses experience (the budgetary base and the earlier choices of participants), role perceptions and associated expectations of choice, and a decentralized decision-making process to reduce the complexity of strategic calculations to a manageable level. For Wildavsky, not only does incremental budgeting have a certain rationality, but also it is in line with the realities of the democratic political process, in which the politics of mutual adjustment appropriately determine those objectives toward which governments should commit public resources.

Drawing on the theoretical constructs of incrementalism, Wildavsky and two of his former students, Otto A. Davis and M.A.H. Dempster, set out to develop models of national domestic budgeting that would describe and explain actual budgetary outcomes through simple linear decision rules. Identifying eight alternative equations to represent decision rules employed by federal budget participants, the authors found that their models were able to "explain or represent the behavior of participants in the federal budgetary process in their efforts to reach decisions in complex situations."[6] They add, "The alternate decision equations can be tried and the most appropriate one used when data on requests and appropriations are available. The appropriate equation explains the data, in that, given a good fit, the process behaves as if the data were generated according to the equation."[7]

Listing every decision rule and its accompanying regression equation would exceed the scope of this chapter, but the following examples give a feel for what the authors regard as the simplicity of their decision rules:

> The agency request (through the Budget Bureau) for a certain year is a fixed mean percentage of the congressional appropriation for that agency in the previous year plus a fixed mean percentage of the difference between the congressional appropriation and the agency request for the previous year plus a stochastic disturbance.[8]

> The congressional appropriation for an agency is a fixed mean percentage of the agency's request for a certain year plus a fixed mean percentage of a dummy variable which represents that part of the agency's request for the year at issue which is not part of the appropriation or request of the previous year plus a random variable representing part of the appropriation attributable to the special circumstances of the year.[9]

Amid the inscrutability of such language to those not empirically inclined, the essence of the best explanatory model called for agencies to request a fixed percentage increase over their base and for the U.S. Congress to take a fixed percentage cut from the request, the basic tenets of incrementalist budgetary strategy.

The Critics of Incrementalism

It is one thing to show that linear equations can approximate the outcomes of the budgetary process and quite another to account for that behavior theoretically. Davis, Dempster, and Wildavsky maintain that the results of their models confirm the incremental thesis of budgeting, at least as it operates at the federal level. Critics, on the other hand, take issue both with the validity of the conclusions drawn from the regression models and with the ties back to the theory of budgetary incrementalism itself.[10]

The work of both John Wanat and John Gist supports the first line of criticism. Using the same models as Davis and his associates but substituting randomly generated data, Wanat comes up with correlations as high as those found earlier and concludes that the presence of high correlations does not support the existence of budgetary decision rules.[11]

Reanalyzing the data used by Davis, Dempster, and Wildavsky, Gist finds that the high correlations in the regression models were the result of a methodological limitation—not controlling for co-linearity in the data, where both independent and dependent variables share common components that account for high correlations.[12]

Notwithstanding such criticisms of empirical methodology, other researchers take issue with the theoretical basis of incrementalism. John Bailey and Robert O'Connor find fault with the "descriptive precision" and "explanatory usefulness" of budgetary incrementalism. Findings suggesting that budgets grow stably over time through relatively small changes to their existing base are cited by proponents of incrementalist theory as evidence that decision makers make choices incrementally. Thus "incrementalism in outcomes" is used as support for "incrementalism in the process." What constitutes incrementalism in outcomes is subject to dispute.

Pointing to findings in which slightly more than half of appropriations reviewed increased by less than 10 percent a year, Wildavsky finds that the outcome supports the incremental thesis. Yet, as Bailey and O'Connor note, the same findings also mean that in about half the cases, appropriations exceeded a 10 percent annual rate of growth. Wildavsky adds that three-quarters fell within a 30 percent increase, hardly what would be considered to fall within the rubric of incremental change.[13]

Even if one accepts that budgeting is associated with stable appropriations patterns over time, apparent stability at the agency level may mask instability at the program level. The use of aggregate budget totals at the agency level may represent a netting of choices made by institutional budget participants across programs, concealing possible competition and tradeoffs among them.

With access to budget requests and decisions at the subagency, agency, central budget office, and presidential levels for the Atomic Energy Commission between 1958 and 1972, Peter Natchez and Irving Bupp examined what they believed to be the competition between programs and policies that takes place within what appears to be the stability of incremental decision making. Examining the programs dealing with high-energy physics, nuclear rockets, nuclear weapons, and thermonuclear research, Natchez and Bupp found considerable differences in their respective patterns of budgetary increase and decrease. If their analysis had been confined to agency-level dollar totals, those fluctuations would not have been apparent.

The Natchez and Bupp findings suggest that budget makers may indeed apply different decision rules to guide their choices at the discrete program level. Restricting the analysis to the agency level of aggregation may hide that variation in choice and give the appearance that a unidimensional decision rule is being used.[14] Other studies analyzing the budgets of the U.S. Department of Defense, the National Aeronautics and Space Administration, and the State Department came up with similar findings.[15]

Still other researchers—recognizing the significant growth in entitlement programs (e.g., programs such as Social Security and Medicaid, under which those who meet statutorily established eligibility standards are legally entitled to receive certain benefits or services regardless of the amounts appropriated) that has occurred since the Great Society years—questioned the theoretical link between the growth in federal entitlement spending and conscious budgetary choice. If spending on entitlements is not subject to control and grows without budget makers having to act on it, can such spending be related in any way to theory of budgetary choice? Incremental strategies become irrelevant to the uncontrollable portion of the federal budget.

Following this line of reasoning, Gist separated uncontrollable federal spending from controllable federal spending, comparing annual increments to the base for each. For uncontrollable spending, Gist used both entitlements and contract and borrowing authority. He found that between 1968 and 1974, while the total budget base grew by $94 billion, the uncontrollable portion grew by $110 billion, so that the controllable portion actually declined.[16]

Gist interprets this finding to suggest that budget makers do indeed go after the controllable base in making budgetary decisions. Unless changes are made in the substantive law governing entitlements, federal budget makers must look elsewhere in the budget to make the reductions they believe are consistent with overall budgetary and fiscal policy.

Moving Beyond Incrementalism

Among the various criticisms of budgetary incrementalism made by researchers, one stands out. It points to the gap between the findings produced by empirical models of incremental decision making and their theoretical underpinnings. The identification and testing of simple decision rules, using total-dollar amounts aggregated at the agency level, produces a picture of budgetary decision making that appears to be oversimplified and even misleading.

The research suggests that budget makers concern themselves primarily with the size of increments in relation to the budgetary base, both in making requests and in acting upon the requests or recommendations of others. We know that agencies tend to pad their requests, expecting that they will be cut back by budget reviewers. The incrementalists further suggest that budget makers apply a limited number of simple incremental decision rules to guide their budgetary choices, irrespective of the program areas in question, the nature of the discrete budget items before them, or the macro-level constraints facing them (whether those be tax or spending limitations at the state and local levels or spending ceilings imposed at the federal level). On the contrary, any theory of budgetary decision making must take such factors into account.

Budget makers at all levels of government are bombarded with innumerable cues that compete to influence budgetary decision making. These cues include the program areas affected, the costs of budget items, the sources of funding involved, the degree of increase or decrease sought or recommended, the relative uncontrollability of the spending, intergovernmental and constituency effects, views of what constitutes the appropriate role of government in society, different standards of judgment employed in defining problems and in evaluating alternative courses of action to resolve them, a sense of appropriate policy priorities, some sense of the prospective efficiency and effectiveness of what is requested or recommended, partisan influences, some assessment of the political feasibility of different budgetary options, the actual choices of those participants deciding earlier in the serial budgetary process, and expectations about how other decision makers will behave in making their own choices.

Budget participants do not attempt to measure their preferences along each of these dimensions of decision making; to take them all systematically into account in a sort of calculus of decision making would overwhelm participants' cognitive ability. Budget makers, however, do respond selectively to these influences, giving heed to some over others. They draw upon cues selectively, depending on the decisions before them. If they regularly turn to certain cues in certain situations, they can be said to follow decision rules. The challenge, then, is to identify the factors that prompt institutional budget participants to adopt certain decision rules in certain situations.

Focusing on Decision Items

Pursuing this line of reasoning, we need to look at the major items considered in budgetary decisions and not at the aggregate dollars requested, recommended, or approved for each government agency, or even for programs or subprograms within those agencies. Such items can be thought of as institutionally supported initiatives to increase, reduce, or reallocate the expenditure authority of an agency's budget base whether they occur across appropriations within the same program, across programs, or even across agencies.

Such decision items at the federal level might be a presidential recommendation to provide the U.S. Department of Defense with additional funds to procure eight new high-cost B-2 bombers, or initiation by the U.S. Senate, in its deliberations on the federal budget, of a program of financial aid to cities to assist them in meeting the rising costs of medical care and social services for the rapidly increasing number of people with acquired immune deficiency syndrome (AIDS).

Decision items can also be recommendations to reduce or eliminate funding for governmental activities. A presidential recommendation to eliminate federal operating subsidies for mass transit presents Congress with a discrete item for decision, as does a presidential proposal to reduce significantly the level of agricultural price supports for certain commodities.

Examples are prevalent in state and local budgeting as well. At the state level, a legislative budget committee's action to earmark state funding for special educational programs for disadvantaged children in major metropolitan school districts forces the entire legislature to act on that item. Similarly, a governor's proposal to close a state mental health institution and increase support for community-based treatment centers puts that choice before the entire state legislature. At the municipal level, a mayor's request for funds to establish a new drug enforcement program in the police department, including the authorization of twenty new positions, confronts the city council with a distinct budgetary choice. Such examples can be multiplied many times over at all levels of government.

Budget participants impose the structure of decision items as they organize the budget into discrete items around which they believe decisions should be made. Although the administrative agencies get the first crack at structuring the budget when they develop their requests, the chief executive and the legislature can alter that structure. The chief executive decides what parts of the request to recommend and how to organize them for presentation to the legislature (except where constrained by law or practice to include all agency requests in the **executive budget** document). The legislature, in turn, decides how it wants to break down the executive budget for review.

True to the basic tenet of incrementalism, the budget base is taken as a "given" unless an institutional participant proposes to alter it in one of the ways mentioned here. Where they are permitted, initiatives in the budget can also create, change, or repeal statutory law, and thus they too are decision items. To qualify as a decision item in either case, the initiative must be officially endorsed by the institution and not merely proposed by one of its members.

All the items in agency budget requests can be considered as decision items in the sense used above because agency leaders have officially endorsed them. These decision items, in turn, are acted upon by subsequent participants in the serial budgetary process—at least as far down the line as the requests survive. It therefore becomes possible to track the fate of decision items throughout the budgetary process. In jurisdictions where agency requests must be included in the executive budget book along with the chief executive's recommendation, it is possible to examine the latter's action on each. Upon receipt of the executive budget, a legislative fiscal or appropriations committee is free to accept, reject, or modify the chief executive's recommendations; when it rejects a recommendation, it may return the decision item to the form originally requested by the agency. The committee can also initiate budget recommendations of its own for which no requests or recommendations have been made either by an agency or by the chief executive. The legislature as a whole faces similar options; it can concur with its committee's recommendation, modify it, or reject it altogether. The legislature can also initiate recommendations that have not yet been considered by any participant coming earlier in the process.

In some cases, an institutional participant may amend a request or recommendation in a way that greatly changes the essence of the decision item. For example, a state appropriations committee might approve a request from its department of public instruction (supported by the governor) to finance twenty new academic subject-matter consultants to work with local school districts. The committee could then further recommend that the new consultants, as well as all consultants already in the department, be placed on program revenue to be supported by user fees paid by the local districts. This recommendation would significantly change the nature of the decision item: not only would it alter the department's relationship with local school districts, but it would also result in a base cut of state funds (substituting program revenue for state general revenue support). In this example, although a major change would be made to the request, the action would not create a new decision item; instead, the item initiated by the department would be changed, albeit significantly. On the other hand, if the whole idea of adding these consultants had been initiated by the legislature itself, another decision item would have been added for consideration.

In another example, the U.S. House of Representatives Appropriations Subcommittee on Transportation might accept the overall spending level recommended by the president for transportation but within that amount shift a high percentage of support from construction of new interstate highways to reconstruction and maintenance of existing state highways. Here the essence of the decision item has been changed; although the appropriation still supports the highway program, the subcommittee's recommendation marks a major change in programmatic emphasis—significant enough to argue that the decision item subsequently bears Congress's distinctive stamp rather than the president's.

Decision items differ not only in the ways they are initiated and chosen but also in their characteristics; some involve the prospective expenditure of hundreds of millions of dollars from the public treasury. This phenomenon, for example, might be seen in a proposal to increase state support for primary and secondary education from 40 percent to 50 percent of available costs. Other decision items that entail no new expenditure of public funds can nonetheless be of major policy significance. For example, a recommendation to eliminate the per capita component of a state's revenue sharing formula and therefore allocate aid exclusively on ability to pay based on each jurisdiction's equalized valuation could result in a significant redistribution of state aid to municipalities and counties, even though no new funds were added to the appropriation. Still other decision items (such as the addition of a clerical position to support an agency's program or the transfer of limited funding from one budget line to another) can have little or no policy significance or fiscal effect.

In addition to knowing the characteristics of decision items, budget makers are attentive to the broader context in which these items are considered. Incrementalist theory suggests that budget makers may view a decision item that calls for a large increase over the base quite differently from the way they see a decision item that includes only a modest request. It also is conceivable that institutional budget participants react differently to decision items from different sources, cabinet agencies, agencies headed by constitutionally elected officials, boards, or commissions. For example, a chief executive may be more inclined to support the requests of cabinet officials than to advocate those coming from elected officials, who may be political rivals.

Serial Budgeting, Interruptions and Adjustments, and Participant Choice

Budget makers also pay attention to the budgetary decisions of the institutional participants who precede them in the serial budgetary process. Documents prepared by staff often track the decisions of prior participants; thus, for instance, members of a state legislature can see what their budget committee did to the governor's recommendation in light of the governor's earlier recommendation. Information such as this is important because the legislature might well be more likely to support the governor's recommendation when its own committee has concurred with it.

Public budgeting, with its serial decision making, is a product of delegation, initiation, and reactive choice. Delegation can be either conscious or unconscious. Conscious delegation is a decision on the part of a budget participant to accept the version of the budget passed on by the immediately preceding institutional participant. Unconscious delegation is really a non-decision in which the version sent forward by a participant remains unaltered because the following participants fail to act on it at all. Those participants do not concur with it affirmatively; they simply do not bother to reject or amend it. The budget item may not even come to their attention; it moves along "unflagged" for review. A forgone opportunity to exercise conscious choice therefore becomes tantamount to agreement. The budget item is sent to the succeeding institutional participants in unaltered form, just as if there had been conscious concurrence.

Budget makers are not willing to delegate their choices across the board. Instead, they are selective about such delegation, relinquishing direct control of that part of the budget that involves little or no policy change or has little or no fiscal effect. Once such a budget item is initiated, chances are good that it will be included in the approved budget. For this relative chaff of the budgetary process, however, a decision by any institutional participant to reject an item altogether just about seals its doom, for it is unlikely that subsequent participants will care enough to reinsert it. Most likely, other participants will not even be aware that the minor decision item had ever been "alive."

Delegation represents a "rational" decision strategy of sorts. It is a way of conserving resources to be invested in budgetary decisions that really matter to budget reviewers. Each institutional participant employs its own criteria in deciding what is important, and because of this selective exercise of delegation and amendatory choice, the final approved budget is a much different product from the document first advanced by the chief executive.

Although there is a distinct seriality to budgeting, budgetary decisions are subject to adjustments based on new and changing information. An interdependence exists among identifiable phases of the budgetary process such as revenue estimating, spending choices, and issues of implementation. New revenue estimates issued by legislative staff well after the legislature has already begun its consideration of the executive's budget recommendations (which were based on earlier executive branch revenue projections) provide important and timely information that most likely would prompt legislators to go back and reconsider the earlier spending recommendations of their fiscal committees. Irene Rubin, a perceptive analyst of budgetary decision making, views this information penetration, and the subsequent adjustments it occasions, as a key feature of what she refers to as "real-time budgeting." It disrupts what otherwise appears to be serial, or sequential, decision making, and prompts decision makers to reexamine assumptions and prior choices and adjust them to the new environmental reality.

Therefore, although budget participants do indeed react to the choices of prior institutional participants in the budgetary process, they must continually reassess their budgetary choices in light of new information. That often means revisiting prior choices and delaying other decisions that should follow in sequence. For Rubin, real-time decision making allows the process to be disrupted, interrupted, and repeated.[17]

The Influence of Macro-Decision Making on Micro Choices

The decision-item approach focuses on what can appropriately be called micro-decision making. Micro-level decisions can focus on the individual decision items considered by budget participants on their line items or on the amounts requested or recommended for agencies, their organizational subcomponents, programs, or subprograms. Macro-decision making transcends agency-specific boundaries and involves a priori choices about how much a governmental jurisdiction should spend and how fast that spending should grow; how much taxing the jurisdiction should do; what the appropriate distribution of budget shares among programs should be; and what an appropriate budget balance or deficit (where permitted) should constitute.[18]

Both micro decisions and macro decisions affect budgetary outcomes, but most students of contemporary budgeting would probably argue that macro-level decisions play a more significant role in shaping public budgets today than they did more than three decades ago, when Wildavsky and his colleagues conducted their research on federal budgeting. Although this generalization probably applies to all levels of government, it is most apparent at the federal level.

As will be shown in chapter 6, Congress's passage of the Budget and Impoundment Control Act of 1974 and its subsequent revisions incorporated within the Balanced Budget and Emergency Deficit Control Act of 1985 (known as the Gramm–Rudman–Hollings Act), the Budget Enforcement Act of 1990, and the Omnibus Budget Reconciliation Act of 1993 pushed macro-policy choices to the forefront of the federal budgetary process. In an attempt to offer a distinctive congressional vision of what the budget should be, and thereby provide an alternative to the president's vision laid out in the executive budget, Congress required itself to pass a budget resolution that set targets for both revenues and expenditures for the coming fiscal year (making a statement about the level of deficit that it is willing to accept), including discretionary spending ceilings for each of the twenty expenditure-oriented functions of the federal government.[19]

Prominently included among them are such big-ticket items as national defense, income security, and transportation. The resolution also sets recommended levels for direct loan obligations, primary loan guarantee commitments, and levels of public debt. Furthermore, Congress requires that any increase in the budget deficit caused by tax cuts or the expansion of entitlements be offset by other additional revenues or cuts in direct spending.

In deliberating over the resolution, Congress necessarily is forced to deal with the overarching issues of public budgeting: deciding both how much to tax and spend and the relative ordering of policy priorities. The resolution also can contain reconciliation instructions directing committees to report legislation that conforms existing revenue or spending laws to the policies adopted in the budget resolution. Legislation developed in response to these instructions is packaged in an omnibus reconciliation bill, which is then considered in both the House and Senate under special rules of procedure aimed at expediting its passage.

Thus congressional decisions about how much to spend on national defense, for example, must necessarily be made both in the context of how much Congress is willing to spend overall and in terms of what share defense should get in relation to the other nineteen functional areas. How much Congress is willing to spend, however, is a function of how much it is willing to tax and what size deficit it is willing to accept. These decisions lie at the very heart of national politics and, once made, greatly constrain subsequent congressional budgetary choices. Choices about how to get the budget items that fall under an appropriations subcommittee's jurisdiction to comply with approved ceilings can still be considered as micro-budgetary decisions; and they may, in part, be made by following incremental rules. The difference today is that they are bounded by a new set of "macro-givens," creating, as Allen Schick has described, a "war between the parts and the whole."[20] The new Republican majorities that swept into the House and Senate as a result of the 1994 national election eagerly turned to macro-level constraints in their plan to eliminate the federal budget deficit by the year 2002, a task that was accomplished by the end of the 1998 fiscal year with the assistance of strong economic growth. Although both parties fashioned budgetary proposals that focused on macro-policy change during the Obama presidency, partisan gridlock and intra-party struggles for ascendency got in the way of using the budget to pursue national policy goals.

Macro-budgeting also intruded on micro-budgeting at the state and local government levels as well. The taxpayer revolt, which started at the local level in the late 1970s and spread to the states, combined with the recession-induced austerity of the early 1980s, created a changed environment for subfederal public budgeting. No longer could agencies count on incremental budgetary growth—the tenor of the times in many state and local governments promoted flat budgets and even some decremental budgeting, where expenditures were budgeted to decline from one year to the next. In many state and local governments, tax or spending limitations kept government growth within bounds. The early 1980s recession created the highest levels of unemployment since the Great Depression and cut significantly into normal state revenue expectations while simultaneously pushing expenditures up for public assistance and social services. The 1990 recession, although less severe than that of a decade earlier, placed new pressures on state and local budgets. In this environment, protectionism often became the name of the budgetary game—warding off budget cuts, staff reductions, and even program elimination. State and local budget officers put the lid on new program creation and existing program growth, and agencies were characteristically called upon to reallocate existing resources to meet new priorities. Budgeting became a zero-sum game in many jurisdictions, as selective increases had to be offset by decreases elsewhere in an agency's budget base. That experience continued following the recession of 2001, as revenues fell short of expenditures in most states, and it was repeated once again during the Great Recession and its near-term aftermath.

Fiscal austerity can conceivably affect budgetary choice in different ways. When it is most severe, budget reviewers may feel they have been given a ready rationale for rejecting all but the most pressing non-entitlement spending. Where budgets must be balanced (at the state and local levels), budgeting can maintain that revenues are merely sufficient—if even that—to cover mandated increases. In this setting, budget reviewers may pay little heed to information offered in support of most requests, and they are not likely to spend much time analyzing budget alternatives. The expectation of a ready-made "no" invites little analytical effort. Conversely, a competing perspective suggests that budgetary analysis is most highly valued in an austere fiscal environment. As the argument goes, tough choices must be made, priorities must be set, and even existing programs and services may need to be cut. By highlighting the implications of alternative choices and assessing the relative efficiency of alternative resource uses, analysis can serve as a useful tool in helping budget participants make those decisions.

Several close observers of budgeting argue that the other extreme—steady and significant revenue growth—tends to be more conducive to incremental decision making.[21]

Lacking tight fiscal constraints, budget makers are able to avoid the difficult priority choices and more readily rely on non-policy decision rules, focusing on requests in relation to the budgetary base. When there are enough revenues to go around, aggregated budgetary choices can be put together through the politics of mutual adjustment. Growing budget surpluses at both the federal and state levels at the end of the 1990s through 2001 provided ample latitude for policy makers to increase spending.

Analysis in Budgetary Decision Making

There are those who advocate the incorporation of policy analysis into budget making as a means of promoting better-informed budgetary decisions regardless of the fiscal environment.[22] Analysis can help decision makers define the problematic, assess the consequences of alternative courses of action, and become aware of the different criteria by which alternatives can be evaluated. At a minimum, advocates view analysis as a filter of sorts that provides decision makers with a sense of which considerations are significant in making different budgetary choices and which are relatively unimportant. They also see analysis as a means of sensitizing budget participants to the fact that there can be more than one criterion or standard of judgment upon which budget requests or recommendations are based. Knowledge of the underlying criterion of judgment provides important information that helps the reviewer to comprehend why a problem is defined in a certain way and why one alternative is preferred over another.

Policy analysis, when used in budgeting, usually does not begin with clearly defined objectives and clarified values, as the rational model dictates; instead, policy analysis often focuses on specific, fairly well-defined issues or problems in the short run, and usually is confined to an examination of a relatively narrow range of alternatives. Budget issue papers, for example, may be produced on a variety of topics. At the federal level, they might examine the appropriateness and implications of existing levels of borrowing and debt, credit programs, and tax expenditures. At the state level, appropriate topics might be the comparative adequacy of public-university faculty salaries, alternative approaches to property tax relief, or the appropriateness of existing public-assistance support levels. Subjects for analysis at the municipal level could include the adequacy of neighborhood police protection, the need for and implications of expanded **user fees**, or options for increasing operating revenues for mass transit. All of these would-be analyses have one feature in common: they attempt to make complex issues more readily understandable to decision makers.

Analyses also tend to be written so as to persuade budget makers and influence their choices. This is particularly true of policy papers or special analyses written in support of executive budget recommendations. Legislative analyses may make recommendations, or they may just review alternatives. Even in the latter instance, the alternatives are often cast in such a way that the preferred option is readily apparent.

Where there is credibility, analysis can influence budgetary choice. Well-reasoned and supported recommendations can sway decision makers, especially when they are premised on a criterion of evaluation prized by the decision makers. For example, a recommendation that defines a budgetary issue largely as a problem of inequity and evaluates budgetary options in terms of the extent to which they improve equity will not go far in swaying a decision maker who sees the problem not in terms of inequity, but as an issue of inefficiency. When preferred options are not premised on shared criteria of evaluation, the analyst faces the considerable challenge of persuading the client that the former's way of viewing the problem and weighing alternatives is better than the latter's.

Such caveats suggest that budgetary choice is in reality political choice. As such, it is significantly influenced by the values and perceptions of political relationships. At the same time, the budget's size and complexity constrain the degree to which analysis can influence budgetary decision making.

Summary and Conclusions

Public budgeting is a complex enterprise. Government budgets not only represent plans to spend large sums of public money; they also serve as key vehicles for public policy making. Budgets can be overwhelming in their size, policy and programmatic diversity, process, structure, specialized nomenclature, and politics. Tight timetables for budget development, review, and action make the decision-making task even more formidable.

Budget makers cope with these constraints by simplifying budgetary decision making. Instead of taking carefully considered positions on all budget elements before them, budget participants selectively turn to decision cues to assist them in making choices. One cue appears to be the extent to which requests and recommendations depart from the budgetary base. A second consists of expectations about how participants will react to the expected choices of other participants. A third involves the characteristics of the individual decision items making up the budget, including their relative policy significance and their fiscal and distributive effects. A fourth can be the persuasive power of analysis that supports a given budget alternative in preference to others. A fifth consists of the influence of macro-level parameters on micro-level budgetary decisions. Macro-level influences can include the state of the economy as well as a priori decisions about aggregate levels of taxing and spending, the existence of tax and spending limitations, and automatic spending mechanisms (such as entitlements and sum-sufficient appropriations) that commit resources outside the normal appropriations process.

Notes

1 Herbert A. Simon, Administrative Behavior (New York: Macmillan, 1958), 1–11.
2 Charles E. Lindblom, "Decision Making in Taxation and Expenditures," in National Bureau of Economic Research, Public Finances: Needs, Sources, and Utilization (Princeton, N.J.: Princeton University Press, 1961), 295–323.
3 Charles E. Lindblom, The Intelligence of Democracy: Decision Making through Mutual Adjustment (New York: Free Press, 1966).
4 Aaron Wildavsky, The Politics of the Budgetary Process (Boston: Little, Brown, 1964).
5 Ibid., 15.
6 Otto A. Davis, M.A.H. Dempster, and Aaron Wildavsky, "A Theory of the Budgetary Process," American Political Science Review 60 (September 1966): 543.

7 Ibid., 542.

8 Ibid., 532.

9 Ibid., 535.

10 Lance T. LeLoup provides a nice road map to the literature critical of incrementalism: see LeLoup, "The Myth of Incrementalism: Analytical Choices in Budgetary Theory," Polity 10 (summer 1978): 488–509.

11 John Wanat, "The Bases of Budgetary Incrementalism," American Political Science Review 68 (September 1974): 1221–28.

12 John R. Gist, "Mandatory Expenditures and the Defense Sector: Theory of Budgetary Incrementalism," Sage Professional Papers in American Politics, vol. 2, series 04–020 (Beverly Hills, C.A.: Sage, 1976).

13 John J. Bailey and Robert J. O'Connor, "Operationalizing Incrementalism: Measuring the Muddles," Public Administration Review 35 (January–February 1975): 64–65.

14 P.B. Natchez and I.C. Bupp, "Policy and Priority in the Budgetary Process," American Political Science Review 67 (September 1973): 951–63.

15 Gist, "Mandatory Expenditures"; Arnold Kanter, "Congress and the Defense Budget: 1960–1970," American Political Science Review 66 (March 1972): 129–43.

16 John R. Gist, "'Increment' and 'Base' in the Congressional Appropriations Process," American Journal of Political Science 21 (May 1977): 351.

17 Irene S. Rubin, The Politics of Public Budgeting, 2nd ed. (Chatham, N.J.: Chatham House, 1993), 258–73.

18 For a discussion of the concepts of micro-budgeting and macro-budgeting, see Lance T. LeLoup, "From Microbudgeting to Macrobudgeting: Evolution in Theory and Practice," in New Directions in Budget Theory, ed. Irene S. Rubin (Albany: State University of New York Press, 1988), 19–42. See Gregory W. Fischer and Mark S. Larnlet, "Explaining Presidential Priorities: The Competing Aspiration Levels Model of Macrobudgetary Decision Making," American Political Science Review 78 (June 1984): 356–71, for a discussion of the interdependence of defense and nondefense program shares at the federal level.

19 There are actually twenty-one functional categories of the federal budget, but the last includes undistributed offsetting receipts and therefore does not qualify as an expenditure-oriented function.

20 Allen Schick, "The Budget as an Instrument of Presidential Policy," in The Reagan Presidency and the Governing of America, ed. Lester M. Salamon and Michael S. Lund (Washington, D.C.: Urban Institute, 1985), 91–125.

21 Barry Bozeman and Jeffrey D. Straussman, "Shrinking Budgets and the Shrinkage of Budget Theory," Public Administration Review 42 (November–December 1982): 509–15; Allen Schick, "Incremental Budgeting in a Decremental Age," Policy Sciences 16 (September 1983): 1–26; Daniel Tarchys, "Curbing Public Expenditures: A Survey of Current Trends," paper prepared for the Organization for Economic Cooperation and Development, October 1982; Irene S. Rubin, "Budget Theory and Budget Practice: How Good the Fit?" Public Administration Review 50 (March–April 1990): 179–89.

22 S. Kenneth Howard, Changing State Budgeting (Lexington, K.Y.: Council of State Governments, 1973); Arnold J. Meltsner, Policy Analysts in the Bureaucracy (Berkeley and Los Angeles: University of California Press, 1976); Charles L. Schultze, The Politics and Economics of Public Spending (Washington, D.C.: Brookings Institution, 1968).

Chapter 3

Budget Organization and Structure

All budgets disclose how revenue is to be raised, in what anticipated amounts, and for what purposes it will be spent. All budgets permit budget makers to set fiscal priorities among competing uses of scarce public resources. In this sense, then, all budgets are policy vehicles; yet differences in governments' programmatic responsibilities, along with the laws under which they operate, either accentuate or limit the extent to which budgets can be used to shape public policy. For example, state governors are better positioned than city mayors to use the budget as an agenda-setting instrument, especially where state law allows substantive legislation to be enacted as part of the budget. Thus governors in those twenty-seven states can include both the statutory and appropriations authority for new programs in the budget bill itself, and then be able to apply the item veto (possessed by governors in forty-four states) to any changes made by the legislature to either. Moreover, the expansive policy reach of the states, grounded in the Tenth Amendment's reserve powers clause, allows governors to use the budget to influence outcomes across a broad range of public policy. Mayors, in contrast, face a budget constructed largely on the services that municipal employees provide to city residents. With upwards of four-fifths of city budgets devoted to salaries and fringe benefits of government workers, and with spending flexibility walled off by myriad special purpose funds, mayors have far less flexibility than governors to carry out major programmatic re-prioritization. Mayors also find themselves with less revenue-raising flexibility than governors possess. As legal creatures of the state, cities can employ only those revenue sources authorized by state law, leaving them heavily dependent on the property tax. In addition, mayors cannot use municipal budgets to create or change local ordinances (comparable to statutory law at the state level); that must be done through separate legislation.

Although all public budgets project anticipated revenues and authorize spending for a specified period of time, budget organization and structure tend to reflect the extent to which the budget can be used as a policy vehicle. All budgets keep track of revenues by their source, such as the individual income tax, corporate income tax, sales and use taxes, motor fuel taxes, and various kinds of user fees. They may also tie revenue sources to specific funds, and restrict the use of revenues in those funds to certain public purposes. For example, state law may require that motor fuel tax revenues be accounted for separately and deposited in a state's highway trust fund, to be used exclusively to finance highway construction and maintenance. Like states, the federal government also makes use of a federal highway fund to segregate motor fuel tax revenues for highway improvements. Fee revenues from hunting and fishing licenses are commonly deposited in a state's conservation fund, to pay the costs of managing wildlife and stocking lakes and streams with fish. In both examples, the budget's underlying accounting structure requires that earmarked revenues be deposited in segregated funds, and be used only for specified purposes. Yet budget structure can also be far less delineated, giving budget makers greater flexibility to tap revenues to cover a broad range of activities. All levels of government employ a general fund, which consists of all revenues not deposited in segregated funds and thus available to be spent on the so-called general purposes of government that cut across agency boundaries. The more revenue sources and spending purposes rolled into the general fund, the greater the budgetary flexibility enjoyed by government officials. Conversely, the greater the use of segregated funds, the less the budgetary flexibility.

Of all general-purpose governments, cities make the greatest use of segregated funds; and that use relates directly to the service structure of municipalities. Cities provide a number of essential services to their residents, such as fire and police protection, street maintenance and lighting, refuse collection, and water and sewerage; but they charge for them differently. While general fund revenues, consisting largely of property and sales taxes, pay most of the costs of police and fire protection, users bear the costs of other important municipal services. For instance, cities commonly charge residents for garbage collection, water, and sewerage services. The user revenues are deposited in separate enterprise funds, and the proceeds are devoted to cover the costs of the services provided. In addition to enterprise funds, cities also utilize special assessment funds, in which revenues charged to residents for exceptional things such as sidewalk repair and ornamental street lighting are devoted exclusively to those purposes.

Just as fund structure can limit budgetary flexibility, so can the way the budget is structured and formatted. All budgets allocate proposed or enacted appropriations authority by objects of expenditure (also referred to as line items) such as salaries, fringe benefits, supplies, small capital items, and the like. And these object classifications are usually broken down even more finely, differentiating, for instance, the discrete elements of fringe benefit costs, including, most significantly, health insurance. Moreover, government agencies build their budget requests along these budget lines, a practice referred to as line-item budgeting. Focusing on fringe benefits, budget officers project increases in health insurance costs for covered agency employees and build those anticipated increases into budget requests. Once part of the approved budget, the expectation exists that the funding authorized for health insurance will be devoted to that purpose, and not used to purchase new laptop computers for agency employees. This combination, then, of making wide use of segregated funds and organizing the budget along object of expenditure lines not only lim-its budget-making flexibility; it also renders the budget more as an accounting document than a policy vehicle.

Focusing the budget this way fosters budgetary incrementalism, discussed in chapter 2. Budget makers direct their attention to what is authorized in the current year—the budgetary base year—and the incremental cost it will take to accommodate expected cost-to-continue increases for each object of expen-diture in the coming year. Budget makers normally include salary increases in the form of pay plan adjustments for all government employees, although they may also target awards for designated groups of employees. Salary increases for state troopers, intended to stem the tide of defections to higher-paid county sheriffs' departments, would be an example of the latter. Some salary adjust-ments have a less discretionary character, reflecting the results of collectively bargained agreements which must be financed according to law. For fringe benefit adjustments, the biggest concern usually centers on the rising cost of employee health insurance coverage.

Beyond addressing the costs of continuing current operations, budget mak-ers also focus on what it will take fiscally to accommodate projected workload increases and support new services. Here, again, budget structure may put the central focus on objects of expenditure: on the salary costs of adding new per-sonnel, on fringe benefits as a standard percentage of salary costs, on supplies and small capital items required to support the new employees, and on large capital items (such as patrol cars for additional law enforcement officers) which might well be handled within the separate capital budgeting process.

Directing attention this way centers on the proverbial budgetary trees rather than the budgetary forest. It, by itself, diverts attention from policy choices about the very goals and objectives of governmental programs, and from prioritized reallocation of resources from one program to another.

Broadening the Budgetary Focus

Budget makers can broaden the budgetary focus in several ways. The most common and important include using performance measures to justify requests for additional appropriations authority, structuring the budget to shift the focus to programs and their objectives instead of budget lines within discrete agencies, and countering incrementalism by reexamining the budget base in competition with new spending priorities. The following discussion describes and compares these significant departures.

Performance Budgeting

Government agencies can incorporate performance measures into their justifi-cation for new resources to meet increased workload or deliver new services. And they can do that in a way that is compatible with the traditional line-item structure. But performance budgeting starts by focusing on activities rather than on budget lines. Budget proposers and reviewers make judgments based on expected performance results, and they devote budgetary resources toward those ends. For instance, a state parole agency might make the case that if the legislature approves its request for forty new parole agents, reducing agent caseload from 50:1 to 35:1, the recidivism (or re-offending) rate could be reduced by a third, yielding sizable net savings to the state when considering the resulting reduced costs of incarceration, let alone the social benefits of increasing the number of offenders who are successfully transitioned back into their community. It is that justification that underlies the request for increased appropriations authority to finance the salaries and fringe benefits of newly hired agents, their associated required supplies, and vehicles for their transportation.

This example of performance budgeting centers on outcomes expected from the infusion of additional budgetary resources. The focus, however, can be on outputs instead of outcomes. A transportation department's budget request to use some of the surplus in the state's segregated highway fund to finance construction of a new high-speed arterial connecting two existing interstate highways can be presented on a cost-per-mile basis. Given x amount of appropriations authority, the department can foresee completion of y miles of new pavement and associated ramps. Shifting the focus to outcome broadens the justification to include considerations such as cost savings resulting from reduced travel time and wear and tear on vehicles, along with reductions in air pollution achieved by lessened stop-and-go traffic.

As can be gleaned from these examples, performance budgeting in either form requires that the projected results of budget activities be measured and related to the costs of producing them. The essential difference lies in what constitutes results.

Both formulations improve the information that budget makers have in making budgetary choices, and they also enhance accountability for the use of public resources. Harkening back to the earlier example of the outcome-justified request for additional parole agents, let's assume that the recidivism rate for parolees did not fall by the projected third but remained essentially unchanged with the addition of the requested new agents. How likely would it be that the legislature in the coming budget session would further reduce the parolee–agent ratio? The agency would likely do well to avoid a reduction in its authorized agent positions.

Although performance measurement can be built into line-item budgeting, as shown above, it can also be incorporated into program budgeting and zero-based budgeting (ZBB). It is to those two budget structures that we now turn our attention.

Program Budgeting

Whereas the organizational locus of performance budgeting is the government agency and the activities *it* carries out, for **program budgeting** it is the broader program that encompasses related activities carried out by potentially several agencies. The starting point for program budgeting is not the activities themselves but the *objectives* to be accomplished through the effective delivery of the activities. Program budgeting recognizes that different agencies, through the activities they undertake, can make valuable contributions toward the realization of the broader program's objectives. Using this wider lens, program budgeting, in its purest form, significantly shifts the focal point of prioritized budgetary decision making from competing activities to competing programs. Yet as we shall see, program budgeting has never been successfully implemented in its purest form.

The Department of Defense made the first substantial effort to institutionalize program budgeting, and the vestiges of that attempt remain today. Introduced in 1961 as the Planning-Programming-Budgeting System (PPBS), program budgeting was based on the premise that all of the department's activities could be grouped into discrete program categories reflecting Defense's various missions, and showing how they collectively contribute to the whole and at what cost. These programs could cut across existing organizational boundaries, grouping like activities together and thus modifying the notion that each agency within Defense has the exclusive prerogative of delivering the programmatic objectives assigned exclusively to it.

As an illustration, the strategic forces program then incorporated nuclear submarines, capable of launching shorter-range nuclear missiles, together with land-based intercontinental ballistics missiles and long-range heavy bombers, capable of carrying nuclear bombs. All three could be said to provide the United States with a nuclear strike force capable of deterring first strikes by other nations. Yet the delivery systems were organizationally assigned to different agencies within Defense. With PPBS, then, the objective was to assemble that package of nuclear strike capability that best met the overarching objective of deterrence at the lowest cost, raising the standard of efficiency as a central criterion of choice along with effectiveness.

In starting with the notion of zeroing in on the goals and related objectives of government and then relating government's various activities to those objectives, the hope is that decision makers will explore alternative ways of realizing those objectives, regardless of organizational lines. Analysis is directed at the desired outcomes and the best way to achieve them. Therefore, analysis must be devoted to measuring the benefits as well as the costs associated with each alternative.

In order to institutionalize PPBS in the federal government and expand its use beyond the Department of Defense, the Bureau of the Budget (BOB) created a budgeting system that it imposed on all executive departments in 1965. Goals, objectives, programs, subprograms, and program elements had to be identified for all agencies. Base budgets had to be restructured along programmatic lines, and requests had to be justified by showing that they represented the most efficient (and adequately effective) use of resources to achieve the desired objectives and their ultimate goals. The BOB developed forms and formats to structure the agencies' analyses, among them the so-called program memorandum (PM) that was to serve as the analytical justification for each program element request. Accompanying the PM was the program and financial plan (PFP), which was to show the financial implications over five years, associated with support of the request. Finally, special analytical studies (SAS) were to be prepared by the requesting agencies on major issues addressed in the budget. These issues were usually identified by the BOB, and their development occurred under its watchful eye.

The use of policy analysis to evaluate alternative solutions to public problems was nothing new; it had been used to inform policy choice well before PPBS was created. What was new was the attempt to incorporate analysis systematically into the fabric of budgeting through program budgeting to make analysis an inherent part of budget development and review. As Charles Schultze remarked,

> Analytical efforts that stay outside of the stream of decisions remain just that—analytical efforts, not instruments for shaping decisions. The crucial element of PPBS is that it operates through the budget process. It seeks to bring analysis to bear on decisions by merging analysis, planning and budgetary allocation. It is a decision structure, and therefore must relate to other elements of the decision process.[1]

The creators of PPBS had great expectations about how it would change decision making in the executive branch and spill over into the congressional arena. Not only would decisions be made in relation to clearly identified goals and objectives; alternative choices would be evaluated using clearly identified criteria. These expectations, however, were never realized in practice. Although forms were created to provide the appearance that analysis was being incorporated into budgetary decision making, beyond its early use within the Department of Defense (where it was promoted by top management), PPBS never really caught on in the federal bureaucracy. By 1969 only three federal departments had made substantial progress toward implementing it, according to the General Accounting Office (GAO),[2] and it never became an accepted part of congressional decision making on the budget. At the executive level, PPBS degenerated into a "paper exercise"—a conformity with form rather than spirit. By the time the Nixon administration came into office, even the attention to form was put aside. In 1971, the Office of Management and Budget (OMB, successor to the BOB) discontinued its requirement that agencies submit PFPs, PMs, and SASs. Except for the continuation of selective special analyses, PPBS as a ubiquitous structure in federal budgeting was allowed a quiet death.[3] Within Congress, Appropriations Committee members, accustomed to line-item budgeting, never became comfortable with program budgeting, retaining their desire for organizationally related "numbers."

Several state and local governments, watching the genesis and growth of program budgeting at the federal level during the 1960s, initiated their own experiments. Help in these efforts came from a Ford Foundation grant, supporting the State–Local Finances Project—an attempt to provide technical assistance to five states (California, Michigan, New York, Vermont, and Wisconsin), five counties (Dade, Los Angeles, Nashville-Davidson, Nassau, and Wayne), and five cities (Dayton, Denver, Detroit, New Haven, and San Diego) in designing and implementing program budgeting systems. Some other governments also implemented their own systems, most notably Hawaii, Pennsylvania, New York City, and Philadelphia.

For the most part, the experience of the state and local governments adopting program budgeting systems paralleled that of the federal government. Some of the forms of program budgeting were incorporated into their budget systems, but nowhere did a PPBS-like system fully survive at the state or local level. Among the states, Pennsylvania has come closest, requiring in 1968 that budget requests be organized by program, objectives be identified for each program, performance measures be employed to gauge the progress made toward meeting the stated objectives, and that total cost figures be used regardless of revenue source. Pennsylvania today employs seven programs, including Education, Health and Human Services, Economic Development, Protection of Persons and Property, Transportation and Communication, Recreational and Cultural Enrichment, and Direction and Supportive Services (for all programs). A look at one of the programs, Health and Human Services, discloses the myriad of agencies involved in conducting activities that contribute to meeting the program's objectives. Notable among them are the departments of Health, Public Welfare, Aging, Labor and Industry, and Transportation.[4]

Although Pennsylvania still requires that the budget be structured by program, the Pennsylvania Legislature demanded that the budget also be organized by agency, and that legislators be provided with a "cross-walk" relating the two. The legislature also amended the program budgeting law to eliminate the requirement that the accounting system governing budget execution be structured along program lines, mandating only that it be done by agency organization and appropriation.[5]

What has remained of the early experiments in most state and local governments is a program structure that parallels departmental organization. Thus program-related numbers are also organization-related numbers. For example, a correctional program might be broken down into a number of subprograms, say, correctional institutions, juvenile institutions, probation and parole, and agency-wide supportive administrative services. And each of those subprograms might parallel agency organization, including separate divisions of adult institutions, juvenile institutions, probation and parole, and administrative services.

To several close observers of public budgeting, it is not surprising that program budgeting failed to become institutionalized. Several reasons are commonly offered:

- It is difficult to come up with program objectives that provide meaningful policy targets and that are widely accepted by budget participants. As Aaron Wildavsky observes, program budgeting fostered the creation of objectives that were either too generalized to provide meaningful direction (so that almost anything could fit within them) or so narrow and organizationally specific that each unit had its own home and did not have to compete with any other. The intrinsic problem, for critics, lies in the assumption that program objectives can legitimately be established by the executive branch at the outset of the budgetary process. They argue that such objectives are necessarily political in nature and can be determined only through the political process of mutual adjustment.[6]
- Despite the inherent problems cited above, critics also argue that budget makers never really knew or learned how to do program budgeting, even though they recognized that it was expected of them. They knew that they had to submit budget requests consistent with the general parameters of program budgeting, using prescribed forms; but the agencies still had to figure out how specifically to evaluate alternatives vis-à-vis program objectives. One description of how the process really worked at the federal level portrays agency attempts at compliance that strayed far from the theoretical model:

> The instructions come down from the Bureau of the Budget. You must have program budget. Agency personnel hit the panic button. They just do not know what they have been asked to do. They turn, if they can, to the pitifully small band of refugees from the Pentagon who have come to light the way. But these defense intellectuals do not know much about the policy area in which they are working. That takes time. Yet something must quickly come out of all of this. So they produce a vast amount of inchoate information characterized by premature quantification of irrelevant items. Neither the agency head nor the examiners can comprehend the material submitted to them. Its very bulk inhibits understanding. It is useless to the Director of the Budget in making his decisions.[7]

- Politically, program budgeting was viewed by both middle- and lower-management agency officials as a tool of top-down decision making. Top agency administrators characteristically exercised the responsibility to determine program structure and set objectives, most often without bothering to broaden the sense of ownership of those objectives across the organization. Similarly, the legislative branch tended to believe that program budgeting strengthened the budgetary hand of the chief executive, who was in a position to influence decisions about program structure, the choice of program objectives, and the choice of analytical approaches to be employed in evaluating alternatives (even though the evidence raises questions about the extent to which executives were able to get it to work that way in practice).

- Budget makers tend to be creatures of habit, who become comfortable with traditional ways of developing and reviewing budgets. Reciprocal expectations about the type of information to be exchanged and the kinds of questions to be asked colored interinstitutional budgetary relationships. Congress, for example, was accustomed to reviewing line-item budgets, first breaking them down along organizational lines and parceling them out to its appropriations subcommittees and then putting them together again in full committee following the norm of reciprocity (by which each subcommittee chair will support other chairs' motions in the expectation that they will reciprocate). Program budgeting complicated this process, partly because of its a priori focus on objectives, but more importantly because it sent Congress a budget organized in a way that was no longer compatible with fragmented congressional decision making. With a few exceptions, state and local legislative bodies clung to the forms of traditional budgeting in much the same way.[8]

Zero-Based Budgeting

While program budgeting was falling out of favor and being abandoned or greatly modified at all levels of government, a "new" form of budgeting was gaining popularity at the state level. That form, called **zero-based budgeting**, originated in the private sector, but within government was first systematically applied in the state of Georgia (although the U.S. Department of Agriculture experimented with a variant of ZBB in the 1960s). Identified with the Jimmy Carter administration, ZBB received national attention as its alleged successes became a prominent element of Carter's campaign for the presidency. In that campaign, the former governor of Georgia promised, if elected, to bring ZBB to the federal government. As touted, ZBB would force all budgets to be examined and justified "from scratch," including all elements of the base. In practice, it did not work that way.

Upon President Carter's election in 1976, the OMB began developing ZBB into a form that could be used by all federal departments. On April 19, 1977, the OMB issued its formal budgetary instructions. Agencies were to break their budgets down into discrete decision units, the lowest level at which meaningful management decisions are made. The instructions left it up to each agency to decide what should constitute a decision unit; it could variously be a program, subprogram, program element, or a cost center. Regardless of the budget level selected, managers had to identify and rank decision packages at four hypothetical funding levels for each decision unit: (1) the minimum level, below which the enterprise would no longer be viable; (2) the maintenance level, that which is required to continue the existing level of operations or services without any policy change; (3) the intermediate level, some point between the minimum and maintenance levels; and (4) the improvement level, requiring additional resources to expand operations or services.[9] In the aggregate then, four budgets were to be prepared, one for each funding level.

The response to ZBB was mixed during the Carter administration. The Office of Management and Budget liked the technique and its products largely because it forced the agencies to place priorities on decision packages, giving the OMB the ready opportunity to cut lower-ranked priorities from the request. Anticipating such behavior, agencies generally attempted to make the case that cuts below current levels would be disastrous to agency programs and that even funding at current levels would result in program erosion through the effects of nonaccommodated inflation. Thus the exercise for agencies became highly guarded and defensive. It also saddled agency budget staffs with much heavier work loads and greatly increased paperwork requirements, all for the purpose, from the agencies' perspective, of giving the OMB ammunition for budget reductions.[10]

Zero-based budgeting is no longer used as a coherent system for federal budgeting today. The Reagan administration retained the requirement that agencies submit alternative budget requests, including one lower than the base, at a percentage decrement prescribed by the OMB.[11] Although that practice continued under the Bush administration, it was discontinued during the Clinton years.

As had happened with PPBS, the status of ZBB as the national government's "new" budgetary system prompted a number of state and local governments to give it a try. Yet they frequently adopted only selective elements of ZBB as it was employed at the federal level. Most commonly, state and local governments incorporated some form of alternative budgeting whereby agencies were required to submit requests corresponding to different target levels, perhaps at 80, 90, 100, and 105 percent of base, so that the tradeoffs among them would be apparent to budget reviewers. This technique fit nicely with the budgetary climate of economic downturn and heightened taxpayer sensitivity in the early 1980s.

In comparison to PPBS, ZBB won greater support from budgeters, agency managers, and legislative reviewers alike, despite the additional workload it entailed for agencies. Zero-based budgeting did not challenge existing budgetary techniques; it could be compatible with line-item budgeting or with variants of program budgeting. Nor did it challenge an agency's basic orientations or prompt a reexamination of its mission or goals and objectives. Instead of promoting top-down decisions, as did PPBS, it encouraged increased involvement of middle and lower management in budget development, even though it posed a threat to them by forcing the identification of lower-priority programs and activities.

Unlike PPBS, where objectives and means toward them were set at the top, ZBB fostered bottom-up budget building. Although budget targets were passed down from the top to successively lower organizational units, the managers at each level predominantly fashioned the decision packages affecting them. This practice followed the premise that these managers, rather than the top administrators, were most familiar with day-to-day operations and therefore best positioned to identify areas where reductions could be made that would least affect program operations. Lower-level managers assembled decision packages to be reviewed by middle-level managers, who in turn sent them on to top-level managers; but the criteria and choices employed at each level largely reflected the preferences of their respective managers. Such broader-based involvement enhanced the legitimacy of what finally went to the central budget office.

These comments must not be taken to imply that all agency managers played the game straight, that they offered up lower-priority programs whose loss would least affect agency operations or services. Instead, fearing that lower-ranked items would prove too tempting to budget cutters, some managers included highly sensitive activities, often those with strong constituencies, into their below-base packages. Of course, this was done with the expectation that more politically sensitive managers at a higher level would remove them and substitute reductions from someone else's unit. Failing that, central budget or legislative reviewers could be counted on to take them out. For example, a bureau within a state department of public instruction might identify financial support for school-crossing guards as a low-priority item that could be reduced as a step toward getting down to a budget level below the base.

Nevertheless, in building decision packages, managers pretty much decided the bases upon which items were included in one package or another. Their decisions could just as well have been made as a product of management experience or "feel" as by analysis.

For the legislative branch, ZBB posed few constraints on decision making while offering some advantages. With ZBB, legislators could go about making budgetary choices as they had in the past. In addition, they got new information on the agencies' and executive branch's relative priorities.

Elements Common to all Public Budgets

Regardless of the structural format adopted to organize presentation of the budget, all government budgets contain certain elements in common, the subject of the discussion that follows. This is not to imply that budgets at different levels of government lack unique elements, but it does suggest that someone close to budgeting at one governmental level would be on familiar ground when perusing the budget of a different level of government. To honor the principle of valid comparison, however, we will restrict this discussion initially to the operating budget, and later consider the separate capital budget (which is used by state and local governments, but not by the federal government).

Budget Authority

All government budgets give agencies the authority to incur financial obligations that can result in actual spending. **Budget authority** can take a number of forms, the most common being appropriations. Appropriations give agencies the authority to obligate and later spend funds for a specific purpose. Although appropriation authority is usually limited to the fiscal year, law can allow unobligated authority to be carried over from one year to the next. With annual appropriations authority, funding not obligated by the close of the fiscal year lapses and is not available in the following year. Lawmakers normally reserve continuing authority for public works projects, such as highway and other types of construction, and for extended research. In addition to continuing appropriations authority, those states that budget **biennially** (for two years rather than one) employ both annual and biennial appropriations, with the latter providing authority over the two years.

Appropriations normally include a dollar limit on the ability of government agencies to obligate public funds. They are referred to as **sum-certain appropriations**. That is the case at the federal level, yet a number of states distinguish between sum-certain appropriations and **sum-sufficient appropriations** (also often called statutory appropriations), which authorize the amount necessary to accomplish a specific purpose, whatever it may total. States typically use sum-sufficient appropriations to cover the cost of interest on debt or provide benefits to individuals who meet statutorily created eligibility standards for public assistance. The amounts for sum-sufficient appropriations in the appropriations schedule are merely estimates of anticipated spending, and place no limitation on the actual amounts required to honor the statutory commitments.

Entitlement authority is the federal government's close equivalent to sum-sufficient appropriations at the state level. It requires the federal government to make payments or provide aid to individuals who meet legal criteria for eligibility, regardless of the cost. The biggest federal programs covered by entitlement authority include Medicaid, Medicare, and social security. Entitlement spending constitutes the largest portion of so-called mandatory spending at the federal level. Mandatory spending, as a category, is controlled by authorizing laws, not by appropriations. Interest on the federal debt is the most costly nonentitlement form of mandatory spending.

All non-mandatory spending falls within the category of **discretionary spending**. Appropriations acts provide the authority for discretionary spending, and, unlike mandatory spending, Congress can decide whether or not to spend, and at what level. Discretionary spending amounts to only slightly more than one-third of all federal spending annually. Defense spending comprises the largest single share of discretionary spending. The rest of federal spending falls into the mandatory category.

The other forms of budget authority include borrowing authority, contract authority, and spending authorized from offsetting collections and receipts.

Borrowing authority, while permitting agencies to incur obligations, requires them to use borrowed funds to make payments. Contract authority permits agencies to incur contractual obligations in anticipation of receipts they will collect at a later time. The authority of agencies to obligate and spend funds derived from collections and receipts paid by clients of a governmental program constitutes still another form of budget authority. Examples of collections authority at the federal level include premium payments made by individuals for Medicare Part B insurance covering outpatient health care, as well as entry fees paid by visitors to national parks. Co-payments which states require Medicaid recipients to pay provide another example. From an accounting perspective, these collections and receipts are treated as negative budget authority, because they are *deducted* from gross budget authority and are available to finance costs that would have to be covered otherwise.

Of all of these types of budget authority, annual appropriations authority is the most restrictive. When the fiscal year comes to an end, appropriations authority expires. This is not a problem if the legislative body approves appropriations for the next fiscal year. When it does not, agency programs reliant on annual appropriations have no continuing authority to obligate and spend public funds. As noted earlier, any unused authority from the prior fiscal year lapses back to the treasury.

Legislatures address this predicament by providing temporary authority, which continues current year spending typically at the prior year's level until legislators can agree politically on a new budget. As its vehicle for providing temporary authority, Congress uses an interim omnibus appropriations bill called a **continuing resolution**. It provides continuing appropriations authority either for a specified period of time or until Congress passes the regular appropriations. The continuing resolution, just as any appropriations bill, must be approved by the president. Congress frequently used it during the Reagan administration, the first term of the Clinton administration, and most of the Bush administration.

Budget Documents

All governmental jurisdictions produce budget documents, which can be categorized by their institutional origin: executive or legislative. We will first discuss the major executive budget documents then turn our attention to those produced by the legislative branch. The discussion will highlight elements common to all levels of government, and note points of significant distinctiveness.

Executive budget documents convey and provide support for the budget recommendations of the executive branch's chief executive, whether that be the president, a state governor, a city mayor, or a county executive. The executive budget may include agency requests together with the chief executive's recommendations relative to them, or it may present only the chief executive's budget recommendations, omitting agency requests. Executive budget documents take various forms, but most include a budget message, a brief overview of budget priorities and recommendations, a comprehensive budget "book" that contains in-depth coverage of budget recommendations, and policy papers supporting major budget recommendations by agency. A separate document analyzing economic conditions and providing a fiscal overview may also be produced, if not included within the main budget book.

The OMB prepares several budget documents, prominently including *The Budget of the United States Government*, *Analytical Perspectives*, *Historical Tables*, and the *Appendix*. The first document is most synonymous with what we consider the federal budget. It includes the president's budget message, a discussion of the economic and fiscal context, a presentation of the president's overall budget priorities, and overviews of the president's budget recommendations organized by agency. It does not include agency requests. *Analytical Perspectives* incorporates a number of analytical background papers on selected topics which the administration wishes to highlight, and which cut across an agency-by-agency focus. Usual topics include aid to state and local governments, research and development, federal receipts and collections, and federal borrowing and debt. *Historical Tables* provide data on receipts (revenues), **outlays** (spending), federal debt, and federal employment from 1940 to the present. The *Appendix* is the source for the underlying budget detail.

On the legislative side, Congress also produces budget documents. The Congressional Budget Office (CBO)—Congress's rough equivalent to the OMB—regularly produces several budget documents. They importantly include the following, discussed in chronological order of their release:

The Budget and Economic Outlook (January) estimates the receipts, outlays, and deficit or surplus that would result from continuing current law through the coming budget period, based on an analysis of the fiscal effects of projected economic conditions. These estimates are commonly referred to as **baseline** budget projections. More will be said about their importance in chapter 6.

Budget Options (February) identifies and describes spending options that members of Congress might consider for each functional area of the federal budget. It also offers revenue options for their consideration.

An Analysis of the President's Budgetary Proposals (March) gives an overview of the president's budget; focuses on policy proposals in the budget that affect revenues, mandatory spending, and discretionary spending; and projects how the president's budget proposals will affect the economy.

In addition to these CBO documents, both the House and Senate Budget Committees generate their own budget documents. They, too, summarize the president's budget, but also contain special analyses of greatest interest to their members. Recent topics have focused on the proposed budget's effects on entitlement programs, and how recommended budget cuts impact each of the states. The House and Senate Budget Committees' documents have more of a partisan flavor than do those produced by the CBO. It's not uncommon for the committees' majority- and minority-party staff to release their own documents. As a sign of partisanship, the Democratic and Republican members have their own committee websites. As might be expected, the party holding a majority of seats on the committees sets the partisan tone for the committees' reports.

Both executive and legislative budget documents can also be found in the states. State budget offices prepare the executive budget containing the governor's budget recommendations to the legislature. Law in most states requires that the executive budget document include agency budget requests along with the governor's recommendations and separate initiatives. This main budget book may present the governor's recommendations variously organized by agency, functional area, program, or a combination thereof. A condensed version, often titled *Budget-in-Brief* or *Budget-at-a-Glance*, may accompany the budget book, as may a separate volume of policy papers or issue briefings that highlight the major policy initiatives endorsed by the governor. The governor's budget message may be released separately, or incorporated with the executive budget document.

Legislative budget staff, whether assigned to appropriations committees or employed by a legislative fiscal office, prepare budget documents for members of the legislature. These documents most commonly include summaries of the governor's budget recommendations in the aggregate, as well as summaries by agency. Where legislative staff organize their summaries by program or functional area, they normally add summaries by agency as well. Beyond descriptive summaries, legislative staff members prepare analytical papers which either suggest options for legislators to consider or make recommendations for alternative legislative actions. Legislative fiscal agencies also keep track of endorsed budget changes made at each stage of the legislative phase of the budgetary process. In addition, they typically publish a summary of the adopted budget.

Executive budget documents for the most populous cities and counties tend to parallel those at the state level, and it is the executive budget documents that take center stage. Local legislative budget documents are far less prominent than those at the state level, and may even be largely limited to briefing papers for city council or county board members. This reality is partly a function of lower fiscal staffing at the local level, but also of the centrality of the executive's budget recommendations in those local jurisdictions with elected chief executives.

Computerized Budget and Accounting Information Systems

Beyond the many documents that support budget requests and describe budget actions, governments use budget and accounting information systems to keep track of all of the detail that constitutes the budget. That keeping track begins with agency requests, and ends with execution of the budget enacted into law. Information systems parallel the organizational structure of the budget. The information system for program budgets must be able to integrate data across agency lines, while providing a "cross-walk" back to the traditional agency basis. Where budgets are structured solely on agency organization, the system must still be able to keep track of budget requests, recommendations, and approved actions by fund, appropriation, organizational unit, and object of expenditure.

The budget system must also be able to aggregate amounts up the agency's organizational hierarchy. An example might be useful here. Take a hypothetical state department of corrections, which operates correctional institutions and includes field supervision of parolees and probationers. Let's presume, for simplicity, that the department is organized into three divisions: correctional institutions, probation and parole, and general departmental administration. The institutional division contains two bureaus: one responsible for institutions housing adult prisoners; the other for juvenile offenders. The state has six institutions for adults and four for juveniles. Separate bureaus for probation and parole exist within the division of probation and parole. Let's assume that the department—based on its analysis of offenses committed, the rate of court convictions, penalties imposed, and the effects on inmate length of stay—requests thirty new correctional officers in the aggregate, and assigns the associated costs for salaries, benefits, and supplies to particular correctional institutions. Let's further assume that the department's request calls for reallocating ten probation officer positions to parole supervision. The state's budget tracking system must be able to reflect these changes to the base budget. Now, let's assume that, based on the state budget office's recommendation, the governor supports twenty of the requested new correctional officer positions, and rejects altogether the reallocation from probation to parole. Again, the budget system must be able to reflect the changes resulting from the governor's action, just as it must be able to capture any successive changes that might be made at the various stages of legislative review process: those in committee; those on the chamber floor; and those resulting from gubernatorial vetoes and legislative overrides of those vetoes.

After the budget is enacted into law, it has to be executed. During this stage, agency officials obligate and spend approved appropriations authority to finance the costs of adding the new officers at the different correctional institutions. Moreover, state law, in our example, may allow the department of corrections, with the approval of the state budget office, to make **budget transfers** from one institution to another during the course of the fiscal year as operational needs dictate. The accounting side of the information system must reflect any changes, and must be able to keep track of spending in relation to available appropriations authority.

As noted earlier, spending in one year may result from budget authority approved in that year or from unused authority provided in previous years. Such is the case at the federal level with authorizations for multi-year public works and research projects. Biennial and continuing appropriations provide carry-over authority at the state level.

Also as noted earlier, the authority for mandatory spending at the federal level comes from authorizing laws, not from appropriations. In the states, sum-sufficient appropriations authorize spending the amounts necessary to accomplish a specific program purpose. Spending is open-ended, the sum of the actual costs of meeting entitlements or interest payments on the debt. The amounts in the appropriations schedule are there as estimates of outlays only. Control lies with ensuring that actual spending is consistent with the authorized program purposes—that, for example, only eligible individuals receive the benefits of entitlement programs.

The Distinctive Features of Capital Budgeting

Most state and local governments have separate **capital budgets** (from their operating budgets) and use distinctive processes to plan for and finance capital projects. In contrast, the federal government has no separate capital budget, and provides budget authority for capital projects through the normal federal budgetary process. Capital projects include the acquisition of land; the construction, renovation, and equipping of buildings; the construction and improvement of highways and roads; and other investments in physical assets that have a reasonably long useful life (such as military hardware at the federal level). The concept of useful life is central to capital budgeting because it recognizes that assets such as new buildings and highways will serve their users for many years after their construction. Yet that construction incurs high costs that must be financed up front, so to speak. As an example, a divided four-lane urban highway, with a concrete surface, can cost up to $12 million per mile to construct. Even though the construction of the state project might be completed in less than two years, the highway can be expected to be serviceable for up to thirty years before it requires major improvement. In financing the project, state officials have two options: pay cash, drawing on appropriations in the operating budget; or borrow from lenders who are willing to finance the project in return for a stream of interest payments and the ultimate repayment of principal. Employing the borrowing option, state officials may decide to sell **revenue bonds** to willing buyers, perhaps pledging motor fuel tax revenues to finance interest payments on the debt. Thus only individuals who buy fuel and potentially use the new highway contribute to debt repayment. Or state officials may decide to use **general obligation bonds** as the financing mechanism, which have the full faith and credit of the general treasury behind the promise that bondholders will be repaid, in recognition of the broad benefits, including economic development, that will accrue to the state from completion of the project. Chapter 10 extends the discussion of capital finance and bonding options.

Even before a decision is made about how to pay for the new project, state officials must first decide whether to undertake that specific project or another.

It might compete with several other candidate highway projects, and potentially with state building projects if state officials are inclined to use general obligation bonding to cover the cost of part or all of the highway project. Capital budget decision makers find themselves having to prioritize among competing projects, and they commonly rely upon a planning and evaluation process to inform their choices.

The state budget office or a facilities management agency may oversee the planning and evaluation process on behalf of the governor at the state level; however, about half the states give that responsibility to a specially designated commission or board which can include the governor or a designee, key legislators, and citizen members who typically have expertise in facilities planning and management. Where the joint commission or board is used, it is that body which prioritizes project selection and makes official recommendations directly to the legislature.[12] Otherwise, the governor submits capital budget recommendations for legislative consideration.

Based on input from the numerous state agencies, capital improvement plans, which can encompass three to ten years, include project descriptions, an analysis of costs and benefits, and a tentative year-by-year schedule. The state body prioritizing projects may adopt formal criteria, perhaps even using a point scale, to prioritize projects, or may simply use consensus or majority vote. But because the legislature makes the ultimate decision on which projects will be funded, it is not surprising that well-placed legislators will try to get their pet projects included in the approved capital budget. While the planning process is often built on objective criteria, the politics of influence can become a more weighty factor in project selection.

States differ in the inclusiveness of their central planning process. Most states delegate highway planning and prioritization to the state highway or transportation department. Although that delegation covers the process of planning and project prioritization, the department's capital budget recommendations still go to the governor, who sends his or her recommendations to the legislature. Some states extend similar delegation to higher education.

Roughly half of the states produce a separate capital budget; the other half combine capital and operating expenditures in one executive budget document.[13] States using joint executive–legislative commissions or boards to develop capital budget recommendations are more likely to produce a separate capital budget document.

Summary and Conclusions

All budgets are policy vehicles in that they reflect budget makers' choices about how to raise revenues and in what amounts, and how to prioritize public spending. However, differences in governments' programmatic responsibilities, and the laws under which they operate, can accentuate or constrain the extent to which budgets can be used to shape policy. Budget organization and structure can also reflect the degree to which the budget can be used effectively as a policy vehicle. The more governments parcel out revenues into separate funds, the less budgetary flexibility budget makers have. Budgets structured on a line-item basis foster incremental decision making by directing attention to the cost components of budget lines and diverting the focus from the budget's contribution to realizing programmatic objectives.

Several efforts have been made to broaden the budgetary focus, most notably including the introduction of performance budgeting, program budgeting, and zero-based budgeting. Performance budgeting incorporates performance measures into the justification for additional budgetary resources, focusing on the activities of government agencies rather than on budget lines. It requires that the projected results of budget activities be measured and related to the costs of producing them. Program budgeting shifts attention from discrete activities to the broader program that encompasses them, potentially including those carried out by more than one agency. The starting point for program budgeting is not the activities themselves but the objectives to be accomplished through effective delivery of the activities. Zero-based budgeting does not force budget makers to build the budget from scratch, as its label suggests. It instead requires them to identify how they would accommodate different levels of funding, starting with a minimum level, below which program operations would no longer be viable, up to an improvement level that requires additional resources to expand operations, as well as including other levels within that range. This exercise has as its primary objective forcing budget makers to clearly identify what cuts should be made at reduced levels of funding.

Regardless of the structural format adopted to organize presentation of the budget, all government budgets contain certain elements in common, including commitments of budget authority of various kinds, assorted budget documents that describe and support budget recommendations and actions, and an accompanying computerized budget and accounting information system that keeps track of all of the detail that constitutes the budget and reflects changes made at each stage of the budgetary process.

Capital budgeting has its own characteristic features compared to operating budgeting. Most state and local governments have separate capital budgets and use distinctive processes to plan for and finance capital projects. Capital projects include the acquisition of land; the construction, renovation, and equipping of buildings; the construction and improvement of highways and roads; and other improvements in physical assets that have a long life. The federal government has no separate capital budget, and capital items must compete for funding within the operating budget.

State and local budget makers have two ways to finance capital budget items: pay cash or borrow funds to cover the costs. Borrowing funds involves selling government bonds to willing buyers. The bonds can pledge the full faith and credit of the jurisdiction's general treasury as security underlying repayment to bondholders, or they can limit resources for repayment to segregated revenues, such as proceeds from the state motor fuel tax.

Although legislative bodies have the ultimate responsibility for approving the capital budget, the task of recommending prioritized projects may fall to the jurisdiction's chief executive officer or to a specially constituted institution including members drawn from the executive and legislative branches, along with residents who have expertise in facilities planning and management.

Roughly half of the states produce a separate capital budget, while the other half combine capital and operating expenditures in one executive budget document. States using joint commissions or boards to develop capital budget recommendations are most likely to develop a separate capital budget document.

Notes

1 Charles L. Schultze, The Politics and Economics of Public Spending (Washington, D.C.: Brookings Institution, 1968), 77.
2 K.E. Marvin and A.M. Rouse, "The Status of PPB in Federal Agencies: A Comparative Perspective," in United States Congress, Joint Economic Committee, Analysis and Evaluation of Public Expenditures: The PPB System (Washington, D.C.: Government Printing Office, 1969), 814.
3 Office of Management and Budget, "Preparation and Submission of Budget Estimates," Circular A-11 (June 1971).
4 Governor's Office of the Budget, Commonwealth of Pennsylvania, The Budget Process in Pennsylvania, www.budget.state.pa.us/portal/server.pt/document/budgetprocess_pdf.
5 Ibid.
6 Aaron Wildavsky, "Rescuing Policy Analysis from PPBS," Public Administration Review 29 (March/April 1969): 189–202; Allen Schick, "A Death in the Bureaucracy: The Demise of Federal PPB," Public Administration Review 33 (March/April 1973): 146–56.
7 Wildavsky, "Rescuing Policy Analysis," 193–4.
8 Haldi Associates Inc., A Survey of Budgeting Reform in Five States (Lexington, K.Y..: Council of State Governments, 1973); Robert L. Harlow, "On the Decline and Fall of PPBS," Public Finance Quarterly 1 (spring 1973): 85–105; Robert D. Lee, Jr. and Ronald W. Johnson, Public Budgeting Systems, 6th ed. (Gaithersburg, M.D.: Aspen Publishers, 1998), 112–13; State–Local Finances Project, Implementing PPB in State, City, and County: A Report on the 5–5–5 Project (Washington, D.C.: George Washington University, 1973).
9 Donald Axelrod, Budgeting for Modern Government (New York: St. Martin's Press, 1988), 296.
10 See Allen Schick, "The Road from ZBB," Public Administration Review 38 (March/April 1978): 177–80.
11 Axelrod, Budgeting for Modern Government, 300.
12 National Association of State Budget Officers, Capital Budgeting in the States, November 1999, 19.
13 Ibid., 15.

Chapter 4

Economics and Politics

Economics and politics are inextricably linked in the fabric of American democracy, and this interrelationship is most evident in the politics of public budgeting. Political leaders often justify their budgetary decisions on economic grounds: that their choices will be good for the economy, will create jobs, or will spur saving and investment. Political challengers take potshots at incumbents who have the misfortune of serving during economic downturns, suggesting that they should be held accountable for economic woes that have occurred on their watch. But beyond the ties to political rhetoric and partisan advantage, the condition of the economy can either constrain or facilitate budgetary choices.

Let's first look at how the economy imposes fiscal constraints on budget makers. In the extreme, an economy that falls into **recession**—a condition in which the real (inflation-adjusted) dollar value of its goods and services declines for two consecutive quarters or more—affects both government revenues and spending. Personal income declines as a result of the increased unemployment that accompanies a drop in the nation's **gross domestic product (GDP)**. As aggregate personal income falls, so does aggregate consumption. This lowered demand soon translates into smaller corporate profits. Thus, both individual and corporate income tax revenues decline as a result of their shrinking tax bases, hitting the federal government hardest given its heavy reliance on income taxes. Although states see their income tax revenues fall, they also feel the drag on sales tax revenues, which on the whole remain the states' primary source of revenue. Local governments that make sizable use of income and sales taxes (when granted these options by their states) feel similar effects. However, those local governments that depend primarily on property taxes are affected less immediately, even though a prolonged recession and slow recovery will typically drive down property values and correspondingly reduce the property tax base.

A recessionary economy packs a one-two punch. Not only does it depress revenues; it also drives up public expenditures. As unemployment rises and personal income declines, more and more people become eligible for government programs that provide need-based assistance. Welfare rolls and unemployment compensation claims rise, as do applications for publicly supported medical assistance. The latter, with medical care costs rising several times above general inflation, puts the greatest pressure on government budgets. The federal government and the states, which cooperate on a number of joint programs of public assistance, feel the fiscal pinch the most.

Conversely, a strongly growing economy generates additional fiscal resources that give budget makers considerable latitude in using them. They essentially have two options: allocating rising revenues to be spent on public purposes, or giving them back to taxpayers in the form of tax cuts. Each offers a much more politically friendly prospect than does the flipside of cutting government programs or raising taxes to replace lost revenues.

Just as the economy can affect budgetary decision making and its associated politics, political decisions can influence the performance of the economy. National policy makers use economic policy to promote solid economic growth without undue inflation. The trick is to expand the economy fully to its potential for production, while being careful not to exceed that potential and run the risk of accelerated inflation and the rising unemployment that characteristically follows. National economic policy makers use two major policy tools toward achieving these ends: **fiscal policy** and **monetary policy**.[1]

The president and the U.S. Congress use fiscal policy to affect the aggregate demand for goods and services and thereby influence the course of the economy in desired directions. In times of economic downturn, fiscal policy makers turn to spending increases and/or tax cuts to stimulate economic growth. When rapid economic growth threatens price stability, they look to spending pullbacks or tax increases to bring inflation down to acceptable levels. Yet because spending reductions and tax increases can carry with them political costs, it is not surprising that politicians have demonstrated a willingness to defer to the Federal Reserve Board, and particularly to its chairman, as the United States' preeminent economic policy maker.

Using monetary policy, the "Fed," as it is commonly called, affects the availability and cost of loans by affecting short-term interest rates and the proportion of deposits that thrift institutions (banks, savings and loans, and credit unions) must keep in reserve. To the extent that Fed policy restricts availability of credit and increases the cost of loans, it dampens the aggregate demand for them. When it acts to widen availability and lower the cost of credit, it encourages increased demand and the heightened commercial activity that follows.

In addition to its traditional focus on adjusting short-term interest rates as economic conditions dictate, the Federal Reserve, in response to the devastating effects of the 2007–9 Great Recession, adopted another policy tool, labeled "quantitative easing," to spur economic development. It consisted of massive purchases of long-term bonds and other assets, such as real estate-based securities, to inject liquidity into the economy by expanding the resources that financial institutions have available to lend, thereby also lowering long-term interest rates. This chapter will later explore the causes of the Great Recession, its economic consequences, and the associated policy response which pushed the boundaries of both fiscal and monetary policy.

Compared to national economic policy makers, state and local policy makers are far less well equipped to influence economic performance. All states, except for Vermont, require balanced operating budgets. So when a state's economy takes a nosedive and revenues fall short of covering budgeted expenditures, governors and legislatures have no option but to raise taxes or cut back spending in line with available revenues—actions that contribute to further economic dampening. Yet even if state legislatures could engage in deficit spending, the reality is that national economic forces tend to overwhelm state economic factors.

Nonetheless, both states and local governments use the resources of government to promote economic development. State legislatures have established economic development agencies whose job it is to entice large manufacturing and service industries to establish new operations, or to expand existing ones, within state borders. States often compete with each other in that regard, employing tax incentives, loans, subsidies, highway improvements, and relaxed regulations as their primary enticements.

Local governments also strive to expand economic activity within their jurisdictional boundaries, and this puts communities in competition with one another. In that competition they use some of the same tools employed by the states, often turning to tax abatements, which can consist of reduced tax rates, deferrals of tax liability, or outright exemption from taxation. Beyond tax considerations, local governments can forgive corporations all or part of their share of the costs of the physical infrastructure needed to support an industrial plant or large service enterprise, including the cost of curbs and gutters, street lighting, and extension of sewer lines. In addition, where permitted by state law, they can offer relaxed regulations to attract development, most commonly in the form of variances from planning requirements and land-use restrictions.

The Roots of National Economic Intervention

The Great Depression of the 1930s tested the conventional wisdom that national economic fluctuations of the business cycle are short-lived and self-correcting. The rapid economic growth of the 1920s, fueled in part by surging investment and stock speculation, gave way to the great stock market crash in the autumn of 1929. Investment plummeted, consumer demand withered, and the ranks of the unemployed swelled. By 1933, more than thirteen million Americans were out of work—about one in four people. America's devotion to laissez-faire capitalism, however, worked against active governmental intervention to jump-start the economy and put people back to work.

America's Great Depression pulled down economies worldwide. Unemployment reached greater heights in Great Britain than in the United States—a fact not lost on British economist John Maynard Keynes. Keynes, best known for his 1935 work *The General Theory of Employment, Interest and Money*,[2] was both an economic theorist and practical activist. He theorized about how economies work, and energetically sought to get top policy makers, including President Franklin Delano Roosevelt, to apply his prescriptions in practice.

Keynes, who worried that the protracted economic downturn showed few signs of self-correcting, offered an explanation for why high unemployment could be an enduring feature of capitalism. In a prolonged slumping economy, consumers are more inclined to save rather than to spend. This resulting slowdown in aggregate demand induces businesses to reduce inventories and postpone orders for new products, thus prompting manufacturers to cut back on production and lay off unneeded workers. This snowballing effect further propels the economy into decline and increases unemployment. Keynes feared that the economy would remain in the doldrums as long as low demand persisted. The policy question became how, when confronted with these forces, to get the economy off dead center and growing again.

The answer, for Keynes, was for national governmental intervention to stimulate demand. As he saw it, both Great Britain and the United States had a large pool of trained workers ready and able to come back to work if only there were sufficient demand for the goods they produced. The problem, though, was how to achieve increased demand in an environment of sustained underemployment of resources. That is where government comes in. National governments can use debt to finance spending beyond their ability to cover costs out of current revenues.

Keynes saw major deficit-financed government spending as the spark that could ignite economic growth, propelling aggregate demand that would revitalize markets and bring the unemployed back to work. Keynes also saw government's obligation to intervene as not limited to recessionary times: An activist government should work to manage aggregate demand whenever market forces prove insufficient to create sufficient demand to keep unemployment at acceptable levels. Although Keynes preferred increased spending as government's foremost instrument to expand demand, he recognized that demand could be fostered through tax cuts. For tax cuts to generate demand, however, those benefiting from them would have to spend their increased after-tax income rather than save it; but in worrisome economic conditions, people are inclined to save rather than to spend. Increased government spending obviates that uncertainty; it translates directly into higher demand.

Keynesian theory also gives national policy makers the expectations and tools to cool down an overheated, inflation-prone economy. The recipe again lies with government action to influence demand, in this case reducing it by decreasing spending or raising taxes. Keynes' primary focus, however, was not on how to slow down an overheating economy, but on how to stimulate an economy operating below capacity, bringing it to full employment and keeping it there.

The major political contribution of Keynesian theory is its justification for governmental intervention in the economy. Classical economic theory prescribes a limited role for government in the economy: to ensure the integrity of the market while not distorting the natural operation of market forces. For the market to function efficiently, government must protect personal property, enforce contractual obligations, and thwart monopolies. Keynes not only legitimized governmental intervention to secure economic prosperity; he honored it. In doing so, his activist orientation has had lasting implications. Those supporting activist government broadened the agenda to include other forms of governmental intervention, including justification for an expanded welfare state.

In focusing on governmental involvement in managing demand to achieve full employment, Keynes did not worry much about the inflationary effects of stimulating the economy beyond its productive capacity because his primary concern was how to mobilize underutilized resources. The former concern fell to his intellectual successors. One prominent disciple, A.W. Phillips, identified an inverse relationship between unemployment and inflation.[3] He found that as unemployment falls, inflation rises, since the growing scarcity of labor drives up wage rates, and higher wage rates inflate the cost of the products or services provided (that is, unless they are accompanied by proportionally increased worker productivity). He found the converse also to be true: inflation drives up the cost of labor, inducing employers to attempt to get by with less of it. Thus, governments face a dilemma. Their efforts to increase aggregate demand can lead to inflation that rises to unacceptable levels. Conversely, their efforts to control inflation can lead to growing unemployment.

The tradeoff apparent in the so-called Phillips Curve reinforced Keynesians' interventionist inclinations. It became incumbent on economic policy makers to anticipate the effects of this tradeoff and to use policy tools to mitigate its negative effects, striving for an acceptable balance between unemployment and inflation. In employing policy tools to achieve that objective, policy makers tend to err on one side or the other. They may be willing to accept a little more unemployment for a little less inflation, or vice versa. That choice represents an inherently political judgment.

Fiscal Policy and the Ascendancy of Monetary Policy for Economic Management

The widespread acceptance of the perceived realities of the Phillips Curve was shaken during the mid to late 1970s, when high inflation coexisted with high unemployment. In 1978, inflation rose to almost 8 percent while unemployment stood at a little over 6 percent, a level well in excess of the Carter administration's policy of 4 percent unemployment. Unemployment remained essentially flat a year later, but inflation increased to 11 percent.

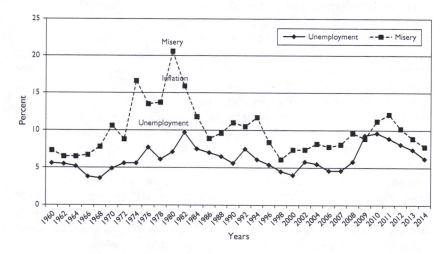

Figure 4.1   Change in the Misery Index, 1960–2014.

Then, the presidential election year of 1980 saw the "**misery index**" (the sum of inflation and unemployment) rise to almost 21 percent—not a good omen for President Carter's reelection prospects (see Figure 4.1).

Although Carter was philosophically inclined to tip the balance on the side of accepting higher inflation to preserve jobs, double-digit inflation was clearly untenable, and it served as a lightning rod for challenger Ronald Reagan in the 1980 presidential campaign. Carter appeared chary about advancing fiscal policy measures to control inflation, worried that they would dampen demand and drive unemployment up even higher—a position that would not sit well with labor-supporting Democrats. With the election just four months away, Carter instead proposed higher federal spending and some last-minute tax cuts. His desire to increase employment prevailed over any concerns he may have had about inflation. Congress took a pass on the proposal in an election year whose outcome looked increasingly clear. The subsequent election of Ronald Reagan paved the way for action. The response took the form of monetary restraint and fiscal stimulus.

Reagan's election, together with the Republicans' newly won control of the U.S. Senate, set the stage for the Fed to pursue a highly restrictive monetary policy. For chairman Paul Volcker and his policy-making colleagues on the Federal Reserve Board, an institution in which banking interests are heavily represented, inflation constituted the most pressing national economic problem. Swift action by the Fed that sent interest rates soaring provided a form of monetary shock therapy that greatly lowered inflation, but at the cost of higher unemployment. By 1982, inflation had fallen to about 6 percent, but unemployment had climbed to 10 percent. By 1986, inflation stood at only 2 percent, a level reminiscent of the early 1960s. Unemployment, over the four years, came down to 7 percent, posing another test of Phillips' thesis.

There is no doubt that the Fed's policy of extremely tight money squeezed excess inflation out of the economy, as it cost 4.7 million net jobs between 1980 and late 1982. But what accounts for the rapid growth in employment that occurred from late 1982 through the early part of 1984, during which the economy added an astounding 7 million net new jobs?[4]

One explanation points to the business cycle at work, from which economic performance rises from trough to peak and then falls back to trough again. The U.S. economy has experienced thirty-four cycles since 1854, averaging one every four and a half years. This explanation suggests that the U.S. economy was due for a period of rapid growth, recovering from its deep trough in 1982.

Another explanation points to fiscal policy. President Reagan came into office with an agenda that included cutting federal taxes, increasing defense spending, slowing the growth in social welfare spending, and reducing federal regulations. In 1981, Congress approved the largest tax reduction up to that time in the nation's history, cutting income tax rates by 25 percent across the board.

At the same time that Reagan set out to reduce the income tax bite, he also worked to boost defense spending significantly. He believed that purchasing power for defense had dropped during the 1970s to a dangerous low, even though it began a modest climb during the late Carter years. For Reagan, the Soviet Union remained a threat that could only be countered by military strength. A turnaround would be costly, and he called for budget increases of 5 percent to 6 percent a year in excess of inflation. Congress responded by increasing real-dollar defense spending by a third during Reagan's first term.

To offset the added costs associated with tax cuts and defense buildup, Reagan sought to decrease domestic spending. His efforts met with mixed success. Although discretionary domestic spending declined in both constant dollars and as a share of overall spending, it continued to rise in current dollars. Means-tested entitlement spending (for which eligible recipients have the legal right to receive benefits) continued to grow in both constant and current dollars.

Considering the above, it is not surprising that the combination of income tax cuts and defense spending gave the economy a decided fiscal stimulus, while adding appreciably to federal budget deficits and mounting federal debt. At face value, the president and Congress appeared to be following the Keynesian formula. Yet Reagan and his key economic policy advisers offered a different formulation of fiscal policy.

As discussed earlier, the persistent "stagflation" of the late 1970s prompted some economists and journalists, influential in Republican circles, to question the adequacy of demand-side Keynesian theory to explain the new economic reality and deal with it effectively. They instead offered a competing model, labeled supply-side economics. For economists Jude Waniski, Arthur Laffer, Robert Mundel, and others, the objective was to rescue the nation from recession and establish the conditions for a sustainable economic recovery without excessive inflation. Instead of spending its way out of recession, as Keynesian theory dictates, "supply-siders" called for the federal government to support public policies that would encourage saving, leading to increased investment.

Recall that Keynes feared saving because it dampened demand. The supply-siders, in contrast, viewed increased saving as providing the investment capital necessary to sustain a long-run recovery in the business cycle. They theorized that the growth in savings would finance the investment that could bring productive capacity in line with rising demand, thus fueling economic growth and keeping inflation in check.

How, though, can government foster increased saving? A major part of the supply-siders' answer in the early 1980s was to cut taxes, giving the largest reductions to those who have the greatest marginal propensity to save—that is, those with the highest incomes. In contrast, as the theory goes, individuals with relatively low incomes are most likely to spend additional after-tax income, not save it, although they would benefit from the greater employment opportunities and higher incomes made possible by the increased investment created by the savings of others (a "trickle down" theory of benefit).

Contrary to the theory's expectations, personal savings declined as a percentage of disposable income during the Reagan presidency.[5] Recipients of the tax cut appear to have spent their higher after-tax income instead of saving it. In fact, it appears that people behaved as Keynesian theory would have predicted. They used the tax cut to spend the nation toward recovery, a stimulus reinforced by large increases in defense spending.

The strong economic growth between 1983 and 1989 gave way to a recession that began in late summer 1990 and continued into the following spring. The economic downturn and sluggish recovery that followed it in the short run caused the federal budget deficit to hit $290 billion at the end of the 1992 fiscal year, despite a slowdown in defense spending that had begun toward the end of the Reagan administration.

The historically high federal budget deficit came to preoccupy both the new administration of President Bill Clinton and the Democrat-controlled Congress. Economic management took a relative backseat to deficit reduction early in the Clinton administration. It is true that President Clinton offered Congress a modest stimulus package shortly after assuming office, but the Congressional Budget Office and most private sector economists warned against its passage as potentially inflationary, since by early 1993 leading economic indicators pointed to an upward swing in the business cycle.

With the Democrats in control of both the presidency and Congress for the first time since the Carter administration, they felt a collective responsibility and political need to deliver on Clinton's campaign pledge to make a sizable dent in what had become a seemingly insurmountable deficit. Their response came through the enactment of a deficit-reduction package of tax increases and budget cuts. The Omnibus Budget Reconciliation Act of 1993 passed without a single Republican vote in either chamber—a dramatic collective gesture of Republicans' political opposition to the package's $240 billion income tax increase. Republican leaders criticized the tax increase as wrongly conceived and ill-timed, threatening the sustainability of economic recovery.

Yet economic growth accelerated throughout the remainder of the decade, with the GDP growing at an average rate of 3.7 percent between 1994 and 1999. Both unemployment and inflation were low by historical standards: For 1999, they stood at 4.2 percent and 2.2 percent, respectively. Moreover, the revenues generated by the combination of higher taxes and economic growth brought the federal budget from deficit to a $237 billion surplus at the end of the 2000 fiscal year.

As the president and Congress focused on deficit reduction and then rode the wave of a rebounding economy (which Republican critics argued took place in spite of the fiscally dampening income tax cuts), the Federal Reserve, following the lead of its chairman Alan Greenspan, remained active in economic management. (Greenspan, first appointed by President Reagan, won reappointment from presidents George H. W. Bush, Bill Clinton, and George W. Bush.) Between August 1990 and August 1993, the Fed, through action by its Federal Open Market Committee, lowered the **Federal Funds Rate** (FFR) from 8 percent to 3 percent, providing robust monetary stimulus. The FFR is the rate at which banks borrow from each other on an overnight basis. Changes in it trigger changes in other lending rates, most importantly in the prime rate—the rate that thrift institutions charge their best customers.

As the economy began to take off, the Fed reversed course and applied the monetary brake in preemptive strikes against inflation. In the short period between early 1994 and early 1995, the Fed hiked interest rates seven times. Thereafter, it kept interest rates fairly constant until 2000, but notched them up modestly in mid-2000 to keep inflation in check.

Signs of an ensuing economic slowdown, leading to recession in 2001, prompted the Feds to reduce the FFR thirteen times between January 1, 2001, and June 25, 2003. During that period the rate fell from 6.5 percent to 1.0 percent, as the Fed injected the greatest monetary stimulus in its history.

Under Greenspan's urging, the Fed began its series of interest rate reductions just days before George W. Bush assumed the presidency. The presidential campaign of 2000 made it clear that both Democratic and Republican Party nominees would pursue a sizable tax cut if elected. Both candidates debated what should be done with a federal budget surplus then projected to exceed $4.5 trillion between the 2001 and 2010 fiscal years—a figure that was revised markedly downward in the months to come. Bush championed a $1.3 trillion tax-reduction package, while his Democratic opponent Al Gore called for net tax cuts of $480 billion. The Republican-controlled Congress threw its support behind the more generous proposal, upping the ante.

The tax law passed by Congress and signed into law by President Bush on June 7, 2001 would cut taxes by $1.35 trillion through December 31, 2010. Reductions in income tax rates would account for about $875 billion of the total, while a phase-out of estate and gift taxes would add another $138 billion. The remainder would come from changes in income tax deductions favoring married couples, child tax credits, pension and IRA liberalization, and favorable tax treatment for educational expenses.

Bush justified the tax cut largely on two grounds: ideology and economic theory. First, he argued that taxpayers deserve to get back money they contributed to the federal surplus because it is their money in the first place and they know best how to spend it. The president grounded his stance on the value of individual freedom; as he posited in a 2001 speech,

> Tax relief expands individual freedom. The money we return, or don't take in the first place, can be saved for a child's education, spent on family needs, invested in a home or in a business or a mutual fund or used to reduce personal debt. We recognize loud and clear the surplus is not the government's money. The surplus is the people's money and we ought to trust them to spend their own money.[6]

Bush's reference to the money that "we . . . don't take in the first place" is highly significant. For Bush, tax cuts are warranted on the principle of constraining the transfer of resources from private hands to government's coffers. This, in part, helps to explain why the president pushed for greater tax cuts even after the surplus turned into deficit.

Second, Bush turned to economic theory in support of tax reductions. Like Reagan before him, he espoused a supply-side approach to fiscal policy. He saw sustained economic growth coming from increased investment, and viewed tax cuts as the vehicle to generate the increased saving that becomes investment. Thus it was consistent for Bush, as it was for Reagan, to structure a tax-cut initiative that gives the greatest benefits to those with the highest propensity to save—in other words, those with high incomes. It should not be surprising that an analysis by the Brookings Institution suggests that the top 5 percent of income-earning households would get about 46 percent of tax savings over the ten-year period once the tax provisions were fully in effect.[7] In terms of equity, however, that distributional share does not appear to be out of line, since the top 5 percent also contribute over half of federal individual income tax revenues.[8]

With the economy having fallen into recession during the first three-quarters of the 2001 calendar year, and with economic recovery in the ensuing years somewhat slower than expected, President Bush successfully pressed Congress to reduce individual income tax rates further and move up the dates on which rate reductions would take effect, increase the per-child tax credit, increase the standard deduction for married couples filing jointly (eliminate the "marriage penalty"), and lower the maximum tax rate applied to dividends and long-term capital gains. These changes, among others—approved by Congress in June 2003—would cost the U.S. Treasury another $350 billion in forgone revenues over a ten-year period.

Although ideology continued to underlie Bush's enthusiasm for additional tax cuts, he also viewed them as good medicine to spur faster economic growth and create jobs. With employment continuing to fall in late 2002 and the first half of 2003, and with critics branding the recovery as "jobless," the president looked to broadened and speedier tax reductions as a further economic shot in the arm.

Economic recovery picked up in the second half of 2003 and grew strongly, adding 7.3 million net jobs by the end of 2006, as the GDP averaged a respectable real growth rate of 3.5 percent between 2004 and 2006.[9] Yet, moving into 2007, leading economic indicators began pointing to a coming economic slowdown, one exacerbated by the surging price of oil. Real growth in GDP fell to 1.9 percent in 2007 and slid into an extended deep recession that began in December 2007 and continued through June 2009, making it the longest recession since the Great Depression. During this period, GDP declined by 4.1 percent, investment fell by 23.4 percent, and non-farm employment dipped by 5.4 percent. Notably, monthly job losses averaged 712,000 from October 2008 through March 2009, the greatest six-month period of lost jobs since 1945, at the end of World War II.[10] Moreover, the median net worth of American families dropped by nearly 40 percent between 2007 and 2010.

Just as business enterprises and households felt the economic consequences of the Great Recession, so did the federal government. The severe drop in economic demand translated into a sharp decline in federal revenues, which fell from 17.9 percent of GDP in fiscal year (FY) 2007 to 14.6 percent in FY 2009. During the same period, recession-sensitive automatic stabilizers, combined with a wave of federal policy initiatives to spur economic demand (which will be discussed below), pushed up federal spending from 19.0 percent of GDP in FY 2007 to 24.4 percent in FY 2009, a post-World War II high. This combination of markedly falling revenues and accelerated spending had the expected effect of driving up the federal budget deficit. Most shocking was the magnitude and the speed of the deficit increase, jumping from $160 billion in FY 2007 to a whopping $1.4 trillion just two fiscal years later.[11]

The Great Recession and No Holds Barred Economic Stimulus and Government Intervention

How did the United States get into this economic mess? How did its economy become so vulnerable to this historic slump? The roots lie in what on the surface looked like good news: a housing boom that broadly supported job growth in housing construction, construction-related manufacturing, real estate sales, and mortgage finance. More and more new home owners were seemingly getting their part of the American dream, and employment got a welcomed boost from housing-related sectors. And as housing values rose, home owners felt more economically secure and more willing to draw out some of their increased mortgage equity to finance other big-ticket item consumer purchases, thus contributing to economic growth. Speculators jumped in, however, buying homes that they never intended to occupy, hoping to "flip" their investments and capitalize on rapidly rising home prices. At the peak of the housing bubble in early 2006, speculative buying accounted for over one-quarter of all housing sales.[12]

A combination of historically low interest rates and liberalized lending practices inflated the growing housing bubble. Lenders increasingly offered alternative financing mechanisms, including adjustable-rate mortgages (ARMs) and interest-only mortgages. The latter especially appealed to those who looked to cash in their capital gains generated by rising prices instead of building principal over the long run. Lenders relaxed traditional lending standards, greatly reducing or eliminating down payments, as well as relaxing income and asset standards for loan qualification. This weakening of standards ushered in a wave of so-called subprime borrowing. Subprime mortgages rose from approximately 7 percent of mortgage originations in 2002 to almost a quarter in 2006.[13] Overall mortgage indebtedness nearly doubled, from $5.3 trillion in 2001 to $10.5 trillion in 2007.[14]

Rising housing prices became the glue that united the interests of those contributing to bubble growth. Borrowers flocked to buy properties before prices rose further, so they would not miss out on the promise of sizable capital gains. Lenders viewed rising prices as a security blanket of sorts, protecting them from potential losses that could otherwise come from delinquent mortgage payments from marginally qualified borrowers. The George W. Bush administration encouraged the growth of an "ownership society," and agencies such as the Federal Housing Administration (FHA), the Federal National Mortgage Association (Fannie Mae), and the Federal Home Loan Mortgage Corporation (Freddie Mac) lent their support to broadening home ownership. Investors, too, got on the bandwagon. Payments from the streams of income generated by mortgage growth became compelling to institutional investors, and **securitization** became the investment vehicle of choice. Securitization also became the vehicle to spread financial risk.

Under traditional lending arrangements, risk was held by the lender. The lending bank held the risk of payment default, although it could sell the mortgages it held to other financial institutions, thereby transferring risk to those buyers. In either case, the holders of the mortgage would be stuck with them, providing a strong incentive to make sound loans. Securitization, in comparison, spread risk widely. With securitization, lending institutions transferred mortgages to a "special purpose entity," which pooled them into so-called collateralized mortgage obligations (CMOs), a form of collateralized debt obligations (CDOs) that could be bought by investors, most typically by large institutional investors. Recognizing that mortgages can carry different levels of risk based on the credit worthiness of the borrowers, the issuing institutions sorted the CMOs into different portfolios of risk and related return, offering purchasers different combinations of risk and reward. It became nearly impossible to tie the mortgages parceled into CMOs back to the original lender. Spreading did not stop there. Big investors in CMOs hedged their bets by buying insurance against default, further shifting risk to large insurance companies.

The para-public agencies, Fannie Mae and Freddie Mac, also got in on the act. Congress created them to add liquidity to real estate markets by purchasing mortgages from lending institutions, thus expanding the capital available to be lent to other borrowers, with an emphasis on increasing the ability of lower income home buyers to get home loans. Both Fannie and Freddie entered the market of securitized mortgage debt, offering CMOs composed of mortgages they purchased. In addition to their mandate to add liquidity to housing markets, both agencies played a major role in guaranteeing mortgages against default, guaranteeing about half of the country's mortgages.[15] Given their mission to enlarge the pool of resources available to be lent to less credit-worthy Americans, both agencies took on added financial risk by providing such guarantees.

The buyers of CMOs tended to be large financial investors, both domestic and international. They included commercial and investment banks as well as public and private pension funds. And in an environment of expanding home sales and rising prices, investors readily added CMOs to their portfolios, enjoying the attractive financial returns. Institutional investors also used them as collateral for other financial transactions. Moreover, credit rating institutions, such as Moody's Investors, Standard and Poor's, and Fitch Ratings, readily gave their stamp of approval to investment in CMOs, contributing to a sense of security. That complacency, however, would soon be displaced by a sense of looming crisis. The real estate bubble was about to burst.

Home prices hit their zenith in April 2006, rising nationally by about 80 percent between 2001 and 2006. Yet that already high rate of increase grew to 150 percent for just four states combined: Arizona, California, Florida, and Nevada. The stage was set for the price bubble to pop, and pop it did. By 2009 home prices had fallen nationally by about a quarter, and by about 40 percent in those four sunbelt states.[16] Cascading prices greatly depressed home building. Whereas single-family housing starts had continued their upward march, reaching a peak of 1.8 million in 2006, they fell drastically to about 400,000 by 2009. At least in the short run, new housing no longer looked to be the ticket to rapid financial gain.[17]

The cash cow for both heavily leveraged mortgage payers and investors in mortgage-backed securities disappeared. Buyers who had bought their homes as prices rose sharply found themselves with mortgage debt that exceeded their home's value. Faced with "negative equity," many home owners stopped making mortgage payments. Those buyers who financed their home using an adjustable-rate or interest-only mortgage, and faced interest rate increases, had the greatest incentive to walk away from their payment obligations.

The financial market was awash with collateralized debt. As the underlying home prices slid downhill, the market value of CMOs fell sharply. So did their value as collateral. Increasingly banks questioned the riskiness of assets they had previously accepted regularly as collateral for loans, and demanded increased collateral to cover them. Financial institutions which had significantly added CMOs to their own portfolios found themselves with much weakened balance sheets, typically unable to meet the demands for higher collateral. The Financial Crisis Inquiry Commission aptly summed up the seeds of crisis:

> Trillions of dollars in risky mortgage-related securities were packaged, repackaged, and sold to investors around the world. When the bubble burst, hundreds of billions of dollars in losses in mortgages and mortgage-related securities shook markets as well as financial Institutions that had significant exposures to those markets and had borrowed heavily against them. This happened not just in the United States but around the world.[18]

It was not long before the financial system seized up and trading nearly ground to a halt. Not only did many financial obligations go unmet, but the balance sheets of large financial institutions turned decidedly negative. Citigroup and Merrill Lynch, with their large holdings of CMOs, were particularly hard hit, writing down the value of their holdings by $24 billion and $25 billion, respectively, by the end of 2007.[19] In that year several major lenders filed for Chapter 11 bankruptcy protection, prominently including New Century Financial, American Home Mortgage, and Ameriquest. All three were big players in subprime loans. Conditions worsened in 2008, and the realistic threat of financial failure spread. In January, Bank of America purchased Countrywide Financial, then the national leader in the volume of mortgages underwritten, saving it from bankruptcy. Bear Stearns, America's third largest investment bank, was also headed toward bankruptcy in early 2008 had JP Morgan Chase not purchased it in March, backed by $29 billion in financing provided by the Federal Reserve Bank of New York to seal the deal. Bank of America went on in September to purchase the struggling Merrill Lynch, keeping it from going under, as it did for Countrywide Financial. One day later, Lehman Brothers, the nation's fourth biggest investment bank, filed for bankruptcy protection after the Federal Reserve Bank of New York refused to extend it a saving line of credit and no prospective purchaser could be found without the Fed's intervention. The fact that Lehman was allowed to fail sent shockwaves throughout the financial community both in the United States and abroad.[20]

With falling values of CMOs, it is not surprising that the financial crisis spread rapidly to the insurance industry, which sold protection against default on the ubiquitous mortgage-backed investments. The world's largest insurance company, American International Group (AIG), faced insolvency, with claims that far exceeded its capacity to honor them. Bankruptcy appeared imminent, but the Federal Reserve once again intervened—this time right on the heels of its refusal to help Lehman Brothers—extending the insurer $85 billion in credit in exchange for a 79.9 percent stake in the company. In effect, the Fed became the largest owner of AIG. This intervention to come to the aid of an insurance company represented a major departure from Fed policy, yet it was done to protect the global financial system from unraveling, given AIG's heavy penetration worldwide. If AIG had failed and the multitude of claims had gone unmet, a contagion of widespread financial failure would have followed.

In addition to the Fed's extraordinary interventions chronicled above, it employed traditional monetary policy by dropping the key short-term interest rate, the Federal Funds Rate (FFR), to near zero (floating between zero and 0.25 percent). The FFR is the rate of interest banks can charge one another for overnight loans and in turn affects the rates charged for other short-term loans. With the FFR at near zero, the Fed found itself with negligible room to use traditional monetary policy to stimulate demand. In response, beginning in September 2012 it took a new tack of pumping liquidity into financial markets by massive purchases of bonds and other asset-based financial securities, a tactic that came to be known as quantitative easing. That policy continued through 2014, and by year's end the Fed held a record $4 trillion in marketable assets, including U.S. Treasury securities.

Congress got in on the act as well, passing the Emergency Economic Stabilization Act on October 3, 2008 upon the strong urging of both Treasury Secretary Henry Paulson and Federal Reserve Chair Ben Bernanke. The act created the Troubled Asset Relief Program, better known as TARP. It authorized the Treasury Secretary to spend up to $700 billion to purchase mortgage-backed securities from teetering banks and to provide an infusion of cash to shore up their financial balance sheets. The Bush administration acted quickly on the latter initiative, providing $125 billion to the nation's nine largest banks in exchange for a corresponding share of stock equity in them. Although not all recipients felt a pressing need for these funds, they all accepted them under mounting pressure from the administration and the Fed. Shortly thereafter, in December, TARP funds were extended to keep two major auto makers, Chrysler and General Motors, financially afloat. In exchange for the $62 billion cash infusion, the federal government received shares of stock in the two corporations, making the federal government a major shareholder. It later fell to the Obama administration to use TARP funds to purchase distressed asset-based securities in the open market.

With the economy still in recession as the Obama administration took office, President Obama turned to more conventional fiscal policy, aimed at injecting demand into the flagging economy. His initiatives, and Congress's response to them, are covered later in the following discussion.

Presidential–Congressional Relations in Fiscal Policy Making

Presidents are much better positioned to influence fiscal policy than monetary policy. As illustrated earlier, presidents set the fiscal policy agenda through their recommendations on taxing and spending. The Council of Economic Advisers (CEA) and the Office of Management and Budget (OMB) are the two major institutions within the White House that assist the president to carry out his leadership role in fiscal policy making. Of the two, the CEA operates at the broadest macro level. Its job is to apprise the president of the state of the U.S. economy and to offer advice about what measures can be taken to improve the nation's economic performance. In addition to its formal responsibility to prepare the president's annual economic report to the nation, the three-member council, and particularly its chair, advises the president on how the economy works, helping the president to sort out complicated economic relationships and be able to handle them in public discourse. Council members also assist in the preparation of presidential speeches on economic matters and help prepare the president for press conferences at which questions on the economy can be expected.

Council members have been drawn primarily from academe, serving a few years in office and then returning to their university appointments. Presidents appoint members for their economic expertise, yet in doing so they look for candidates who share their views on the proper role of government in the economy. However, the CEA is not divorced from politics of partisanship.[21] Members and top-level staff assistants realize that they have a duty to give the president sound analysis drawn from their academic and professional expertise; at the same time, they are not disinterested in the president's political fortunes. They share an interest in making the president look as good as possible in the public arena. That combination can translate, on the one hand, into offering frank assessments of the condition of the economy and how the administration's economic policies are working and, on the other, into putting a positive gloss on the administration's accomplishments. A careful reading of annual economic reports shows their public relations value to the president.

Compared to the CEA, the OMB is the operational arm of presidential fiscal policy. Fiscal policy direction must be translated into concrete taxing and spending choices, decisions that are influenced by the OMB director and top administrators, but also by other key White House advisers. They include presidential assistants for national security and domestic policy, along with the president's chief of staff. Among the president's closest White House advisers, the chief of staff generally exercises the broadest reach across policy areas and is best positioned to mix political counsel with policy advice. In George W. Bush's administration, however, that role went to Karl Rove, whose job it is to advance the president's policy agenda in a way that advances the president's political fortunes.

In addition to White House advisers, the president is able to tap the expertise and counsel of cabinet agency heads. Moreover, each cabinet department characteristically has an undersecretary or assistant secretary responsible for policy development and analysis. But since presidents realize that agency heads normally function as advocates of their programs and administrative turf, the job of screening counsel and resource requests and reconciling differences and conflicts falls to White House advisers. On budgetary matters, for example, the OMB director may suggest that a cabinet secretary does not fully understand the inter-program and interagency effects of a given budgetary request or the overall fiscal constraints under which the executive budget is formulated.

Although the U.S. Constitution gives Congress the power to tax and spend, Congress is not well situated to set the nation's fiscal policy agenda. That continues to be true even after reform of the federal budgetary process that aspired to bring greater coherence and coordination to congressional budgeting (which is discussed briefly below and in depth in chapter 6). But it is true now for a different reason than it was before reform.

Before the reform of the federal budgetary process in 1974, Congress possessed little institutionalized ability to substitute its collective vision of national fiscal policy and budgetary priorities for that of the president. Congressional decisions on taxing and spending were decentralized and fragmented, built on a foundation of "contained specialization."[22] Congressional subcommittee and committee leaders enjoyed considerable autonomy in their decision making. No plan of congressional action informed committee choices. Congress's imprint on taxing and spending became the production of numerous and often discrete unconnected choices. In a manner of speaking, the finished quilt of decision making was a product of its many individual squares.

While Congress lacked a collectively endorsed blueprint for its taxing and spending actions, entitlement spending grew rapidly—without Congress needing to make annual decisions on appropriations. Entitlements are requirements in federal law, applied to certain programs (such as social security, Medicare, and Medicaid), that individuals who meet eligibility requirements for federal assistance receive cash benefits or services regardless of the cost. With this automatic spending feature, largely a creation of Great Society legislation, entitlement spending grew three times faster than discretionary spending (that is, that part of the federal budget for which Congress is required to enact annual appropriations to finance federal spending) between 1960 and 1974 alone.[23] Spending seemed to be out of control, and Congress appeared to have no agreed-upon strategy to deal with it.

Congress turned to budgetary reform to bring coherence to congressional budget making and to provide a means of controlling the rapid growth of spending. Facing a president greatly weakened by the Watergate scandal, Congress passed the ambitious Congressional Budget and Impoundment Control Act of 1974 by overwhelming margins of 80 to 0 in the U.S. Senate and 401 to 6 in the U.S. House of Representatives. Members hailed the act as "a historic legislative development," providing a "new process by which Congress determines national spending priorities."[24] Notably, Congress was to set these priorities within the backdrop of its own fiscal policy directions on taxing and spending, not those of the president's administration. It would be assisted in this effort through the creation of new budget committees in both the House and Senate and by staff assistants in the newly created Congressional Budget Office (CBO). Congressional leaders conceived of the CBO as Congress's own alternative to the White House's CEA and OMB.

The reform legislation also created two procedural devices to guide congressional decision making: the **concurrent budget resolution** and **reconciliation**. The first embodies Congress's fiscal game plan for the legislative session, establishing aggregate-level ceilings on budget authority and outlays (actual expenditures) and projecting revenues to be available based on forecasts by CBO and the resolution's assumptions about tax law, including planned changes in current law. Comparing planned expenditures and anticipated revenues, the resolution yields a projected level of deficit or surplus. Macro choices precede micro choices.

Following passage of the concurrent resolution (which must be passed in identical form by both chambers but does not require the president's approval), each new budget committee parcels out budget authority and outlay targets to its chamber's other committees to guide them in their budgetary decision making. When the resolution calls for changes in entitlements, the budget committees instruct the committees having jurisdiction over the entitlement programs in question to approve legislation that would implement the resolution's provisions. Similarly, the tax writing committees—the House Ways and Means Committee and the Senate Finance Committee—are charged with acting on the tax changes called for in the resolution.

Working within the aggregate ceilings and instructions contained in the budget resolution, the committees exercise their respective discretion in reporting authorizations, appropriations, and changes in tax law. Yet the authors of reform realized that conditions can change from the passage of the concurrent resolution to action by the committees, and that committees may feel compelled to reflect those changes in their decisions. They also appreciated that not all committees would be politically able to muster the support of their members to comply fully with the resolution's provisions. If committees failed to comply, the budget committees, under direction from legislative leaders, could then roll the changes needed for compliance into a single piece of legislation termed a reconciliation bill, which would then be reported to the floor for a single vote, bypassing the recalcitrant committees. Reconciliation was intended to give legislative leaders ultimate leverage in bringing congressional actions in line with Congress's original blueprint.

In practice, the reformed process did not work in the way its authors intended. Reconciliation soon ceased to function as a procedural tool internal to Congress, one that the legislative branch uses to put the final touches on its own fiscal alternative to that of the president. Instead, presidents since Reagan have used reconciliation as an eleventh-hour device to bring congressional budgetary decisions closer in line with presidential priorities, in a sense co-opting a process designed to serve Congress's own decision-making needs.

David Stockman, President Reagan's first OMB director, set the precedent for using Congress's reconciliation process to advance an administration's policy goals. Drawing upon the support of the Republican majority in the Senate and a coalition of Republicans and conservative Democrats (the so-called blue-dog Democrats) in the House, Stockman and his White House colleagues hurriedly drafted omnibus reconciliation legislation that contained major changes in entitlements that the administration wanted, late in the 1981 session.

Presidential administrations that followed Reagan's continued the practice of using reconciliation as the vehicle of choice for putting the president's imprint on major deficit-reduction and tax-cutting packages. Deficit reduction was the focal point of the Omnibus Budget Reconciliation Acts of 1990 and 1993, enacted during the elder Bush and Clinton administrations, respectively. George W. Bush, by comparison, employed reconciliation as his instrument for attaining large tax cuts. The first use, resulting in the Economic Growth and Tax Reform Reconciliation Act of 2001, appeared primarily motivated by the president's ideological commitment to return to the taxpayers a good part of the federal budget surplus existing at the time. As the economy quickly worsened, fell into recession, and then went through an initially slow recovery, the Bush administration, in urging further cuts and the speeding up of existing ones, shifted its emphasis to the fiscal policy effects of tax reduction. As the administration argued in true supply-side fashion, the provisions in the Jobs and Growth Reconciliation Act of 2003 would help to accelerate and sustain economic growth, as they fostered investment that would raise the nation's potential GDP. They would also offer further evidence of the administration's commitment to tax relief.

Toward the end of President Bush's second term, economic growth gave way to recession, leading to depths not encountered since the Great Depression. Although monetary policy, including the Federal Reserve's innovative departures from its traditional policy tools, assumed most of the burden to ward off economic collapse and foster increased demand, economic policy makers turned to fiscal policy as well. The Bush administration had used TARP funds to help stabilize financial markets and keep General Motors and Chrysler operating during their financial reorganizations; it was the Obama administration that used fiscal policy to stimulate economic growth. President-elect Obama and his economic advisers worked with the leadership of the Democrat-controlled House and Senate to shape legislation that would use both spending increases and tax relief to stimulate economic growth. The major components of the stimulus package, enacted as the American Recovery and Reinvestment Act of 2009 and passed without a single Republican vote, included $144 billion in increased federal aid to the states, to reduce employee layoffs and service cuts that would otherwise be required under state requirements to balance their budgets. Another $144 billion went to infrastructural improvements aimed at buttressing construction-related employment. Authorized tax cuts and credits added $288 billion to the package's total cost of $787 billion, an amount criticized by liberal economists as not nearly enough to provide the needed stimulus. One prominent critic, Nobel prize-winning economist Paul Krugman, put it this way at the time:

> While Mr. Obama got more or less what he asked for, he almost certainly didn't ask for enough. We're probably facing the worst slump since the Great Depression. The Congressional Budget Office, not usually given to hyperbole, predicts that over the next three years there will be a $2.9 billion gap between what the economy could produce and what it will actually produce. And $800 billion, while it sounds like a lot of money, isn't nearly enough to bridge that chasm.[25]

The Obama administration and Congress faced a pressing fiscal dilemma in 2010, when at year's end the so-called Bush tax cuts were scheduled to expire. If Congress allowed the tax cuts to expire, taxpayers would face considerably higher tax bills—not the fiscal recipe to improve upon, or even sustain, what was tepid economic growth. In response, the lame-duck Congress, with Democrats still in the majority in both chambers, passed the Tax Relief, Unemployment Insurance Reauthorization, and Job Creation Act of 2010. It included a two-year extension of the Bush tax cuts for all taxpayers, even though the president preferred ending the cuts for those making over $250,000 a year. The act also extended unemployment insurance benefits for thirteen months, and provided a temporary reduction from 6.2 percent to 4.2 percent in employees' share of the social security payroll tax.

The 2010 mid-term election gave Republicans control of the House, and reduced the Democrats' majority in the Senate. That shift, coupled with an increase in fiscally conservative Tea Party membership, refocused Congress's sights on the federal budget deficit, which had grown sharply as a result of reduced revenues and increased spending, reaching $1.3 trillion at the end of FY 2011. Moreover, the need to raise the nation's debt ceiling by late summer 2011 gave Republicans, joined by fiscally conservative Democrats, a lever to push for deficit reduction in return for their support of an increase in the debt ceiling. The result, the Budget Control Act of 2011, committed Congress to $917 billion in cuts over ten years—cuts that would be made across the board if Congress could not decide how to prioritize them. Congress couldn't, and the cuts began to be implemented.

Fiscal stimulus gave way to deficit reduction. Prior stimulus, from both monetary and fiscal policy, had helped the economy reverse its trajectory, giving the business cycle a decided push in the upward direction. With the United States in 2015 experiencing decent GDP growth, falling unemployment, and rising equity markets, the proverbial economic corner appears to have been turned, as the Great Recession slides into history.

The Federal Reserve and Traditional Monetary Policy Making

Unlike fiscal policy, for which Congress exercises its constitutional power to tax and spend (although the president sets the national agenda), Congress has vested the authority for monetary policy in an independent agency, the Federal Reserve. The Fed was created by Congress in 1913 and is governed by a seven-member board, with its members appointed by the president for staggered fourteen-year terms, subject to confirmation by the Senate. The Board of Governors is augmented in its policy-making functions by the presidents of the twelve Federal Reserve banks, who are appointed by regional governing boards, subject to approval by the Board of Governors (see Figure 4.2). The twelve Federal Reserve banks and their twenty-five branches carry out a variety of financial and regulatory functions, including serving as a depository for the banks in their district, distributing the nation's currency and coin, operating a nationwide payments system (involving interbank check clearing), and regulating member banks and bank holding companies. Federal Reserve banks also serve as fiscal agents of the U.S. government, performing several

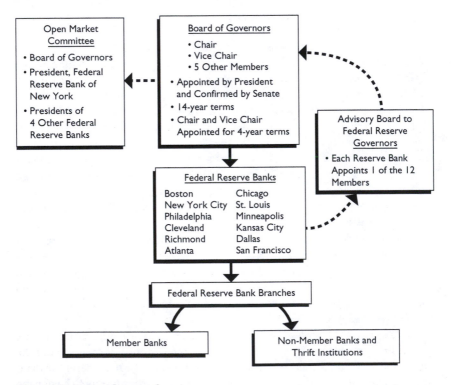

Figure 4.2 Federal Reserve System.

services for the Department of the Treasury that include maintaining the Treasury's funds account; clearing Treasury checks; and conducting auctions of Treasury securities as well as issuing, servicing, and redeeming them.[26]

The presidents of the Federal Reserve banks, in addition to providing executive leadership for these functions, have representation on the highly important Federal Open Market Committee (FOMC). The FOMC is composed of the seven members of the Board of Governors and five of the twelve Federal Reserve bank presidents. The president of the Federal Reserve Bank of New York is a permanent member, and the four other presidents serve rotating one-year terms. As noted earlier, the FOMC functions as the Federal Reserve's principal monetary policy maker, whose actions affect the interest rates charged by financial institutions in the United States. It does so by buying and selling federal securities on the open market in amounts calculated to raise or lower interest rates by a desired percentage. When the Domestic Trading Desk at the Federal Reserve Bank of New York sells Treasury securities through about three dozen large-volume dealers to the highest bidding banks and other financial institutions, it draws reserves from the banking system, thus shrinking the availability of lendable funds. Conversely, when it buys government securities at the lowest price the market will bear, it pays for them by adding reserves to the banking system, thus increasing the capacity of banks and other depository institutions to make loans. Interest rates rise as reserves shrink, following the law of supply and demand. They fall as reserves expand.

The committee's open market operations target the FFR, the rate at which depository institutions charge one another for overnight loans. Overnight borrowing allows the borrowing institution to acquire resources beyond its existing reserves to meet the immediate needs of its customers while still meeting reserve requirements (the percentage of deposits that depository institutions must keep in cash or as non–interest bearing balances in Federal Reserve banks). When the FOMC acts to raise or lower the FFR, other short-term interest rates tend to rise or fall accordingly, including the prime rate—the rate that lending institutions charge their best commercial customers.

Although the FOMC acts by majority vote, its chairman exercises disproportionate influence over its decisions. The committee's decisions are typically unanimous or nearly unanimous. There were no more than two dissenting votes on any FOMC monetary policy vote under Greenspan since 1992,[27] and if opponents to the chairman's policy recommendations were to gain enough support to produce close and contentious votes, the chairman would likely step down from office. That prospect was never an issue during Greenspan's tenure.

Greenspan's long service as chairman ended on January 31, 2006, as the economy consolidated a period of strong economic growth. During his tenure, Chairman Greenspan became the personification of the Federal Reserve Board and the international model of the successful central bank leader. Under his watch, the economy survived the October 1987 stock market crash, the comparatively mild recessions in 1990–91 and 2001, the 9/11 terrorist attacks on New York City's World Trade Center, and a sharp decline in equity prices during 2000 and 2001.

Greenspan's successor, Ben Bernanke, assumed the Fed chairmanship at a time of substantial job growth, low unemployment, high worker productivity, and low core inflation. That tranquil economic climate was soon to change, however, as a national bubble in home prices was about to burst. Setting four consecutive records for home sales from 2000 through 2004 before leveling off in 2005, the growing demand for housing pushed up prices dramatically.[28] Not wanting to be left on the outside looking in, buyers rushed to get into the market, lured by what they thought was the promise of continued price increases. Speculators did their part to drive up prices, since one-quarter of the sales nationally went to investors who did not intend to occupy their newly acquired properties.[29] Lenders, for their part, were more than willing to finance this home-buying spree, as they lowered their standards for borrower qualification and increasingly offered mortgage options including interest-only loans and adjustable-rate mortgages.

But, as noted earlier in the chapter, the bubble in demand-driven price increases did indeed pop. Prices fell just as holders of the new mortgage instruments confronted rising interest rates. Marginally qualified or unqualified borrowers became delinquent in their mortgage payments, or defaulted, and increasingly faced foreclosure. Borrowers found themselves with mortgage obligations that exceeded the value of their dwelling. Lenders lost expected cash flow and assumed ownership of the housing market's growing number of "white elephants."

The economic chaos entrapped investors, as well—a fact that ironically minimized the economic impact on commercial banks and other mortgage lenders. Most originators of mortgage loans sold them to other parties, commonly investment banks, rather than holding and servicing them. The investment banks packaged the acquired mortgages into so-called collateralized debt obligations (CDOs) and marketed them to investors, who looked to earn a favorable rate of return on their investment. However, with falling home values and growing delinquencies and defaults, the value of these securitized investments fell. Not only did investors lose money, but investment banks held CDOs whose market value fell and could be liquidated only at a sizable discount. In this environment, lenders became much more conservative in their lending practices, many reverting to traditional criteria for borrower qualification. Banks also became more circumspect in their willingness to loan money to other banks. Investment banks, saddled with write-downs of unpaid debt obligations, soon became cash-strapped, as investors proved less willing to inject new cash to increase liquidity.

In response to these snowballing conditions, the FOMC, under Bernanke's leadership, lowered the FFR from its June 29, 2006 high of 6.25 percent to 0.25 percent on December 16, 2008. These actions in 2008 alone included two reductions of three-quarters of a percentage point, and three others of one-half of a percentage point each.

Following Chairman Bernanke's lead, the governors of the Federal Reserve Board applied another dose of monetary medicine, permitting investment banks to borrow directly from the Fed at its established discount rate, the same rate of interest charged to commercial banks. The Fed allowed investment banks to provide investment-grade securities and CDOs as collateral behind the loans. From Bernanke's perspective, these combined actions represented not a bailout of the banks, but protection against economy-wide fallout. He saw increased liquidity as a necessary but temporary ingredient in stemming the economic contagion.

As the above discussion illustrates, Congress has given the Fed a great deal of freedom in making monetary policy. Although Congress created the statutory authority under which the Federal Reserve operates, and therefore can change it, federal law shields Fed policy makers from direct control by the president or Congress. The president appoints members of the Federal Reserve Board, but the length and staggered nature of their terms make it difficult for a president to appoint a majority of board members, even though high member turnover can enable a two-term president to do so. Moreover, the addition of Federal Reserve bank presidents to the FOMC, joining presidential appointees, further distances the president from the committee.

The fact of institutional separation should not lead to the conclusion that the president lacks influence on monetary policy. The president's "bully pulpit" is his greatest non-legal resource. Presidential statements garner attention, and when presidents highlight their visibility, political actors and the media pay attention to both the message and the political forces behind it. Federal Reserve chairs want presidential support for their boards' policies and do not relish presidential criticism. That does not mean, however, that the Fed does whatever the president wants. Nevertheless, a rather weak pattern of political responsiveness does appear to exist, characterized by increased monetary stimulation prior to a presidential election, followed by a more restrictive policy to dampen inflationary tendencies after the election.[30] Still, economic conditions appear to exercise the greatest influence on the Fed's willingness to change interest rates.

Recent history paints a mixed picture of influences on monetary policy. The 1980 election year does indeed provide support to the so-called political business cycle. Two months after he took over as chairman, Paul Volcker pledged to Congress that the Federal Reserve would significantly raise interest rates as a primary weapon against inflation, which had hit double-digit proportions in 1980. Yet the FOMC actually lowered the FFR by 5 percentage points between April and October of 1980, giving credence to those who labeled the FOMC as the "Committee to Reelect the President."[31]

As the election neared, President Jimmy Carter's Republican challenger, Ronald Reagan, continued to hit inflation hard as a major campaign issue.

The 1980 election not only gave Reagan a landslide victory but also swept conservatives into Congress, giving Republicans control of the Senate for the first time since the years of President Dwight D. Eisenhower. Political support existed for a more restrictive monetary policy, a mood that the inflation-weary Federal Reserve Board quickly embraced in the months immediately following the election. The FOMC hiked the FFR by over 6 percentage points between October 1980 and January 1981 alone. The Fed's implementation of monetary shock therapy was under way with a vengeance.

Nearly a decade later, Richard Darman and Nicholas Brady, George H.W. Bush's OMB director and Treasury secretary, respectively, took issue publicly with Greenspan's unwillingness to urge the FOMC to lower interest rates and stimulate recovery from the recession of the early 1990s. Greenspan, however, voiced his determination to stay the course and support measured rate reductions that would keep inflation in check as the economy grew out of its economic trough—an illustration at odds with the political business cycle thesis.

The experience of the 1996 and 2000 presidential election years also fails to support the thesis. In the months preceding the 1996 election the FOMC kept the FFR pretty much stable, and the committee acted to increase rates in the months leading up to the election of 2000, responding to continued strong economic growth. Although the FOMC sharply decreased the FFR in the face of the 2001 recession and the following slow economic recovery, it turned around and raised the rate during the period of accelerated economic growth that preceded the 2004 presidential election. With economic recovery strongly under way, the Bush administration voiced no concerns about the gradual tightening. Thus it appears that economic conditions, not presidential politics, have exercised the greatest influence on Greenspan-led monetary policy making.

Both the George W. Bush and the Obama administrations collaborated closely with the Federal Reserve toward containing the contagion of the Great Recession. The administrations' Treasury secretaries and Fed officials jointly urged the cooperation of top bank executives in improving banks' financial positions, and they worked in concert to elicit congressional support for economic stimulus. Chairman Bernanke became a fixture at congressional hearings.

Outside of congressional calls for the Fed to pursue a certain policy tack desired by congressional leadership, Federal law limits Congress's oversight authority. Unlike most federal agencies, the Federal Reserve System does not rely on congressional appropriations for its financial support. Instead, it gets its revenue from three primary sources: (1) the interest it earns on U.S. securities held in its accounts; (2) the fees charged for its services to financial institutions; and (3) the interest paid by depository institutions that borrow directly from Federal Reserve banks. This last source (referred to as discount borrowing), once a sizable share of revenue, has dwindled over time as financial institutions have turned to other financial institutions—not to the Fed—for loans. Fed policy has reinforced that inclination. The Fed requires that would-be borrowers exhaust alternatives in the private sector before borrowing from a Federal Reserve bank, and it charges a higher interest rate for discount borrowing than can be obtained for an overnight commercial loan.

This financial independence from Congress removes the regularized oversight of the annual appropriations process and the associated scrutiny that subcommittees give agencies. Federal law does, however, require the Federal Reserve chair to report twice a year to the congressional banking committees on the state of the economy and the course of monetary policy followed. But Congress has no authority, under existing law, to intervene and legislate monetary policy.

Congress could change the authorizing statutes that give the Fed its arm's-length freedom, but several factors mitigate Congress's inclination to change the current system. First, the Federal Reserve enjoys a high degree of legitimacy in the American political system. Its widely perceived effective performance over the past two decades has strengthened its grip on favorable public opinion. Second, it has a solid foundation of constituency-based support in Congress, drawn from districts that contain major banking interests, traditionally strong supporters of Fed independence.[32] Third, the technical demands of monetary policy making, with its complex models and seemingly endless data, limit the feasibility of close congressional oversight. Fourth, the Federal Reserve provides a political shield for members of Congress. Poor economic performance can be blamed on Fed policies. Conversely, members can readily share the public accolades that follow strong economic performance. Federal Reserve independence allows members of Congress to deflect negative fallout, while basking in economic success.

Summary and Conclusions

The economy affects politics, and national policy makers use policy to foster solid economic growth without undue inflation. National economic management takes two forms: fiscal policy making and monetary policy making. Fiscal policy is the province of the president and Congress. The president sets the fiscal policy agenda, and Congress approves the tax and spending initiatives that embody the enacted fiscal policy. To stimulate a stagnant economy by injecting added demand into it, Congress either increases federal spending or cuts taxes. When the objective is to use fiscal policy to increase spending, Congress enacts tax cuts aimed at those taxpayers who are most likely to spend the increased after-tax income rather than save it. When the objective is to increase investment, Congress enacts tax cuts directed at taxpayers who have the highest propensity to save the increased after-tax income, not spend it, since saving is required to finance investment.

Monetary policy, by comparison, operates at greater arm's length from the president and Congress. The Federal Reserve Board, through its Federal Open Market Committee, employs several policy instruments to affect the availability and cost of credit—most prominent among them the sale or purchase of federal securities on the open market. When the Fed sells securities, it draws reserves from lending institutions; when it buys securities, it adds to the reserves available to be lent. As reserves constrict, interest rates rise. As they expand, interest rates fall. It is these market transactions that are employed to effect changes in the FFR, the rate at which banks borrow from one another on an overnight basis. Changes in the FFR affect other short-term interest rates.

During the Great Recession, after the Fed lowered the FFR to near zero, it turned to unconventional measures to stem financial collapse and raise economic demand. These included injecting cash into teetering financial institutions and the automotive industry, as well as buying bonds and other financial securities in the open market to lower long-term interest rates—a policy labeled quantitative easing.

Neither the president nor Congress can veto the Fed's monetary policy choices, although Congress could change the authorizing statutes that grant the Federal Reserve its considerable independence. Yet Congress is not likely to do so. The Fed enjoys a high level of public confidence, and Americans look at it as the frontline in the struggle for sustained economic growth with high employment and price stability.

The relative success of economic policy makers in accomplishing their objectives has direct implications for budgetary decision makers. Strong economic growth not only greatly increases personal income; it also fattens public treasuries. Budget makers have more resources to work with: to reduce existing budget deficits, finance new programs, expand existing ones, or give some of the added revenue back in the form of tax cuts. Economic decline decreases personal income, reduces tax revenue, and increases spending on human service programs.

Notes

1 The discussion of economic policy making in this chapter incorporates and revises material written by the author and included in James J. Gosling, Economics, Politics, and American Public Policy (Armonk, N.Y.: M. E. Sharpe, 2008). It appears with the permission of the publisher.

2 John Maynard Keynes, The General Theory of Employment, Interest and Money (N.Y.: Harcourt Brace, 1964).

3 A.W. Phillips, "The Relation between Unemployment and the Rate of Change of Money Wage Rates in the United Kingdom," Economica 25 (November 1957): 263–99.

4 Bureau of Labor Statistics, U.S. Department of Labor, http:data.bls.gov/SurveyOutputServlet

5 Paul Krugman, Peddling Prosperity (N.Y.: W. W. Norton, 1994), 126.

6 President George W. Bush, Remarks by the President in Tax Cut Bill Signing (Washington, D.C.: The White House, June 7, 2001).

7 William Gale and Samara Potter, "The Bush Tax Cut: One Year Later," Brookings Policy Brief 101 (Washington, D.C.: Brookings Institution, June 2002).

8 Tax Foundation, Summary of Federal Individual Tax Data, 2001, www.taxfoundation. org/article/summary-latest-federal-income-tax-data-0.
9 Bureau of Economic Analysis, U.S. Department of Commerce, News Release: Gross Domestic Product, March 29, 2007, Table 1.
10 Christopher J. Goodman and Steven M. Mance, "Employment Loss and the 2007–2009 Recession: An Overview," Monthly Labor Review (April 2011), 5.
11 Jesse Bricker, Arthur B. Kennickell, Kevin B. Moore, and John Sebelhaus, "Changes in U.S. Family Finances from 2007 to 2010: Evidence from the Survey of Consumer Finances," Federal Reserve Bulletin, 98, 2 (June 2012).
12 Stan J. Liebowitz, "Anatomy of a Train Wreck: Causes of the Mortgage Meltdown," Independent Policy Report (Oakland, CA: The Independent Institute, 2008).
13 The Financial Crisis Inquiry Commission, The Financial Crisis Inquiry Report (Washington. D.C.: Government Printing Office, January 2011), 70.
14 Ibid., 7.
15 Liebowitz, "Anatomy of a Train Wreck," 3.
16 The Financial Crisis Inquiry Report, 87.
17 Bureau of the Census, Department of Commerce, www.census.gov/construction/ nrc/historical_data
18 The Financial Crisis Inquiry Report, xvi.
19 Ibid., 256.
20 The Federal Reserve Bank of St. Louis, The Financial Crisis: A Timeline of Events and Policy Actions, www.stlouisfed.org/Financial-Crisis
21 Paul Krugman, "Failure to Rise," New York Times, February 13, 2009, A31.
22 Roger Porter, "Economic Advice to the President, From Eisenhower to Reagan," Political Science Quarterly 98 (Fall 1983): 403–26; Edwin C. Hargrove and Samuel A. Moorley, eds., The President and the Council of Economic Advisers: Interviews with CEA Chairmen (Boulder, C.O.: Westview, 1984).
23 Aaron Wildavsky, The Politics of the Budgetary Process (Boston: Little, Brown, 1964), 58.
24 Office of Management and Budget, The Budget of the United States Government, 1961 (Washington D.C.: Government Printing Office, 1960); The Budget of the United States Government, 1975 (Washington D.C.: Government Printing Office, 1974).
25 Committee on the Budget, United States Senate, Congressional Budget Reform (Washington, D.C.: Government Printing Office, 1976), 8.
26 The Federal Reserve System: Purposes and Functions (Washington, D.C.: Board of Governors of the Federal Reserve System).
27 Federal Reserve Bank of New York, Fedpoint, June 2003, www.ny.frb.org/ aboutthefed/fedpoint/fed48.html
28 The National Association of Realtors, www.realto.org/Research
29 Sue Kirchoff, "Bubble or Not, High Home Prices Can Hurt," USA Today, May 10, 2005.
30 Richard H. Timberlake, Monetary Policy in the United States: An Intellectual and Institutional History (Chicago: University of Chicago Press, 1993), 356–7; Thomas D. Willett, Political Business Cycles (Durham, N.C.: Duke University Press, 1988).
31 Timberlake, Monetary Policy in the United States, 350.
32 John T. Wooley, "The Politics of Monetary Policy: A Critical Review," Journal of Public Policy 14 (1994): 57–85.

Chapter 5

Taxing and Spending

Political office holders—whether motivated by ideology, partisan interests, constituent pressures, self-preservation, or the desire for advancement—make choices that shape public policy. As suggested in chapter 2, the mix and relative saliency of such factors change with the issues before them. Politicians establish priorities, both individually and as members of collective bodies. Budgetary choices lay those priorities bare. Public spending is a highly reliable map of policy priority and political influence.

Those who make the choices do not have to pay for them out of their own pockets. The public pays. Although it is also true that the public derives benefits from what government does, neither those benefits nor the burden of paying for them are distributed evenly across society. Making choices on behalf of others, policy makers decide who should benefit and who should pay. Some people will inevitably pay more and benefit less, and vice versa. The optimal situation for those paying the bill is to benefit greatly while paying little. Conversely, a taxpayer's worst nightmare is to pay heavily while receiving few or no benefits in return.

Who Benefits and Who Pays

Some benefits from public spending can be clearly individualized: a payment under Temporary Assistance for Needy Families (TANF); a government-financed medical service; government-supported work training; an educational loan guaranteed by the federal government or by a state; or a price-support subsidy to dairy farmers. In these cases, only particular individuals who meet certain requirements can be beneficiaries; those who do not meet the requirements go without the benefits. At the same time, all taxpayers contribute to financing the benefits received by some, even though many of those taxpayers, given a choice, would not elect to contribute to them. A number of those who receive benefits are likely to pay no taxes at all.

The circle of those who benefit from government activities can be drawn progressively wider. Those who ride city buses, for example, benefit because their fares are subsidized by all general municipal taxpayers. However, it can be argued that even those who never ride buses benefit from mass transit. The displacement of would-be automobile drivers cuts down on road and highway congestion and reduces air pollution caused by motor vehicle emissions. Similarly, all municipal residents can be said to benefit from garbage collection—both in having their own refuse removed and in enjoying a cleaner and healthier environment. Where garbage collection is financed from general taxes, all taxpayers support the service. Nevertheless, people who generate more garbage than others benefit disproportionately. Likewise, all municipal residents benefit from police and fire protection, but some actually use the services more than others.

We all benefit from government efforts to purify drinking water, improve air quality, and provide national security. Since we all drink water, breathe air, and enjoy secure national borders, such benefits can be said to be indivisible. Individuals or categories of people are not singled out for benefit; the benefits inhere equally to all, constituting a public good.

Within this broad spectrum from individualized benefits to general benefits, government policy makers determine not only what public services should be provided and for whom, but also who should pay for them. For example, a city council might establish the policy that no general revenues should be used to support bus operations, so that operating costs must be covered fully from fares. Such a policy recognizes that users benefit directly from the service and that they should pay for it. Looking at the matter from a different perspective, another city council could take the position that all municipal residents should help to finance mass transit because of its broader benefits to the community at large. The council might also note that many in the community have no transportation except mass transit and that government has a social obligation to keep fares affordable to the less fortunate as a public good. Accordingly, the council might require a mix of financial support—part coming from fares and part from property tax revenues.

Similarly, a city council might decide that garbage collection financed by general revenues should be limited to one standard-size receptacle per residence. Beyond that, the council would require residents to pay special fees for additional containers or for bulky items.

Public spending can affect individuals, communities, and private industry differently, depending on the ways in which the revenues are raised. Each of the major forms of raising revenue affects taxpayers differently, and the choice of which to use can greatly alter the benefit–payer relationship. For example, government insistence that highway construction, repair, and maintenance be funded exclusively from motor fuel taxes, vehicle registration fees, and other revenues related to highway use (without the addition of any general-purpose revenues) would put the onus of highway finance clearly on the shoulders of motor vehicle users. With this choice, the person who does not own a motor vehicle contributes nothing toward building and maintaining highways. Conversely, to the extent that any general-purpose revenues are appropriated for these purposes, nonusers are put in the position of financially supporting users. Moreover, to the extent that revenues earmarked to support highway-related spending are used to pay for non-highway purposes, highway users bear the direct financial burden.

Yet even within the same category of taxpayer—in this case highway users—different classes of users can be called on to provide disproportionate levels of financial support, depending on how that support is exacted. Because heavy trucks do much more damage to highway surfaces and structures than passenger vehicles, state policy makers typically charge truck owners higher fees and taxes to operate heavy trucks on public highways. Policy makers commonly graduate registration fees on the basis of a vehicle's weight; they may also charge a higher tax on diesel fuel than on gasoline to ensure that trucks pay more (even though diesel car drivers have to pay more as well). If all vehicles were charged the same registration fee and motor fuel tax, automobile operators would have grounds for arguing that they were paying far more than their fair share given their marginal contribution to highway deterioration.

To look at another example, if state law permits municipalities to impose a local income tax, municipalities that do not impose this tax place a heavier burden on property taxpayers. A municipality adopting an income tax may have the option of taxing both residents and nonresidents who work within the municipality's borders. The logic of taxing nonresidents recognizes that they use some city services, although not the full range of services that residents use. Nonresidents who work within a municipality but live in surrounding communities place additional burdens on city services associated with commuting; their added numbers during the workday also place added pressures on such basic services as sewage treatment, trash collection and street cleaning, and traffic direction and police protection. Nonresidents may also benefit from city-subsidized cultural and social events. In the absence of the local income tax, residents would be obliged to cover costs not met by user fees. It could, nevertheless, be argued that nonresidents should not pay local income tax at the same rate as residents because residents receive an even broader range of service benefits than those who live outside of the city.

Besides determining those who benefit from public spending and those who pay for it, government policy makers decide the size of individualized benefits and how much should be spent on benefits that are less readily divisible. Moreover, within notable constraints, public policy makers also determine how fast government spending should grow and which revenue sources should finance that growth.

Several factors push up public expenditures: inflation, population growth and its attendant claims on public services, growth in the number of individuals who meet previously enacted benefit entitlements, the creation of new public programs, and the expansion of existing ones, to name a few. Spending pressures associated with inflation manifest themselves in higher prices for supplies, purchased services, and capital goods, as well as higher expectations and demands for salary increases on the part of public employees who want to preserve their purchasing power.

Population growth increases demands on basic government and education services. Depending on the nature of that growth, it can also burden social welfare services—particularly when individuals who meet eligibility standards are deemed to have the right to collect approved benefits irrespective of the amounts appropriated to finance them. Finally, the enactment of new programs to meet emerging needs obviously brings with it new expenditure claims, as does the expansion of existing programs.

As the adage goes, "there is no such thing as a free lunch"; someone has to pay to finance spending increases. Either additional revenues must be raised or expenditure cuts must be made elsewhere, with the freed-up revenues reallocated to finance the areas of growth. The quest for additional revenues again raises the question of who should pay to support increased spending, and the identification of reductions in the base budget raises the issue of whose existing benefits should be reduced. Clearly, however, not all expenditure cuts will necessarily result in a reduction of public benefits; some may merely necessitate increased efficiencies in administration and service provision. But after a point, base cuts can no longer be accommodated by efficiency or productivity improvements; services or other benefits must be reduced.

Government Spending

Any assessment of the history of government spending in the United States is greatly constrained by the lack of consistent records of state and local government spending before the twentieth century. Federal expenditures have demonstrated a pattern marked by significant increases in support of war efforts, peaking during the course of military campaigns and then dropping dramatically at the end of hostilities, but always to a level higher than that found before entry into war. As Table 5.1 shows, federal expenditures rose from $63 million in 1860 to nearly $1.3 billion by 1865, the height of the Civil War. However, by 1870 federal spending had decreased by 76 percent, reaching $310 million—still nearly four times higher than it was just ten years earlier.

Similar shifts in federal spending accompanied U.S. involvement in World War I, World War II, and the Korean War. Although not shown in the table, federal spending rose from $700 million in 1916 to $18.5 billion in 1919, falling off to $6.4 billion in 1920. Federal spending continued to fall during the 1920s as an expanding domestic economy replaced a war-driven economy, but the Great Depression of the 1930s spurred federal domestic spending, particularly during the period from 1934 to 1936. The administration of Franklin Delano Roosevelt and the U.S. Congress created and expanded federal programs aimed at ameliorating the effects of record national unemployment, including programs assisting dependent children, the elderly, the blind, and farmers (through price parity).

Table 5.1   Federal Government Expenditures, Selected Fiscal Years, 1805–2015

(In $ millions)

Year	Amount	Year	Amount	Year	Amount
1805	11	1880	268	1955	68,444
1810	8	1885	260	1960	92,191
1815	33	1890	318	1965	118,228
1820	18	1895	356	1970	195,649
1825	16	1900	529	1975	332,332
1830	15	1905	567	1980	590,941
1835	18	1910	694	1985	946,344
1840	24	1915	761	1990	1,252,994
1845	23	1920	6,403	1995	1,515,742
1850	40	1925	3,063	2000	1,788,950
1855	60	1930	3,440	2005	2,471,957
1860	63	1935	6,412	2007	2,728,686
1865	1,298	1940	9,468	2010	3,457,079
1870	310	1945	92,712	2012	3,537,079
1875	275	1950	42,562	2015e	3,900,989

e = estimate.

Source: Office of Management and Budget, Budget of the United States Government, FY 2015, Historical Tables, Table 1.1; Historical Statistics of the United States, Colonial Times to 1970, Part 2 (Washington, D.C.: Bureau of the Census, U.S. Department of Commerce, 1975), 1114–15.

World War II both put people back to work—in military uniforms or in industries supporting the war effort—and exacted increased resources from them to finance the country's major involvement in the war. The Allied Forces' victory allowed U.S. spending to drop by 1950 to nearly half of what it had been in 1945, although U.S. participation in the Korean War pushed federal spending up again in the early 1950s.

With the end of the Korean War, the U.S. Treasury had amassed a base level of revenues that became available to support growing federal domestic programs aimed at advancing the nation's domestic infrastructure, assisting veterans in their return to civilian life, and accommodating the needs of a rapidly growing populace for government services; although, as will be shown later in this chapter, the greatest pressures for increased domestic spending were also felt at state and local levels. Funding was also available to finance increased military spending at a time when there were no armed conflicts, but the country was pursuing its Cold War with the Soviet Union (even though the percentage of federal spending for national defense has dropped dramatically since the Korean War). Finally, the Vietnam War era provides an exception to this established pattern of federal spending. Contrary to prior experience, federal spending rose during and after the war.[1]

Different measures can be used to compare government spending. One measure is current dollars. This does not, however, take into account changes in the purchasing power of the dollar over time; nor does it capture a sense of the level of government spending in relation to the changing size of the economy or to a changing population. A 5 percent increase in expenditures, for example, means one thing at a 10 percent rate of inflation and quite another at a 2.5 percent rate. In the former, the increased spending is insufficient to cover price increases and the higher level of spending is able to purchase less, not more, from one year to the next. In the latter, the spending increase is more than adequate to cover the increased costs and represents a 2.5 percent increase (i.e., one-half of the increase covers inflation and the other half is growth in real purchasing power).

Increased government spending produces different economic effects in a growing economy from those it sparks in a level or contracting economy. When government spending grows more slowly than the gross domestic product, the economy is more than able to finance the growth without placing increased demands on available resources; however, when government spending grows faster than the economy, new resources are required to finance that growth— resources the economy is not producing. This places an increasing drain on existing resources.

To incorporate these considerations explicitly into comparisons at federal, state, and local levels, government spending will be compared using **current dollars, constant dollars**, and as a percentage of the gross national product (GNP) before 1954 and the gross domestic product (GDP) thereafter. Given the availability of uniform and consistent data, comparisons will begin with the 1929 fiscal year, the year preceding the Great Depression.

As Table 5.2 illustrates, total government spending increased by 838.5 percent between 1929 and 1954 (the end of the Korean War). If constant 1982 dollars (spending converted to its 1982 purchasing power) are used, the percentage increase drops to 496.7 percent. When spending is presented as a percentage of GNP, growth over the twenty-five-year period is reduced to 162 percent.

Table 5.2 shows that increases in federal spending account for a very large proportion of the growth in government spending. As a percentage of the GNP, federal spending increased nearly nine times faster than state spending. The federal government was clearly the preeminent spender between 1929 and 1954, as the Great Depression and two wars primed this spending. In contrast, local government spending decreased as a percentage of the GNP.

Direct government spending since 1954 can be meaningfully broken into seven discrete periods: 1954–64, 1964–74, 1974–81, 1981–8, 1988–2001, 2001–7, and 2007–11 (with 2011 as the most recent year for which spending data for the state and local government component were available at the time of this writing).

The year 1964 marks a departure from the gradual economic growth of the previous decade, associated with transition to a domestically driven economy—one built around providing educational benefits and employment for returning veterans and education for their post-World War II "baby boom" offspring. Between 1954 and 1964, as Table 5.3 shows, the growth in state

Table 5.2 Government Expenditures for 1929 and 1954 Compared (in $ billions)

	Total			Federal			State			Local		
	1929	1954	% Change	1929	1954	% Change	1929	1954	% Change	1929	1954	% Change
In current $	10.4	97.6	838.5	2.7	70.3	2,503.7	2.1	12.8	509.5	5.6	14.5	158.9
In constant 1982 $	60.8	362.8	496.7	15.8	261.3	1,553.8	12.3	47.6	287.0	32.7	53.9	64.8
As percentage of GNP	10.0	26.2	162.0	2.6	18.9	626.9	2.0	3.4	70.0	5.4	3.9	−27.8

Note: Federal aid to state and local governments counted as federal expenditure. State aid to local governments counted as state government expenditure.

Sources: Significant Features of Fiscal Federalism, 1988 ed., 2 (Washington, D.C.: Advisory Commission on Intergovernmental Relations, 1988), 22.

Table 5.3 Direct Government Expenditures, Selected Fiscal Years, 1954–2011

	1954	1964	1974	1981	1988	2001	2007	2011	Average annual percentage change						
									1954–64	1964–74	1974–81	1981–88	1988–01	2001–07	2007–11
Total government expenditures (in $ billions)															
In current dollars	107.5	199.1	495.1	1165.2	1891.3	3758.6	5389.9	6762.7	8.5	14.9	19.3	8.9	7.6	7.2	6.4
In constant 2000 dollars	763.0	1047.9	1612.7	2094.9	2570.1	3672.7	4473.3	4904.7	3.7	5.4	4.3	3.2	3.3	3.6	2.4
As percentage of GDP	26.4	28.6	34.4	36.6	37.1	37.9	37.2	43.5							
Federal government expenditures (in $ billions)															
In current dollars	70.9	118.5	269.4	678.2	1064.5	1863.8	2728.7	3603.1	6.7	12.7	21.6	8.1	5.8	7.7	8.0
In constant 2000 dollars	502.9	623.8	877.4	1219.4	1446.5	1820.6	2263.1	2613.2	2.7	4.1	5.6	2.7	2.0	4.7	4.1
As percentage of GDP	16.8	16.5	19.4	21.1	20.9	19.1	18.8	23.2							
State and local government expenditures (in $ billions)															
In current dollars	36.6	80.6	225.7	487.0	826.8	1894.8	2661.2	3159.6	12.0	18.0	16.5	9.7	9.9	6.7	4.7
In constant 2000 dollars	259.8	424.2	735.2	875.6	1235.0	1851.5	2210.2	2291.5	6.3	7.3	2.7	5.9	3.8	2.9	0.9
As percentage of GDP	9.6	12.1	15.0	15.5	16.2	18.8	18.4	20.3							

Sources: Office of Management and Budget, Budget of the United States Government, FY 2015, Historical Tables, Tables 1.1 and 1.3; Bureau of the Census, U.S. Department of Commerce.

and local spending exceeded the growth in federal spending. In fact, federal spending decreased as a percentage of the GDP, as defense spending garnered a shrinking percentage of the federal budget. As a counterbalance, federal domestic spending was buoyed by the creation and expansion of new federal programs to aid primary, secondary, and higher education, and to finance the interstate highway systems.

Local governments faced perhaps the greatest challenge of the period in building the infrastructure necessary to support a burgeoning population, expand basic municipal and county services, and educate a growth cohort that spread from the primary grades through high school. The states faced a similar challenge: population growth created the need for new highways, for expanded natural resource management and protection, and for social services. States also began to increase their financial assistance to local school districts during this period, although not to the extent experienced during the next decade.

Of all the periods, 1964–74 represents the greatest post-World War II growth in constant-dollar government spending. Three forces drove spending up between 1964 and 1974: the Great Society program, the Vietnam War, and the continued population pressures exerted by the second wave of the post-World War II baby boom. Domestic policy in the 1960s was characterized by President Lyndon Johnson's call for a Great Society to improve the quality of life in the United States for all people. The federal government articulated national policy goals for the Great Society and offered the inducement of greatly increased federal aid to entice state and local participation. Programs directed at improving the lot of the less fortunate in society formed the core of the federal initiatives, for a Great Society was defined by the Johnson administration and the Democrat-led Congress as one that ensured an adequate quality of life for its needy. At President Johnson's behest, Congress enacted into law most of the proposals designed by the administration's social architects, including programs providing financial aid to poor families with dependent children (a major broadening of the fledgling children's aid program of the Roosevelt administration) and to people who were aged, blind, or disabled but did not qualify for social security; medical care for the needy not qualifying for social security; subsidized public housing; community rehabilitation and development; job training; and need-based aid for students pursuing higher education. While domestic discretionary and means-tested spending increased its share of total expenditures, defense's share shrank.

Yet, in spite of this markedly increased federal financial commitment, state legislatures were not to be outdone. Often following gubernatorial initiatives, they expanded state aid to local governments and used rapidly growing state revenues to equalize the distribution of such major state aids as shared revenues, general school aids, and mass transportation assistance. (**Equalization** involves distributing financial assistance in relation to need rather than population or a proportional return to the contributing source.) As a result, state aid to local units of government increased three and a half times between 1964 and 1974.[2] Moreover, states raised their own levels of support for social welfare programs, matching—and in some cases exceeding—the percentage of growth in federal assistance.

Local spending, in comparison, increased at less than half the state rate in constant dollars. The revenue substitution offered by greatly expanded federal and state aid clearly contributed to the relative slowdown in local spending financed by local resources. Even with that increased intergovernmental aid, local spending still managed a 38 percent increase in constant dollars.

The period from 1974 to 1981 has been characterized as the "Great Slow-Down in State and Local Government Spending."[3] The increase in annual constant-dollar state and local spending dropped by two-thirds compared to the 1964–74 period. Federal spending, in contrast, grew over twice as fast as state and local government spending in real terms. Domestic spending, particularly spending devoted to entitlement programs and to interest on the federal debt, led the increases. National defense spending continued to contract as a percentage of total federal expenditures, in 1979 reaching its lowest point since World War II.

Faced with major spending increases at the state and local levels during the latter half of the 1960s and the first half of the 1970s, voters increasingly voiced their displeasure over higher state and local taxes. The so-called taxpayer revolt began in California in 1978 with the passage of Proposition 13, a citizen initiative that cut local property tax revenues by half. Taxpayer activism spread quickly to other states, and by 1981 sixteen states had imposed some form of fiscal limitation on their local governments, limiting rate increases, the actual levies themselves, or expenditure growth.[4]

Although the immediate object of the revolt was the increased property taxes occasioned by skyrocketing property assessments, particularly in southern California, the revolt spread to the state level. At about the same time, Ronald Reagan was building his presidential campaign on pledges to reduce the federal tax bite, restrain the aggregate growth in federal spending, reduce federal aid to state and local governments, and cut back the federal government's regulatory penetration of society. His decisive victory was perceived widely as a mandate for restraint in taxing and spending. By the beginning of the 1980s, austerity had become the political watchword at all levels of government, and the "spenders" and "tax raisers" were popularly out of vogue.

The Reagan presidency left its mark on government spending in the 1980s. Although federal spending continued to grow in both current- and constant-dollar terms, it did so at a reduced rate. Yet significant shifts in federal spending occurred within this framework of spending restraint. National defense spending, after consistently dropping as a percentage of federal expenditures since the Korean War, increased from 23.3 percent in 1981 to 27.3 percent in 1988. Net interest paid on the federal debt increased as well, rising from 10.1 percent in 1981 to 14.3 percent in 1988. These relative increases occurred at the expense of domestic spending. Domestic discretionary spending saw its share of federal budget outlays fall from 20.1 percent to 14.8 percent. Means-tested entitlements were squeezed as well, as their share fell from 7.6 percent to 7.2 percent. This was the only period during which these entitlements' share fell.

Overall, the period from 1981 to 1988 was a time of rebounding constant-dollar spending for state and local governments, with local spending showing the steepest increases. It is misleading, however, to generalize about the period as a whole. The recession of 1981–2 depressed the economies of most states (except the oil-producing states, which benefited from the sharply rising price of oil), forcing state legislatures to cut budgets and increase taxes. It also exerted upward pressure on state spending for public welfare programs.

Local government spending was less affected by the recession. The property tax fared better than the more elastic sales and income taxes, and the recession affected local government spending less than it did state spending (although counties, because of the composition of their budgets, experienced more pressure for increased public assistance spending than did municipalities). But local spending also started from a more depressed base than did state spending, struggling through four years of real-dollar decline.[5]

With economic recovery well under way in most states by 1984, state and local government policy makers increased state spending to address needs and respond to demands that were not met earlier in the decade. Governors and legislators in the states most hurt by the recession, which had to raise taxes (often simultaneously making midyear budget reductions), finally found themselves with adequate revenues to increase spending. By 1986, their state treasuries had accumulated sizable surpluses. Several Midwestern industrial states continued that condition to the end of the decade, while most states in the Northeast found their fortunes reversing. Conversely, by mid-decade, lawmakers in the oil-producing states, which had enjoyed economic prosperity early in the 1980s, found themselves forced to reduce spending and raise general-purpose taxes to compensate for falling revenues from petroleum-based taxes. By decade's end, their fortunes had improved somewhat.

In the aggregate, the period from 1984 to 1988 saw renewed and sustained state and local spending, which rose by 22 percent in constant dollars, making up for lost ground. Growth in local spending, as chapter 8 shows in greater detail, was largely funded by increased local revenues. State aid in relation to local **own-source revenue** (revenues raised directly by a given government) increased only for school districts between 1984 and 1988, while it fell for both cities and counties.[6]

The thawing of the Cold War in the late 1980s provided Congress with the opportunity to reduce federal spending on national defense significantly. Seizing that opportunity, Congress cut defense spending in constant dollars between 1988 and 2001, and saw its percentage of federal spending drop from 27.3 percent in 1988 to 16.4 percent in 2001. The so-called defense dividend, combined with lower interest rates and major deficit-reduction packages approved by Congress in 1990, 1993, and 1997, greatly reduced the preceding period's sharp rise in net interest payments. These two factors, however, were countered by rapid growth in domestic spending, including both entitlement and discretionary spending. Still, constant-dollar federal spending rose by only 2 percent annually between 1988 and 2001, and federal spending declined as a percentage of GDP.

In contrast, state and local spending rose in relation to GDP. Required state matching for growing entitlement programs, along with pressures for other increased spending engendered by the 1990–1 recession, pushed spending up in the early years of the decade. Later, strong economic growth during the second half of the 1990s provided the financial means for policy makers to satisfy demands for further increased spending. At the local level, rising school-age populations and court orders aimed at closing gaps between state funding for richer and poorer school districts put the most pressure on local government spending.

That pattern soon changed. The United States' military engagements in Afghanistan and Iraq increased national defense spending by $171 billion between the 2001 and 2006 fiscal years, raising defense's share of federal spending from 17.4 percent in 2002 to 19.6 percent in 2006. Yet spending shares also rose sharply for means-tested entitlements (reflecting the increased demand for spending on human service programs during the recession and its immediate aftermath), offset by declining shares for social security and net interest.

State and local governments also felt the spending pressures generated by heightened homeland security. States, with their heavier reliance on sales and income taxes when compared to local governments, faced the brunt of revenue shortfalls that necessitated budget cuts in the aftermath of the recession of 2001: Forty states reduced their enacted budgets by almost $12 billion in the 2003 fiscal year alone. Even with an improving economy in 2004, eighteen states were still forced to make $4.8 billion in cuts after their budgets were enacted into law.

As economic growth continued at a brisk pace in 2005 and 2006, states were variously able to increase spending, cut taxes, and replenish their rainy-day funds. The improved economic times encouraged budget makers to restore cuts made during the down fiscal years of 2002 and 2003 and enact tax and fee reductions totaling $2.1 billion for FY 2007. Rainy-day fund balances across the states soared, reaching a thirty-year high as a percentage of expenditures.

Revenues continued to grow during the 2007 fiscal year, rising about 3 percent faster than in FY 2006, and revenues exceeded budget projections in thirty-eight states. Only one state, Wisconsin, was forced to reduce its enacted budget in midyear.[7]

As Table 5.3 shows, state and local government constant-dollar spending slowed considerably between 2001 and 2007 compared to the previous twenty-five-year period, returning to growth levels reminiscent of the 1974–81 period.

But of all the seven periods examined, constant-dollar state and local government spending hit bottom from 2007 to 2011, rising only nine-tenths of a percent as state and local government budgets felt the fiscal effects of the Great Recession. Fortunately for budget makers, greatly increased federal aid offset the depth of the cuts that would have been necessary absent the large infusion of federal assistance. See chapter 9 for a discussion of federal aid and its consequences for state and local governments.

Government Revenues

All states (except Vermont) and all general-purpose units of local government must enact budgets that are in balance, for which projected revenues equal or exceed budgeted expenditures. No such requirement exists for the federal government. Thus, for the states and localities, revenues have pretty much paralleled expenditures over time. Between 1929 and 1954, state and local revenues grew faster than expenditures by about 2 percent. In contrast, revenues grew much more slowly than expenditures at the federal level (1,590 percent and 2,504 percent, respectively), producing the frequent deficit spending that occurred during the Great Depression and World War II eras.[8]

With the exception of brief periods of revenue surplus, federal revenues continued to fail to keep pace with spending for most of the next six decades, with the largest constant-dollar deficits found in the early to mid 1980s, the early 1990s, the early to mid 2000s and during the years of the Great Recession, with deficits spiking during the 2009–12 fiscal years. State and local governments, which further improved their financial position during the period from 1954 to 1981, saw that position erode from 1981 through 1994 and then recover strongly through 2000, only to face prospective revenue shortfalls as a result of the recessions of 2001 and 2007–9.

Tax Revenues

The federal government gets 87 percent of its on-budget receipts from taxes. In comparison, taxes comprise 74 percent of state own-source general revenue and 62 percent of local own-source general revenue. The lower revenue contribution from taxes for local governments reflects their relatively greater reliance on user fees.[9]

Of all taxes paid in the 2011 fiscal year, the federal government collected 53 percent, the states 27 percent, and local units of government 20 percent. Since fiscal year 1954 the federal share of tax revenue has decreased as the shares of state and local governments increased, the greatest increase occurring at the state level (see Table 5.4). In fiscal year 2011, seventy-four cents of every federal tax dollar came from the individual income tax, up from forty-seven cents in 1954. The corporate income tax added another twelve cents in 2011, down from thirty-four cents in 1954.

Table 5.4   Government Tax Revenues, From Own Source, for Fiscal Years, 1954 and 2011 (in $ millions)

	1954		2011	
	Amount	Percentage of total	Amount	Percentage of total
Total tax revenues	84,580	100.0	2,828,844	100.0
Federal tax revenues	62,493	73.9	1,484,674	52.5
State tax revenues	11,129	13.2	762,379	27.0
Local tax revenues	10,958	12.9	581,791	20.6
Federal tax revenues				
Individual income tax	29,542	47.3	1,091,473	73.5
Corporate income tax	21,101	33.8	181,085	12.2
Excise taxes	9,945	15.9	72,381	4.9
All other taxes	1,905	3.0	139,735	9.4
State tax revenues				
Individual income tax	1044	9.0	259,613	34.1
Corporate income tax	772	7.0	41,280	5.4
Sales and gross receipts tax	6,573	59.3	369,476	48.5
Motor vehicle taxes	1,098	9.9	21,536	2.8
All other taxes	1,642	14.8	56,229	7.5
Local tax revenues				
Income tax	122	1.1	25,680	4.4
Sales and gross receipts tax	703	6.4	94,503	16.2
Property tax	9,557	87.2	431,528	74.2
All other taxes	576	5.3	21,283	3.7

Note: Figures **exclude** social insurance taxes and retirement receipts. Figures do not add exactly due to rounding.

Sources: Office of Management and Budget, Budget of the United States Government, FY 2015, Historical Tables, Table 2.1; Bureau of the Census, U.S. Department of Commerce, Quarterly Summary of State and Local Government Tax Revenue, www.census.gov/govs/www/qtax.html; Bureau of the Census, U.S. Department of Commerce; Significant Features of Historical Federalism, 1989, ed. 2 (Washington, D.C.: Advisory Commission on Intergovernmental Relations, 1989), 32–3.

At the state level, individual income tax revenues showed the greatest jump of any tax source between 1954 and 2011, rising from 9 percent to 34 percent of tax revenue. The corporate income tax's share declined from 7 percent to 5 percent. Sales, gross receipts, and motor vehicle taxes fell as a percentage of total tax revenue, dropping from 59 to 49 percent, but in 2011 sales and gross receipts taxes still generated the highest percentage of state tax revenue.

At the local level, the property tax lost ground to both the income tax and the sales tax. Property taxes comprised 74 percent of local tax revenues in 2011, down from 87 percent in 1954. Sales and gross receipts tax revenues increased to 16 percent, up from 6 percent in 1954, and the local income tax share increased from 1 percent to 4 percent over the fifty-seven-year period. The relative increase of sales and income tax revenues would no doubt have been even larger had more states permitted their municipalities, counties, and school districts to impose such taxes. Local governments are legally creatures of the states and can exercise only those powers granted to them in state constitutions or statutes. If neither permits local governments to employ the sales or income tax, neither tax is available to them. Chapter 8 discusses the extent to which local governments use both taxes.

With its heavy reliance on the individual income tax, the federal government is well positioned to benefit from the increases in personal income that accompany economic growth. It also benefits from having a national pool of taxpayers, so that economic slumps that depress income growth in some parts of the country are offset, at least partially, by greater prosperity in other parts. When the economy is in a national slump, the federal government can resort to increased deficit spending. The states, on the other hand, have less opportunity to balance declines and growth within their borders, and, as noted, all but one must operate under balanced budgets.

States differ significantly in their ability to raise revenues. Some enjoy much higher levels of per capita personal income than do others. Consequently, their taxpayers not only offer a higher income base to tax but also show a greater propensity to make discretionary purchases subject to sales tax. Although these states can be said to rank high in tax capacity, they may operate under tax laws that exact actual taxes at levels well below that capacity. In such cases, they rank low in tax effort. **Tax capacity** can be thought of as the amount a state would raise if it applied a national average set of tax rates to commonly used tax bases. **Tax effort** can be thought of as the ratio of a state's actual tax collections to its tax capacity.[10]

From these concepts and the appropriate measures associated with them, it is possible to compare states in terms of both tax capacity and tax effort. With the exception of Alaska, which ranks first in both tax capacity and tax effort, no other state's effort matches its capacity. That should not come as a surprise: It should be expected that states having taxpayers with comparatively lower ability to pay would have to raise their tax effort if they wished to spend at a level higher than their revenue-raising capacity allows.

The Concept of Tax Expenditures

Despite the nomenclature, a discussion of so-called **tax expenditures** is properly part of a discussion of revenues. Tax expenditures should be thought of as forgone revenues that would have been collected had special provisions not been included in federal, state, or local income tax codes. Such provisions allow taxpayers who qualify to exclude or deduct income from taxation, to defer tax liability, or to claim tax credits that provide a dollar-for-dollar reduction in the bottom-line taxes owed.

Prominent examples of tax expenditures include income deduction for mortgage interest, as well as property taxes paid on owner-occupied residences; oil and gas depletion allowances (which allow the deduction of a portion of the income associated with oil and natural gas extraction, in recognition of the progressive depletion of available supplies); deductions for certain business-related expenses; credits for child care; and the deferral of tax liability for incomes set aside, within specified limitations, for retirement.

Depending on your perspective, tax expenditures can be viewed either as incentives that bias options in a manner consistent with the public interest or as loopholes that permit fortunate individuals or corporations to escape paying their fair share of taxes. Deductions benefiting property owners have broad popular support because they reduce the tax liability of a wide spectrum of taxpayers and thereby encourage home ownership. Those same taxpayers, however, may view oil depletion allowances as a special-interest "rip-off." Itemized deductions, at the federal level, reduce taxable income by over 12 percent, shrinking federal tax revenue accordingly.[11]

The states, which pattern a significant part of their income tax structure on that of the federal government, make considerably greater use of tax expenditures than do local governments, which have relatively simple income tax provisions (where income tax is permitted at all). Unfortunately, no empirically based estimate of the magnitude of state or local tax expenditures has yet been made.

Nontax Revenues

Governments also derive revenues from sources other than taxes. When users of government services pay directly for the benefits they receive, the charges are called **user fees**. Only those receiving the service bear the cost of its provision.

User fees can be voluntary or mandatory.[12] They are voluntary when individuals or corporations may decide whether or not to accept a governmental service; they are mandatory when such discretion does not exist. Voluntary fees include such items as admission charges at a public museum or zoo, where individuals are charged only if they want to gain admission. Similarly, greens fees on municipal golf courses are charged only to golfers who use the facilities. On the other hand, mandatory fees are charged to all presumed users. Garbage and sewage collection charges are normally mandatory on the presumption that residents produce garbage and sewage that need disposal.

With other fees, it is not so clear whether they are voluntary or mandatory. Postal charges seem to be voluntary; individuals who elect to send mail and packages are charged only when they do so. Yet few of us have any choice except to use postal services. Fees for the use of mass transit also appear voluntary, but for many people mass transit represents the only available means of mobility other than walking. If they are to get to and from work, they have little choice.

The U.S. Department of Commerce treats other government fees as taxes instead of user fees, although they possess all the distinctive properties of user fees. Good examples are motor vehicle fuel taxes, registration fees, and driver's license fees. These are tied directly to motor vehicle use. Anyone who does not operate a vehicle pays no fuel tax. If a vehicle is in continuous storage, it does not need to be registered. Similarly, anyone who never drives needs no driver's license. All three charges are usually classified as voluntary payments. Individuals, in theory, can elect not to own and operate motor vehicles; but the structure of U.S. society is such that almost no one who can afford a car elects to forgo it.

Some user fees look like payments for benefits received but also can be said to contribute to the public good. The persons who pay the fees receive distinct benefits, but society also benefits in determinable ways by such collective use. Mass transit again provides a good example. Nonusers of mass transit benefit by others' use. Assuming that a significant percentage of mass transit commuters would otherwise drive, their choice of mass transit reduces both highway congestion and air pollution. This public good serves as a rationale for some general taxpayer support of public transportation.

Special assessments, although not always classified as user fees, are levied on a modified principle of payment for benefits received. Local units of government most commonly employ special assessments to help finance infrastructure improvements such as sewer extensions; sidewalk, curb, and gutter installation; or the construction of utilities, streets, or interchanges serving new commercial developments. A home owner whose property abuts the improvement site often pays a sizable share of the cost, on the principle that the owner benefits disproportionately from the improvement. Others benefit as well as those who enjoy the improvements as they pass through but pay nothing.

Interest earnings and proceeds from the sale of government-owned property represent the two other major forms of nontax general revenue. Nongeneral government revenues largely come from employees' contributions toward their retirement, employer contributions for unemployment compensation, employee and employer contributions for social security and Medicare, consumer payments to government-owned utilities, and receipts from government-owned liquor stores.

Criteria for Evaluating Taxes and User Fees

Several criteria can be used to evaluate both taxes and user fees. Other criteria are appropriate only for evaluating one or the other. Those applicable to both include adequacy of yield in relation to costs of administration, relative ease of administration, effects on economic behavior, political acceptability, and equity.

Yield in Relation to Costs of Administration

The primary purpose of a tax or user fee is to generate revenue to support the operations and programmatic activities of government. Obviously, those that produce high yields at low administrative costs are to be preferred. Conversely, taxes or user fees that produce relatively little revenue in relation to cost of administration are usually to be avoided—unless they have been instituted largely for other purposes, for example to bias individual choices in what are deemed to be socially desirable directions (as discussed below under the criterion of effects on economic behavior).

Ease of Administration

Taxes or fees should be unambiguously calculable, so that taxpayers and tax collectors alike can readily determine what is owed. They should also be collectible, for it does little good to establish taxes or fees that can easily be evaded. Some taxes become difficult to collect because of the lack of valid and reliable information about transactions subject to taxation.

Effects on Economic Behavior

Taxes and fees shift resources from private to public use. Economists argue that revenue-generating instruments should not alter the payers' behavior in ways that jeopardize the attainment of economic goals. In other words, they should capture revenues while distorting economic activity as little as possible.[13]

Governments may also institute taxes and user fees to bias individual choice. For example, a surcharge on downtown parking will not only raise municipal revenue but also may serve to discourage drivers from bringing their cars into an already congested central business district and thereby prompt commuters and shoppers to make greater use of mass transit. Other effects on individual behavior may not be the result of policy design. For instance, high income tax rates can depress entrepreneurial activity and remove any significant economic gain from additional income earned at the highest tax bracket. When individuals choose leisure over work, potential tax revenues are forgone.

Political Acceptability

A tax or fee that meets the above criteria but meets with widespread opposition is not likely to be adopted. Taxes have to be tolerated. In addition to these criteria, taxes are usually evaluated in terms of their equity, and user fees in terms of the principle of "payment for benefits received."

Equity

Equity can be defined as treating like cases alike and different cases in an appropriately different manner. Under this definition, government policy makers must give good reasons for different treatment. Policy makers must show that it is appropriate and not just arbitrary. Put differently, people expect taxation to be fair.

Economists speak of both horizontal and vertical equity.[14] **Horizontal tax equity** presumes equal treatment of taxpayers who have equal capacity to pay. **Vertical tax equity** concerns the appropriate relationship between the relative taxes to be paid by persons with different abilities to pay. Here the comparison is of unequals (rather than equals, as with horizontal equity), and the focus is the extent to which their tax obligations should differ. The vertical equity criterion looks at the relationship between income and the relative incidence of the tax burden. A tax is considered **progressive** if its rate increases as ability to pay rises. Those with progressively higher incomes thus pay a higher percentage of their incomes in taxes. A tax is **regressive** if its proportional burden is inversely related to ability to pay. Regressive taxes derive a higher proportion of receipts from those with lower incomes. A **proportional tax** applies the same rate to all levels of income. Unlike a progressive tax, it does not gradually increase as incomes rise above set brackets; the same rate is applied to all income levels. As a consequence, those with higher incomes pay greater amounts in taxes, but they pay less than they would under progressive taxation.

The individual income tax that incorporates progressive tax rates is considered the fairest tax, scoring highest on vertical equity. The individual income tax is further related to ability to pay by the existence of personal deductions, through which tax liability is reduced for every person financially dependent on the income earner or earners—disproportionately benefiting those with relatively lower incomes.

The sales tax tends to place a greater burden on those with lower incomes, since they are likely to spend a relatively higher percentage of their incomes on items subject to a sales tax—particularly when the tax is applied to necessities, such as food and utilities. Exempting these necessities makes a sales tax less regressive.

Finally, the property tax (limited here to real property taxes imposed on land and structures built on the land) is progressive in the sense that it increases as the value of the property increases. Indeed, the value of real property can be used as a measure of wealth, and property taxes are the closest approximation of any tax in the United States to a wealth tax. However, the value of real property is not always a good indicator of its owner's ability to pay. Many elderly citizens own houses bought when their incomes were much higher. In such cases, the tax can be considered regressive.

Comparing taxes at the federal, state, and local levels, federal taxation is the most progressive overall, since almost 69 percent of federal tax revenues come from the individual income tax. By comparison, both state and local taxes are more regressive. States rely most heavily on the sales tax, and local governments place greatest reliance on the property tax. State programs of "circuit-breaker" property tax relief reduce the burden of property taxes on lower-income taxpayers. The most common form of circuit-breaker relief allows those with lower incomes to take a special credit on their income taxes for a certain percentage of their paid property taxes. Unlike local governments, states hardly use the property tax at all.

Summary and Conclusions

Public budgets cut through political rhetoric and therefore disclose policy priorities. They force policy makers to "put their money where their mouths are." Yet those who make decisions about spending do not have to pay the bills; the public pays. The public also benefits from government spending. However, the benefits are not evenly distributed across society, and neither is the burden of paying for them. Therein lies the strain inherent in the politics of taxing and spending.

Beyond taxing and spending to provide services to its citizenry, a government may also tax and spend to influence the economy in desired directions. Among all governments in the United States, the federal government is best able to influence the economy. Smoothing out the business cycle has long been a central objective of U.S. economic policy. Unlike the federal government, state and local governments are not well positioned to employ fiscal policy successfully. They must balance their budgets and may not run deficits financed by credit, and their economies are too easily penetrated by either the national economy or regional economic conditions.

Government spending has grown steadily in the twentieth century. It increased by 839 percent between the beginning of the Great Depression and the end of the Korean War (by nearly 500 percent measured in constant dollars), with the federal government accounting for the greatest portion of the increase. The stimulative federal policies of the Depression era, along with U.S. involvement in World War II and in the Korean War, primed federal spending. During that period, state spending rose only about one-sixth as fast as federal spending in per capita constant dollars. In contrast, local government spending remained essentially flat.

With the end of the Korean War, state and local spending grew faster than federal spending through 1964, as federal spending decreased as a percentage of the GNP and as state and local governments expanded services to meet the needs of families with baby boom offspring. Government spending took off during the subsequent ten-year period, pushed rapidly upward by the Great Society initiatives, the Vietnam War, and the continued population pressures exerted by the second wave of the post-World War II baby boom. State spending rose as fiscal federalism greatly increased federal spending and, through matching grants, brought state spending along. At the same time states pursued their own spending initiatives, significantly expanding financial assistance to local units of government, particularly aid to local school districts.

The period from 1974 to 1981 constituted a major slowdown in state and local spending. Federal spending outpaced state and local spending. Domestic spending, particularly entitlement spending, led the way.

The period from 1981 to 1988 represents a time of rebounding state and local spending. The growth rate of federal spending slowed a bit, although inconsistent patterns could be seen below the surface. National defense spending rose both in constant dollars and as a percentage of GDP. At the same time, the growth rate of domestic discretionary spending declined significantly.

The "peace dividend" brought about by the thawing of the Cold War, along with lower interest rates, kept the annual constant-dollar increase in federal spending down to 2 percent between 1988 and 2001, the lowest of any period examined and below the annual increase in GDP. In contrast, state and local spending rose as a percentage of GDP during this period, before dropping off sharply between 2007 and 2011 as a result of the Great Recession. Federal spending as a percentage of GDP increased markedly, reflecting its stimulative fiscal policy, as well as increased federal aid to assist hard-pressed state and local governments.

In financing spending, both the federal government and the states have become much more dependent on the personal income tax since the Korean War. In turn, the federal government has become less dependent on the corporate income tax or on sales and gross receipts taxes. States have come to rely less on sales and motor-vehicle-related taxes, although sales taxes remain the single largest component of state tax revenue. Local governments have made less use of the property tax and have increased their reliance on sales and income taxes, where permitted by their states. Most recently, though, the property tax has made a modest comeback.

Notes

1 Robert D. Lee Jr., and Ronald W. Johnson, Public Budgeting Systems, 4th ed. (Rockville, M.D.: Aspen, 1989), 29–30.
2 U.S. Advisory Council on Intergovernmental Relations, Significant Features of Fiscal Federalism, 1989 ed., book 2 (Washington, D.C.: U.S. Advisory Council on Intergovernmental Relations, 1989), 20.
3 John Shannon, "The Great Slowdown in State-Local Spending—Will It Last?" Presentation to the Task Force on Local Government, Washington, D.C., February 22, 1982.
4 Richard D. Bingham, State and Local Governments in an Urban Society (New York: Random House, 1986), 308.
5 Tax Foundation, Facts and Figures on Government Finance, 30th ed. (Washington D.C.: Tax Foundation, 1995), 6.
6 U.S. Bureau of the Census, Government Finances in 1987–88 (Washington, D.C.: Bureau of the Census, U. S. Department of Commerce, 1990), 7; see also earlier editions of this publication.
7 National Association of State Budget Officers, Budgeting Amid Fiscal Uncertainty (Washington, D.C.: National Association of State Budget Officers, 2004); National Association of State Budget Officers, Fiscal Survey of the States (Washington, D.C.: National Association of State Budget Officers, December 2006), vi–viii; Fiscal Survey of the States, December 2007, viii-ix, 1.

8 U.S. Advisory Committee on Intergovernmental Relations, Significant Features of Fiscal Federalism, 1988 ed., book 2 (Washington, D.C.: Advisory Council on Intergovernmental Relations, 1988), 26, 34.

9 Bureau of the Census, State and Local Government Finances by Level of Government and by State: 2012, www.census.gov/govs/local; Office of Management and Budget, Budget of the United States Government, FY 2015, Historical Tables, Table 2.1.

10 Advisory Council. These concepts and associated indexes were developed by the Intergovernmental Relations (ACIR) and the subject of their report, 1988 State Fiscal Capacity and Effort (Washington, D.C.: ACIR, August 1990).

11 Eric Toder and Daniel Baneman, "Distributional Effects of Individual Income Tax Expenditures: An Update," Tax Policy Center, February 2, 2012.

12 Lee and Johnson, Public Budgeting, 61.

13 John L. Mikesell, Fiscal Administration: Analysis and Applications for the Public Sector, 5th ed. (Fort Worth, T.X.: Harcourt Brace College, 1999), 300–1.

14 Ibid., 286–93.

Chapter 6

National Budgeting

Debate over the federal budget cuts to the heart of national politics, and well it should. The federal budget indicates how much our national government is willing to spend on public purposes, sets substantive policy priorities within overall spending levels, and determines the amount that must be borrowed in order to finance approved spending levels. The federal budget can also affect the taxing and spending decisions of state and local governments.

Among its various functions, the federal budget also serves as a policy tool to transfer resources from the private sector to the public sector, or vice versa. Taxation takes resources from the private sector to finance spending for public purposes. However, most public expenditures put resources back into private hands, albeit not necessarily and not often returning them to those from whom they were taken, and certainly not in the same proportion. Each new federal budget sets the transfer balance in the aggregate, while the previous budget serves as a **baseline** for current action.

The federal budget not only establishes how much our national government is willing to spend on public purposes but also identifies our nation's relative policy priorities. Its programmed resource commitments cut through political rhetoric, clearly illuminating the policy choices of budget makers. Budget recommendations and spending decisions can be compared—both in actual dollars and in percentage increases or decreases—for different substantive policy areas. It is thus possible to compare spending commitments for each policy area, such as national defense, foreign assistance, public welfare, and education.

The federal budget also indicates the extent to which the federal government is willing to borrow to supplement tax and fee revenue in order to fund approved spending levels. When aggregate national spending choices exceed available revenues, the resulting deficits make it necessary to borrow to close the gap and provide resources adequate for budgeted obligations. Inordinate deficits can crowd private borrowers out of national credit markets when the supply of available credit is insufficient, potentially retarding domestic investment and, in turn, national economic growth.

In addition to its effects on the national economy, the federal budget can also affect the taxing and spending decisions of state and local governments.

Sizable cuts in federal aid force state and local policy makers to decide whether to raise their own taxes or fees to replace lost federal revenue. State and local policy makers can elect to reduce expenditures not covered by federal revenue, making room to continue spending on the federally aided programs at existing levels. They can also reduce the programs that are experiencing federal cuts to levels supportable by the remaining federal funding, or they can eliminate them altogether. In addition, under significant federal reductions, state policy makers face the decision whether to increase aid to local units of government and thereby soften the local impacts of federal aid reductions; however, when cuts in federal aid affect both state and local governments, the state's fiscal flexibility is reduced. State policy makers then must weigh local government needs along with state needs, and must decide which to satisfy and how. Again, as with local governments, the primary options available are raising additional own-source revenues and cutting expenditures.

Increases in federal aid may also significantly affect state and local spending, particularly when federal law requires state or local funds to match the federal assistance. In those instances, state and local policy makers are forced to place priorities on their spending decisions. Do they approve the matching funds to secure the federal money, though this action may leave them with insufficient resources for higher-priority programs? Of these two scenarios, state and local, officials would no doubt prefer the happier problems posed by expanding federal aid—problems that were characteristic of the 1960s and most of the 1970s—to those occasioned by contracting federal assistance.

The federal budget thus provides a fiscal and substantive public policy plan for the country. It provides a composite statement of the direction government should take over the coming fiscal year, put in the context of a longer-term strategy. The federal budget thus can be seen as a vision for the country in setting forth a policy agenda. It lays out, in macro terms, the major dimensions of that vision: how much the federal government should spend, and for what; how much it should tax, and who should bear the burden of that taxation; and how much it should go into debt.

From a different perspective, the federal budget can also be viewed as an amalgam of many disjointed decisions made on a vast array of budget items adjusted at different phases of the budgetary process. The first characterization regards federal budget making as a policy-driven process; the second views it as mechanistic and programmatic. The first sees the whole shaping the parts; the second sees the whole only as a composite of its parts.

Although contemporary federal budgeting has elements of both, the up-front debate about policy direction has dominated the politics of budgetary decision making over the past two decades, even though the appropriations committees continue (but with increased constraints) to determine how to allocate their slice of the larger budget pie. In the charged, highly partisan political environment of contemporary federal budgeting, it is the larger or macro debate that has become most deeply ideological and highly contentious. At its core are profound differences over the size and role of government in U.S. society. Key elements in that debate include whether recipients should pay more in support of Medicare (a program that provides a measure of health care security for older Americans who have contributed toward that end during their working years); whether a guaranteed federal safety net should make cash assistance, food stamps, and health care available to needy Americans who meet income and asset eligibility requirements, or whether these programs should lose their entitlement status and be turned over to the states; whether environmental protection standards should be lowered and enforcement reduced; whether the federal government should play a bigger role in setting K-12 educational policy and providing financial assistance; and whether and by how much taxes should be cut, and for whom.

Macro Choices and the Transition from Budget Deficit to Budget Surplus, and Back to Budget Deficit

Over the past three decades large federal budget deficits have colored budgetary decision making, with the exception of a brief interlude of budget surpluses from fiscal years 1998 through 2001. Although partisan politics shaped the debate about policy priorities, that debate took place within the larger issue of how to deal with highly visible and politically wrenching budget deficits. As the federal budget deficit soared in the early and mid-1980s (see Table 6.1), so did partisan squabbling over what to do about it. Despite procedural budgetary reforms commonly known as the Gramm–Rudman–Hollings legislation (discussed in detail later in this chapter), the U.S. Congress and the president were unable to agree on major budgetary initiatives that would dramatically stem the deficit tide. That fact is not without irony, since conscious policy choices had earlier contributed to the growing budget deficit. After all, Congress approved President Ronald Reagan's proposals to cut individual income tax rates by 25 percent across the board and to increase defense spending by 5–6 percent a year (after inflation) during Reagan's first term. Even though the Reagan administration was able to slow the growth rate of domestic spending, the combined fiscal force of these first two initiatives was too great to overcome (see Table 6.2).

A strong economic recovery from the 1981–2 recession helped to keep the federal budget deficit from rising any higher by mid-decade, and continued solid economic growth in the latter half, coupled with increased congressional restraint in defense spending, caused the deficit to decline. That good fortune was all too temporary, however, as still another swing of the business cycle pointed to an ensuing economic slowdown by the decade's end. Facing projections of a rapidly rising deficit and increasing media criticism for not doing anything about it, President George H.W. Bush and the Democrat-controlled Congress agreed in October of 1990 on a deficit-reduction

Table 6.1   The Changing Budget Deficit, Selected Fiscal Years, 1974–2018 (in $ billions)

Fiscal year	Receipts	Outlays	(Deficit)/surplus
1974	263.2	269.3	(6.1)
1975	279.0	332.3	(53.3)
1976	298.0	371.7	(73.7)
1977	355.5	409.2	(53.7)
1978	399.5	458.7	(59.2)
1979	463.3	504.0	(40.7)
1980	517.1	590.9	(73.8)
1981	599.2	678.2	(78.9)
1982	617.7	745.7	(127.9)
1983	600.5	808.3	(207.8)
1984	666.4	851.8	(185.4)
1985	734.0	946.3	(212.3)
1986	769.1	990.3	(221.2)
1987	854.2	1,004.0	(149.8)
1988	909.2	1,064.4	(155.2)
1989	991.1	1,143.7	(152.6)
1990	1,031.9	1,252.9	(221.0)
1991	1,054.9	1,324.2	(269.3)
1992	1,091.2	1,381.5	(290.3)
1993	1,154.3	1,409.3	(255.0)
1994	1,258.5	1,461.7	(203.2)
1995	1,351.7	1,515.7	(174.0)
1996	1,453.0	1,560.4	(107.4)
1997	1,579.2	1,601.1	(21.9)
1998	1,721.7	1,652.4	69.3
1999	1,827.4	1,701.8	125.6
2000	2,025.1	1,788.9	236.2
2001	1,991.0	1,862.8	128.2
2002	1,853.1	2,010.8	(157.7)
2003	1,782.3	2,159.8	(377.5)
2004	1,880.1	2,292.8	(412.7)
2005	2,153.6	2,471.9	(318.3)
2006	2,406.8	2,655.0	(248.2)
2007	2,567.9	2,728.6	(160.7)
2008	2,523.9	2,982.5	(458.6)
2009	2,104.9	3,517.6	(1,412.7)
2010	2,162.7	3,457.0	(1,294.3)
2011	2,303.4	3,603.0	(1,299.6)
2012	2,450.1	3,537.1	(1,087.0)
2013	2,775.1	3,454.6	(679.5)
2014e	3,001.7	3,650.5	(648.8)
2016e	3,567.9	4,099.0	(531.1)
2018e	4,029.8	4,443.1	(413.3)

e = estimate

Source: Office of Management and Budget, Budget of the United States Government, FY 2015, Historical Tables, Table 1.1.

Table 6.2 Federal Government Expenditures by Major Function, Selected Fiscal Years, 1954–2016

Year	National defense	Nondefense discretionary	Means-tested entitlements	Social security	Medicare	Net interest	Other
Amount (in $ billions)							
1954	49.3	6.7	2.2	3.4	NA	4.8	4.5
1964	55.0	24.1	5.0	16.2	NA	8.2	16.1
1974	80.7	57.5	20.2	55.0	11.3	21.4	40.6
1981	158.0	149.9	52.2	137.9	42.5	68.8	98.1
1988	290.0	173.5	78.1	216.8	87.7	151.8	100.3
1994	282.3	259.1	173.4	316.9	162.5	202.9	110.1
1998	270.2	281.9	204.8	376.1	213.6	241.1	116.5
2002	349.0	285.4	280.6	452.1	256.8	170.9	164.6
2004	459.1	441.1	328.6	491.5	301.5	160.2	146.1
2006	520.0	496.7	354.3	543.6	378.6	226.6	204.7
2008	612.4	522.4	426.5	612.1	452.0	252.8	171.8
2010	688.9	658.3	562.6	700.8	516.8	196.2	247.7
2012	670.5	615.6	534.0	767.7	544.6	220.4	281.2
2014e	612.4	561.9	637.3	852.3	600.4	223.4	256.2
2016e	584.2	568.7	750.5	947.4	662.3	317.6	375.2
Percentage distribution (Totals greater than 100% do not account for Undistributed Offsetting Receipts)							
1954	69.5	9.4	3.1	4.8	NA	6.8	6.4
1964	46.4	20.3	4.2	13.7	NA	6.9	13.6
1974	30.0	21.3	7.5	20.4	4.2	8.0	15.1
1981	23.3	22.1	7.7	20.3	6.3	10.1	14.5
1988	27.3	16.3	7.3	20.4	8.3	14.3	9.4
1994	19.3	17.7	11.9	21.7	11.1	13.9	7.5
1998	16.4	17.1	12.4	22.8	12.9	14.6	7.1
2002	17.4	19.2	14.0	22.5	12.8	8.5	8.2
2004	19.8	19.2	14.3	21.4	14.0	7.0	6.8
2006	19.6	18.7	13.3	20.5	14.3	8.5	7.7
2008	20.5	17.5	14.3	20.5	15.2	8.5	6.1
2010	19.9	19.0	16.3	20.3	12.7	5.7	6.9
2012	19.0	17.4	15.1	21.7	13.0	6.2	7.7
2014e	16.8	15.4	17.5	23.3	13.8	6.1	6.8
2016e	14.3	13.9	18.3	23.1	13.6	7.7	8.9

e = estimate
NA = Not Applicable

Source: Office of Management and Budget, Budget of the United States Government, FY 2015, Historical Tables, Tables 8.1, 8.3, and 16.1.

package that included both spending cuts and, significantly, tax increases—the latter happening after President Bush proclaimed on national television to the American public, "Read my lips—no new taxes." Unfortunately for Bush, the economy fell into recession in late 1990, which reduced projected revenues and increased recession-sensitive entitlement costs. These combined effects wiped out all of the would-be gain promised by the compromise package, and the federal budget deficit rose to over $290 billion by the end of the 1992 fiscal year. To make matters worse, the gross federal debt cracked the $4 trillion level, up from $1.1 trillion just ten years earlier.

At the time of his inauguration, President Bill Clinton faced a projected federal budget deficit well in excess of $300 billion. During his campaign for the presidency, Clinton had championed deficit reduction and spoken of the likely need for a tax increase to do the job—a position that placed him at odds with Bush, who admitted publicly that his support for the 1990 tax increase had been a big mistake that, if reelected, he would not repeat. In pondering the need for a tax increase, Clinton was well aware of the tax choices of preceding administrations. He knew that the large Reagan-engineered income tax cut of 1981 had removed more than $300 billion from 1990 fiscal revenue. He also knew that between 1982 and 1990 Congress had enacted a dozen tax increases that augmented revenues by about $250 billion by the 1990 fiscal year, largely through increased social security taxes, motor vehicle fuel taxes, and other non-income taxes. In balance, he inherited a smaller revenue base than did Reagan.[1]

President Clinton also recognized that the top 1 percent of income earners got the lion's share of the real after-tax personal income growth produced by a strongly recovering economy and the 1981 reduction in the top income tax rate. He further knew that although the tax changes of the 1980s removed most poor families from the income tax rolls by raising the personal exemption and standard deduction and by providing an earned income tax credit for low-income workers with children, increased payroll taxes for social security and Medicare pretty much canceled out their gains.[2]

These realizations appear to have influenced President Clinton's choices about how to raise revenue in pursuit of a reduced budget deficit. Of the $433 billion in deficit reduction over five years approved by Congress in 1993 at the president's behest, the Congressional Budget Office (CBO) projected that $240 billion would come from tax increases. Yet what is most salient here is the way in which that additional revenue was to be raised—with the bulk coming from an increase in the top income tax rate from 31 percent to 36 percent, along with a 10 percent surcharge on taxes due on incomes over $250,000. At the other end of the income spectrum, Congress, again at the president's behest, expanded the earned income tax credit for low-income workers. The vote on the Omnibus Budget Reconciliation legislation reflected the highly partisan nature of the debate, as Republicans failed to give it a single vote in either chamber. Strong Democratic unity produced a meager two-vote margin in the U.S.

House of Representatives; in the U.S. Senate, it took Vice President Gore's tie-breaking vote to win passage.

The 1994 election dramatically changed the partisan balance in Congress. The Republicans won control of both the House and the Senate. Both the Republican congressional leaders and the rank and file saw the 1994 election as a mandate to reduce the size of government and its programmatic and regulatory reach. The House Republicans, led by their new speaker, Newt Gingrich, pursued that mission with apostolic zeal. Buoyed by the national attention given to their "Contract with America," the House Republicans pushed their Senate counterparts to cooperate in enacting a late-session reconciliation bill that was faithful to the principles outlined in the Contract and consistent with the congressional budget resolution passed earlier. The Republicans' agenda included going after entitlement spending at the same time as calling for new tax cuts. In pursuing the former, Republican leaders pointed to a 1994 CBO study that projected entitlement spending growing three times faster than inflation through the end of the twentieth century without major reforms,[3] following a period of steep increases accelerating after 1988, as Table 6.2 clearly shows. In seeking the latter, they saw tax cuts as ideologically consistent with their desire to transfer resources from public into private hands, reversing what they viewed as the failed policy of tax increases approved in 1993.

Both the Republican-stamped budget resolution and the reconciliation bill for fiscal year 1996 included provisions that, if signed into law by the president, would balance the federal budget by the end of the 2002 fiscal year. Its $664 billion in deficit reduction over seven years included spending cuts of $887 billion and increased corporate tax revenues of $18 billion resulting from the elimination of corporate tax breaks, offset by personal income tax cuts of $241 billion. Prominently included among the spending cuts were major reductions in federal spending for Medicare ($201 billion), Medicaid ($117 billion), and welfare ($82 billion). Republicans supported the bill overwhelmingly; only five Democrats voted for it in the House, and none cast a yea vote in the Senate. President Clinton, in turn, vetoed the bill. He also subsequently vetoed the Defense Authorization Act, as well as appropriations bills funding the U.S. Department of the Interior and the Environmental Protection Agency.

Clinton's veto messages portray the deep normative divisions existing at the time. In rejecting the reconciliation bill, the president especially took issue with its cuts in his recommended funding levels for Medicare and Medicaid, its income tax reductions, its cuts in the Earned Income Tax Credit Program available to the working poor, its elimination of the Direct Student Loan Program, and what he saw as a number of objectionable natural resource and environmental policy changes that would weaken governmental protection. The president's veto of the Defense Authorization Act registered his opposition to continued congressional support for so-called Star Wars weapons development and procurement. He objected most strongly to the act's required deployment of a missile defense system capable of intercepting missiles aimed at all of the fifty states. Not only did he take issue with the associated cost implications of developing and deploying such a system, but he also saw it as a threat to continued nuclear reduction treaty talks with Russia. Inherently, he questioned its need in a changing world free of the Cold War and its perceived threats. For Clinton, the mid-1990s were a time to realize the "peace dividend" further, a dividend that had been paying off for several years (as Table 6.2 also illustrates); he was not anxious to reverse that trend.

Congress's and the president's inability to reach agreement on a policy vision for the United States created governmental instability for much of the 1996 fiscal year. With only seven of thirteen appropriations bills enacted into law by the calendar year's end, another three passed by Congress but vetoed by the president, and another three still in Congress, many federal agencies and programs were forced to rely on continuing resolutions to keep operating and for federal employees to be paid. In all, a record twelve continuing resolutions were required before Congress and the president reached a compromise budget agreement in late April, which provided spending authority for the remainder of the fiscal year. During the protracted budget battle, breaks in coverage forced the shutdown of government agencies and the furloughing of federal employees for two stretches, the longest lasting from December 16, 1995 to January 6, 1996.

Polls suggest that the public tended to blame the Republicans for the stalemate and government shutdown. Clinton skillfully reinforced that perception and used the presidential podium to paint the Republican leadership as extreme. Political moderates, in response, called on Congress and the president to turn from confrontation and work closer together to address pressing national problems, including further deficit reduction. Getting the message, the president and Congress essentially agreed to continue spending at the current level and to await the outcome of the 1996 elections as an indicator of voter sentiment.

As the election neared, Clinton lent his support to Republican-initiated welfare reform legislation that eliminated the Aid to Families with Dependent Children (AFDC) entitlement program and replaced it with discretionary block grants to the states, giving voters further evidence of their ability to work together and enact legislation favored by the public. National opinion polls registered widespread voter approval, and both the president and Congress took credit for "ending welfare dependence." Not everyone shared that enthusiasm, however. Liberal Democrats viewed the end of entitlement as an unwelcome departure from the traditional values of the party. The welfare reform package divided Democrats not only in Congress but also in the Clinton administration.

Along with their growing hopefulness that the president and Congress finally recognized the need to cooperate and accommodate their respective interests if progress were to be made on matters the public cares about, Americans were also increasingly optimistic about the national economy and their own fortunes. Both Clinton and congressional incumbents benefited from this state of affairs. The president won reelection easily and the Republicans maintained majorities in both chambers, although they suffered some losses in the House. Voters did not use the electoral opportunity to take sides, to answer unambiguously whether they supported the "Republican Revolution" or Clinton's more moderate stance, as many observers had expected. Instead, voters seemed to sanction the status quo of divided government—a relationship that appeared to be working better as of late. In that environment, both the president and Congress appeared less willing than before to rock the political boat.

Democrats seemed content to ride the waves of prosperity for a time, and Republicans looked to make further gains in polishing their quickly tarnished image. Both parties' agendas became less ambitious and controversial, centering primarily on further reducing the federal budget deficit. The Democrats' attention to the details of deficit reduction, however, soon became diverted by growing allegations of influence peddling and campaign finance irregularities, directed at both the president and vice president personally. Yet the issue never became the scandal that the Republicans had hoped it would become. Political accommodation and the strength of the economy helped to keep Clinton's approval rating at historically high levels. This confluence of fledgling, but unrealized, scandal and public support for the outcomes of political accommodation set the stage for further cooperation on deficit reduction. For Clinton, a major further deficit-reduction package would deflect the public's and the media's attention away from allegations of campaign finance abuse and reinforce the public's perception of him as a leader who could work with the other party in Congress to get things done. For the Republicans, it would help to repair further their popular image as hard-liners who preferred ideological purity to getting things done.

On May 2, 1997, Clinton and Republican congressional leaders reached agreement on further deficit reduction aimed at balancing the federal budget by 2002, an agreement subsequently enacted into law in late July 1997. The margin of congressional approval was especially noteworthy given the record of partisan divisiveness and rancor marking congressional debate and action on previous deficit-reduction packages. The House passed the tax portion of the plan by a lopsided vote of 389 to 43, punctuating its vote with a hearty round of applause, and the Senate followed with a nearly unanimous vote of 92 to 8. In a similar fashion, the House voted 346 to 85 in favor of the spending package, and the Senate followed suit with an 85 to 15 vote.

With the 1997 deal, the White House could claim that the path to a balanced budget reflected the values and priorities of the president and his supporters, including increased spending for education, environmental protection, expanded medical assistance coverage for uninsured children in low-income families, restored public assistance benefits for legal immigrants, and tax incentives for businesses to hire welfare recipients. Overall, the budget agreement would allow domestic discretionary spending to increase by $70 billion over the five-year period, capping its growth at projected inflation—a looser cap than the spending freeze that preceded it. The president and his advisors were careful to label the higher domestic spending as vital domestic investment.

Republican leaders, in turn, could point to $95 billion in net tax cuts, prominently including a reduction in the tax rate on capital gains, a $500 per-child tax credit, a doubling of the estate tax exemption, and a liberalization of the deductibility of independent retirement accounts, making them available to higher-income taxpayers. Republicans could also take credit for putting Medicare on a sounder financial footing through controls on reimbursements to hospitals and health care providers, along with increases in the premiums paid by middle- and upper-income beneficiaries. These changes would produce a projected reduction in entitlement spending of $115 billion—savings that would offset the cost of increased domestic spending and tax cuts. In addition, both parties could highlight new tax credits for lower- and middle-income taxpayers to offset the costs of higher education, even though many of the more ideological Republicans voiced their preference for other forms of tax relief that would contribute more directly to economic growth.

A year later, in the fall of 1998, Congress continued its bipartisan support of the budget, with the House passing that year's omnibus budget act by a margin of 333 to 95 and the Senate supporting it by a vote of 65 to 29. The 1998 deal gave the president and the Democrats more in discretionary spending than Clinton had requested in his February budget submission, and it included the president's hard-fought $1.2 billion initiative to aid local school districts in reducing class size in the early grades. For Republicans, the omnibus spending bill contained an increase in defense spending and funding for new antidrug programs.[4]

The 1999 budget session presented the president and Congress with a dilemma. Although revenue projections pointed to a likely surplus in excess of $100 billion by the end of the 1999 fiscal year, budget makers faced tightened limitations on spending. The president and Congress could rightfully claim that they had begun to win the battle against the deficit, yet because of congressional caps on spending they had little legal leeway to increase spending to meet needs that had been squeezed by deficit-reduction measures. In response, Congress turned to budgetary gimmicks, reminiscent of the earlier Gramm–Rudman–Hollings era. Primary among them was Congress's willingness to label $20.8 billion in new fiscal year 2000 spending as "emergency spending," keeping it outside the caps. New spending for such diverse purposes as "Y2K" computer problems, increased agricultural price supports, embassy security, missile defense, and increased military spending were all folded in under the emergency exception.

By the end of the 1999 fiscal year, the federal budget surplus had grown to $125.6 billion, and forecasters expected the surplus to approach $200 billion by the end of the 2001 fiscal year. Yet the tough spending caps approved in 1997 continued in place. Faced with this macro-constraint, would Congress resort again to gimmicks to meet the statutory spending limits? No. Instead it changed the law.

Box 6.1 illustrates both Congress's predicament and its newly found solution. Confronting a cap of $541.1 billion on discretionary spending, both Democratic and Republican congressional leaders publicly pronounced that limit as unrealistic and politically unattainable. It would take a limit of $611 billion just to maintain the current spending program at the projected rate of inflation. Continuing strong economic growth would produce ample revenues both to increase spending beyond the caps and to generate an enlarged surplus. With wide support, Congress passed a continuing resolution that allowed it to spend $600.3 billion in the 2001 fiscal year, still less than what it would take to compensate for the lost purchasing power attributed to inflation.

Box 6.1   Discretionary Spending in an Environment of Budget Surplus, FY 2001

$541.1 billion	Cap Imposed in 1997
$600.3 billion	2001 Congressional Resolution
$611.1 billion	Inflation Adjusted
$625.7 billion	President Clinton's Revised Request
$640.2 billion	Revised Cap (October 25, 2000)
$635.0 billion	Outlays Approved by Congress

But as negotiations within Congress, and between Congress and the president, began to unfold, it became readily apparent that political pressures would break that lid. Not to be outdone by Clinton's revised request for $625.7 billion in domestic spending, Congress raised the ante just before the 2000 elections and set the discretionary spending cap at $640.2 billion. In its ensuing lame-duck session Congress approved $635 billion in discretionary spending for fiscal year 2001, as conservative Republicans, worried that their party was going too far in accommodating the president's spending desires, pulled back their support for the additional spending.[5] Nevertheless, the budgetary restraint of the past had clearly been broken. Strong economic growth swelled revenues, providing budget makers with comfortable room to make up for the constrained spending opportunities of the past two decades and to continue to amass a sizable surplus, which rose to $236 billion at the end of the 2000 fiscal year.

Attention passed from spending restraint to how to handle the surplus. Although the public debate included major alternatives such as cutting taxes, fiscally shoring up the social security and Medicare trust funds, and paying down the national debt, it became clear that an increasing share of the surplus would go toward higher domestic and defense spending. The spending caps had been broken, and revenue constraints had disappeared, or so it seemed late in the calendar year 2000, even as economists warned of an impending slowdown in economic growth.

By early 2001, after George W. Bush's presidential electoral victory in November, both President Bush and the Republican leadership in Congress were calling for large income tax cuts to give back some of the surplus to taxpayers. A slumping economy prompted congressional Democrats to support a tax cut as a Keynesian tool of fiscal stimulus, yet expressing their desire to negotiate with the Bush administration and GOP leaders over the size of the cut and its distribution. The resulting legislation, passed by Congress on June 7, 2001, produced a tax cut of $1.35 trillion through 2010. The House passed the conference report by a vote of 240 to 154, with 28 Democrats joining 211 Republicans and one independent in support. No Republican voted against it in the House. The Senate approved the report by a vote of 58 to 33, with 12 Democrats joining forces with 46 Republicans in support. Only two Republicans voted with the Democrats in opposition.

As was discussed in chapter 4, most of the tax-reduction package— $843 billion over ten years—resulted from changes in personal income tax brackets and lowered rates, which proved most attractive to congressional Republicans (especially reductions in the top rates applied to the highest tax brackets). Republicans also overwhelmingly supported phasing out estate tax, which proponents skillfully labeled "the death tax."

Along with rate cuts that greatly benefited upper-income taxpayers, the legislation dropped the lowest tax rate from 15 percent to 10 percent, an action attractive to Democrats. Other ingredients that garnered some Democratic support include doubling the $500 per child tax credit, instituting a tax credit for adoptions, and providing tax relief for two-income married couples who pay more income tax filing a joint return than they would if they were unmarried and living together.

Congress enacted the tax cut legislation in an environment of a worsening economy—one which, as it was later recorded, fell into recession during the first three quarters of the 2001 calendar year. With reduced gross domestic product (GDP) came lowered personal income and lowered individual income tax revenue. Sluggish economic recovery that followed shortly after the recession caused tax revenues to continue to fall below estimates. Not only did the economic downturn depress revenues but it also caused spending on entitlement programs for the needy to rise significantly. Moreover, the September 11, 2001 terrorist attacks soon prompted increased spending on homeland security and military engagements in Afghanistan. And just three months following the attacks on U.S. soil, riding on the public's growing approval rating of President Bush, Congress passed the president's No Child Left Behind national educational reform initiative, committing the federal government to new domestic spending. The U.S. invasion of Iraq beginning in March 2003 added greatly to defense spending and contributed to a rapidly growing federal budget deficit, which hit $412 billion at the end of the 2004 fiscal year.

Between the 2001 and 2004 fiscal years, federal budget outlays increased by 23 percent. Federal spending rose from 18.6 percent of GDP in fiscal year 2001 to 19.5 percent in 2004. Defense spending rose by $146 billion between the 2001 and 2004 fiscal years—an increase of 48 percent. Domestic discretionary spending added $115 billion over those years, rising by 36 percent.[6]

Accelerating economic growth in 2004, after a slow recovery from the 2001 recession, generated a wave of revenue increases that contributed substantially to a falling federal budget deficit, which hit $162 billion at the end of the 2007 fiscal year. That drop occurred in spite of the rising costs of the United States' continuing military involvement in Iraq and Afghanistan—which pushed defense spending up from $456 billion in FY 2004 to $553 billion in FY 2007—and the ongoing revenue loss resulting from the Bush tax cuts. But with economic growth slowing in FY 2008, and interest costs tied to the federal government's debt-financed injection of capital into struggling financial institutions projected to rise sharply, the CBO forecast a return to budget deficits exceeding $400 billion for the 2008–2010 fiscal years.[7] In fact, the deficits were much higher, jumping sharply to $1.4 trillion in FY 2009 and remaining at about $1.1 trillion through FY 2012 (see Table 6.1).

The Great Recession (discussed comprehensively in chapter 4) was the culprit. Yet although the monetary policy of the Federal Reserve became the nation's primary weapon to generate increased demand and reverse the economy's course, presidential economic policy made its contribution as well. The Bush administration, late in President Bush's second term, championed federal intervention to prevent the collapse of the nation's financial system. Congress followed the president's lead and passed the Emergency Economic Stabilization Act in October 2008. It authorized the Treasury to provide cash infusions to struggling banks, as well as to purchase mortgage-backed securities that had lost considerable value, as an effort to stem the tide of collapsing value. The Bush administration also used these TARP funds to keep two major vehicle manufacturers, Chrysler and General Motors, operating during their financial reorganizations.

Bush's successor, Barack Obama, urged Congress to employ fiscal policy as a means to stimulate demand and thereby promote economic growth. Shortly before assuming the presidency, his transition team worked with the Democratic leadership in Congress to shape and subsequently enact the American Recovery and Reinvestment Act of 2009, at a cost of $787 billion. The package included tax relief intended to spur consumption; financial assistance to the states to limit budget cuts made necessary by state balanced budget requirements; and federal support of infrastructure, with its associated job creation.

With Republicans gaining control of the House of Representatives in the 2010 mid-term elections, they turned their attention to reducing the federal budget deficit. Republican leaders used the need to raise the nation's debt ceiling by late summer 2011 as leverage to push deficit reduction, culminating in Congress's passage of the Budget Control Act of 2011, which committed Congress to $917 billion in cuts over ten years and resulted in automatic across-the-board spending reductions, referred to as sequesters, which began in January 2013.

Buoyed by his reelection in 2012 in the context of an improving economy, President Obama turned to tax policy in the wake of budget cuts. With a bipartisan vote that garnered eighty-nine yea votes in the Senate and got the support of fifteen Republicans in the Republican-controlled House, Congress passed the American Taxpayer Relief Act of 2012, signed into law by the president on January 2, 2013. It prevented the so-called Bush tax cuts from expiring altogether, which they were scheduled to do at the end of calendar year 2012. Instead, it eliminated them only for single income tax filers earning $400,000 or more annually, and for joint filers earning $450,000 or more. The legislation also raised the top tax rate on capital gains from 15 percent to 20 percent for income tax filers at or above those income levels. In addition, it raised the estate tax from 35 percent to 40 percent for estates valued at $5 million or more. These measures increased revenues from where they would have been had the Bush tax cuts been extended in their entirety, and did so equitably—at least in the eyes of the Obama administration—but they cost the Treasury money in continuing to provide cuts to those with incomes below the floors for elimination.

Most significantly, the combination of spending cuts and an improving national economy prompted the Office of Management and Budget to forecast a decline in the federal budget deficit to $513 billion in FY 2016, down sharply from its $1.4 trillion apex in FY 2009 (see Table 6.1). In a more recent estimate the CBO forecast the deficit to fall to $467 billion in FY 2016, projecting growth in the nation's GDP of a respectable 2.9 percent in both of the 2015 and 2016 fiscal years.[8]

Structuring the Process of Budget Deliberation

Although the president gets the first shot at using the budget to set national priorities, Congress structures the process by which it reviews the president's budget recommendations and identifies and deliberates on its own budgetary actions. The president's budget is just that—the president's statement of the direction he wants the federal government to take in taxing and spending—and that sense of direction reveals something of the president's view of what should be government's role in the economy and society more broadly.

On the executive side, the Budget and Accounting Act of 1921 made the president responsible for developing and presenting the budget to Congress; it also gave the president the necessary tools to get the job done. First, the law required government agencies to send their budget requests to the president, who decides whether to incorporate them into the executive budget as requested or to modify them. Before 1921, agencies sent their estimates of budgetary needs directly to congressional committees without presidential review or recommendations. Second, the act created an executive budget office—the Bureau of the Budget (since renamed the Office of Management and Budget, or OMB)—to assist the president in preparing the budget. At its inception, the budget office was charged with reacting to agency requests and recommending courses of action on each to the president. Since then its role has greatly expanded, and today the OMB not only develops the president's budget but also acts as a presidential clearing house for all proposed legislation initiated by executive branch agencies.

The director of the OMB today holds cabinet officer status. The director has become much more than a manager of the presidential budget staff; he or she is a key policy architect within the president's small circle of top policy strategists. This observation is not intended to suggest that cabinet members do not shape policy choices within their respective departments or that the influence of some—such as the secretaries of state, the treasury, or defense—does not stretch beyond their agency boundaries. However, unlike cabinet members, who have policy and administrative authority over their agencies and who are charged with helping to shape and advance presidential policy in their substantive areas, the OMB director is responsible for shaping and advancing presidential policy across agency jurisdictions. In that respect, the budget director shares a purview similar to that of other key presidential aides, including the chief of staff, to whom the OMB director traditionally reports. The complexity and technical demands of the budget nevertheless place the director in a unique position. The budget director controls the "numbers," and the creative use of numbers can constrain the advice of others and channel presidential choice. The director is in the enviable position of sketching the big budgetary picture and envisioning how the many pieces to the budgetary puzzle fit together and interrelate. The director can suggest that a cabinet secretary does not really understand the inter-program and interagency effects of a given budgetary recommendation. He or she can also point out that an agency head lacks a ready appreciation of the overall fiscal constraints under which the presidential budget is being formulated. With that kind of ammunition, the OMB director has formidable resources that can be employed to transcend narrower agency-specific interests.

Scholars have traditionally characterized congressional involvement in national budgeting as decentralized and fragmented, built upon a foundation of "contained specialization."[9] Before the congressional budgetary reforms of 1974 (discussed below), Congress had little institutionalized ability to substitute its collective vision of national priorities for that of the president. Although its leaders may have spoken of congressional priorities, those priorities were largely defined along committee and subcommittee lines. There may have been a House Ways and Means Committee position on Medicare or a Defense Appropriations Subcommittee position on the expansion of nuclear-powered submarines, but budget participants and observers alike would have been hard-pressed to identify an overarching congressional position on such issues as how much Congress should tax and spend on the one hand, and how much should be committed to each of the discrete substantive policy areas in the budget on the other.

In the absence of an explicit policy plan, it became difficult to speak in terms of a congressional alternative to the president's budget. Therefore, although Congress did certainly modify the president's recommendations—sometimes in dramatic ways—it followed the president's blueprint for spending, making incremental adjustments on the margins. Congress's budgetary imprint could best be seen after the fact, as an endorsement of the many discrete actions promoted by its subcommittees and committees. The resulting quilt of congressional action was the product of its decisional squares, and the quilt was sewn together through the politics of adjustment and reciprocity.

While Congress lacked a collectively endorsed plan for its budgetary actions, entitlement spending grew without Congress even needing to make annual spending decisions. Entitlement spending is uncontrollable because once entitlement legislation becomes law, all persons who legally qualify for federal assistance have the right to receive it. The federal treasury is obligated to pay the bill regardless of congressional expenditure estimates for the program. Therefore, major entitlement programs are, in reality, beyond the control of the appropriations process. Congress can change the entitlement itself, by deleting or modifying the statutory authorization, but as long as the authorization remains on the books the resulting costs must be covered. With this automatic spending feature, entitlement spending grew faster than any other part of the budget, increasing three times faster than non-entitlement spending between 1960 and 1974.[10] Spending seemed to be out of control, and Congress appeared to have no agreed-upon strategy to control it or to guide its own spending choices.

Along with these factors, the Democrat-led Congress in 1974 found itself in a power struggle with President Richard Nixon over his reprogramming of appropriations and his use of executive **impoundments**. **Reprogramming** is the use of funds for a purpose other than the one for which they were appropriated. Nixon's diversion of foreign assistance funds to finance the U.S. invasion of Cambodia provided the most dramatic illustration of this practice and provoked contention over what Congress viewed as presidential abuse of power. On the domestic front, Nixon incurred congressional rancor by impounding (not using) funds Congress had appropriated for specific programs that were in disfavor with the Nixon administration. By refusing to allot to federal agencies the amounts appropriated, the OMB, at Nixon's behest, effectively prevented the funds from being spent for the purposes intended by Congress. The impoundment of funds intended for community development and low-income housing programs, waste treatment facilities, and farm assistance programs struck a highly sensitive nerve in Congress.

In response to the president's perceived misuse of administrative budget controls, and as a means to bring coherence to its own budget making, Congress passed the Congressional Budget and Impoundment Control Act of 1974 by an overwhelming vote of 80 to 0 in the Senate and 401 to 6 in the House, just one month before President Nixon resigned from office under threat of impeachment. In the aftermath of the Watergate scandal, Nixon's weakened administration provided Congress with an opportunity to retrieve some of the authority over budget control it had given the president. Congress also sought, through changes in the congressional budgetary process, to equip itself to use the federal budget as a policy vehicle in pursuing its own vision. If successful, Congress could then advance its own comprehensive fiscal and policy priorities as a coherent alternative to the president's.

The 1974 Budget Act

Congress itself described the Congressional Budget and Impoundment Control Act of 1974 as a "historic legislative development," providing a "new process by which Congress determines national spending priorities."[11] These were to be Congress's priorities, not necessarily those of the president. Congress was to set these priorities in light of its own fiscal policies, deciding what constitutes an appropriate level of surplus or deficit on the basis of the nation's economic conditions and needs.

Although the act did not require Congress to create an alternative to the president's budget with the same form and level of detail, it did significantly modify the congressional budgetary process, creating structures and procedures to give Congress the ability to make appropriations decisions (after it had first recommended overall levels of revenues, spending, surplus or deficit, and public debt). The spending total was to be broken down into the same twenty functional spending areas into which the president's budget was then divided (such as national defense, international affairs, agriculture, income security, and the like), as is shown in Box 6.2. Congressional staff, in turn, developed "crosswalks" that could be used to apportion the recommended spending targets to each of the thirteen appropriations subcommittees. Box 6.3 shows the twelve appropriations subcommittees and the associated bills under their jurisdiction.

Box 6.2 Functional Budget Categories

(050)	National Defense
(150)	International Affairs
(250)	General Science, Space, and Technology
(270)	Energy
(300)	Natural Resources and Environment
(350)	Agriculture
(370)	Commerce and Housing Credit
(400)	Transportation
(450)	Community and Regional Development
(500)	Education, Training, Employment, and Social Services
(550)	Health

(570)   Medicare
(600)   Income Security
(650)   Social Security
(700)   Veterans Benefits and Services
(750)   Administration of Justice
(800)   General Government
(900)   Net Interest
(920)   Allowances
(950)   Undistributed Offsetting Receipts

Box 6.3   The Twelve Federal Appropriations Bills

Agriculture
Commerce, Justice, Science
Defense
Energy and Water Development
Financial Services and General Government
State, Foreign Operations
Homeland Security
Interior, Environment
Labor, Health and Human Services, and Education
Legislative Branch
Military Construction, Veterans Administration
Transportation, Treasury, Housing and Urban Development

The reform legislation changed the federal budgetary timetable, including the federal fiscal year (see Table 6.3). It created new budget committees in the House and Senate, each with its own staff, along with the new Congressional Budget Office (CBO). With the CBO, Congress intended to free itself from technical dependence on the executive branch by creating a congressional counterpart to the OMB and the president's economic staff. Those who drafted the act reasoned that Congress would need to be able to develop its own economic projections and credible estimates of revenues and expenditures if it were to forge an independent direction in budgeting.

The act also created the procedural devices of budget resolutions and reconciliation as instruments of coherent budgeting. Budget resolutions, like laws, must be adopted in the same form by both houses of Congress. However, unlike laws, congressional budget resolutions require no presidential action, and cannot be filibustered in the Senate. The Budget Act provided for two distinct concurrent resolutions. In the first, Congress recommended aggregate levels of budget authority, outlays (or anticipated levels of expenditure), and

Table 6.3 The Federal Budgetary Timetable

Action	Prior law	Gramm–Rudman–Hollings	Current law
President submits budget request	End of Jan.	First Monday after Jan. 3	Not later than first Monday in Feb.
Congressional Budget Office (CBO) reports to budget committees on fiscal policy and budget priorities	April 15	Feb. 15	Feb. 15
Committees submit report and estimates to budget committees	March 15	Feb. 25	Within six weeks of president's budget
Senate Budget Committee reports current budget resolution to floor	April 15	April 1	April 1
Congress completes action on budget resolution	May 15 (first resolution)	April 15	April 15
	Sept. 15 (second resolution)	May 15	House may consider appropriations bills in the absence of an approved concurrent resolution
House Appropriations Committee reports last regular appropriations bill		June 10	June 10
Congress completes action on reconciliation bill	Sept. 25	June 15	June 15
House completes action on regular appropriations bills	7th day after Labor Day	June 30	June 30
"Snapshot" of economic indicators, laws affecting spending and revenues and projected deficit taken by Office of Management and Budget (OMB); CBO report advisory only		Aug. 15	
OMB reports to Congress and the president on whether the deficit is projected to exceed the G-R-H target; also reports on the content of the sequester order, if required		Aug. 25	
President issue preliminary sequester order based on OMB report		Sept. 1	

(Continued)

Table 6.3 (Continued)

Action	Prior law	Gramm–Rudman–Hollings	Current law
Fiscal year begins	Oct. 1	Oct. 1	Oct. 1
Sequester order takes effect		Oct. 1	
OMB issues revised report reflecting congressional action taken after earlier reports, including any legislation passed after the president's Oct. 1 order		Oct. 5	
CBO issues (advisory) final sequester order			10 days after adjournment
OMB issues final sequester order			15 days after adjournment
President issues final sequester order based on report		Oct. 15	15 days after adjournment
OMB issues compliance report on sequester order		Nov. 15	

revenues—yielding a projected surplus or deficit. Congress also recommended spending levels for each of the functional program categories discussed earlier. The first resolution had to be adopted before either chamber could consider any legislation providing new budget authority (including authority to borrow or contract), new spending authority, or changes in revenues or public debt.

Following passage of the first resolution and the associated parceling out of budget authority and outlay estimates to the relevant committees and subcommittees, Congress was to have less than four months for those committees to complete action on all spending bills. If the committees reported bills that were not in accord with the resolution's limits, Congress gave itself the opportunity to pass a second resolution that brought the terms of the first resolution into line with the committees' actions, in a sense retroactively blessing the earlier excesses. Congress could also use the second resolution to revise spending, revenue, and debt requirements that departed from both the first resolution and the aggregate actions of the spending committees (the appropriations committees in both chambers, as well as the Senate Finance Committee and the House Ways and Means Committee for certain programs).

The second resolution, in such instances, could include "reconciliation instructions" to specific committees, directing them to report legislation to change existing laws (including entitlement and statutory tax provisions) to comply with the terms of the second resolution. Upon receipt of the reported legislation, the budget committee was authorized to roll the changes into a single bill, called the reconciliation bill, which would become law when passed by both chambers and signed by the president. If any committee failed to report legislation directed by the reconciliation instructions, however, the budget committee was empowered to initiate the required legislation itself. Therefore the second resolution, with its reconciliation instructions, was to be treated by the committees as binding. The first resolution was to represent a statement of congressional intent, albeit one to be taken very seriously and one that was already the product of heated debate and political accommodation within Congress.

The architects of the new congressional budgetary process strove to create structures and procedures that would give Congress control of the budget—control over its use as a tool of both fiscal policy and substantive policy priority setting. They wanted the budget to be the product of a plan agreed upon by the whole Congress and not an ex post facto amalgamation of the choices of autonomous spending committees. For that aspiration to become a reality, some of the entrenched power of the spending committees had to be wrested away and shared with members of Congress who did not have the good fortune to sit on them. Inevitably, the spending committees insisted that any redesign of the process had to preserve their authority to set appropriations levels and place conditions on spending for the areas under their jurisdiction. At the same time, members of the spending committees came to appreciate their colleagues' desire to set budgetary direction and restore Congress's collective power over the budget. All members of Congress had the right to vote on revenue and spending bills, but most thought their voices were heard too late in the process—after bills' terms were crafted in committee and after partisan compromises had already been reached. They also believed committee choices came too early, before Congress had an opportunity to relate each bill to the whole of spending, taxing, and substantive policy direction.

The spending committees believed that the act contained procedural constraints that would stem the growing interference of the authorizing committees, which increasingly seemed to be eroding the power of the spending committees by granting budget authority (most commonly the authority to borrow or enter into contracts) in the authorizing legislation itself.[12] By creating budget committees to map out directions for the other committees while not usurping their long-institutionalized functions, and giving each chamber the opportunity to act collectively on the proposed resolutions, the act provided a widely accepted new point of inter-institutional balance within Congress.

It is important to note in this regard that the Budget Act did not do away with any congressional institutions participating in the budgetary process. The substantive standing committees, such as the House Armed Services Committee or the Senate Labor and Human Resources Committee, continued to act on new program authorizations. The revenue committees, the Senate Finance Committee and the House Ways and Means Committee, continued to write and review changes in federal tax law and certain entitlement legislation, and the appropriations committees of both chambers continued to report appropriations. The newly created budget committees were given responsibility to propose an integrating direction for committee action and to monitor the other committees' budget resolutions, setting out their respective chambers' spending and revenue targets for the coming fiscal year. The budget committees were positioned to shape and monitor Congress's strategic plan for budgetary policy.

The halls of Congress rang with enthusiasm about the new congressional budgetary process. Congress believed it had struck a major blow to obtain independence in national budget making. To many close observers, however, congressional performance under the Budget Act fell far short of those initial high expectations. Louis Fisher of the Congressional Research Service notes that "rarely has a statute missed goals by such wide margins without being repealed or severely amended."[13]

An assessment of the appropriateness of Fisher's critique must begin with a summary of the goals of the act, both explicit and implicit. They can be divided into two categories: procedural and substantive. Procedurally, the act was intended to provide a forum for Congress to debate macroeconomic policy and decide broad issues of budgetary policy. Substantively, Congress expected (or hoped) that the new procedures would also enable it to (1) restrain spending; (2) reduce deficits; (3) control backdoor spending; (4) eliminate continuing resolutions by enacting appropriations on time; and (5) control presidential impoundment.[14]

An evaluation of the act after ten years of experience yields a mixed report card. Spending was not restrained between fiscal years 1976 and 1985, the last year before Congress modified its budgetary procedures by passing the Gramm–Rudman–Hollings Act. Between those years, federal spending rose 20 percent faster than gross personal income in this country.[15] Although no one can know what would have happened without the act, Louis Fisher argues that a number of procedures associated with it have actually encouraged spending. They include "the existence of the Budget Committee as another access point for members of Congress and lobbyists rebuffed by the authorization and appropriations committees, the use of 'current services' and 'current policy' to adjust the spending levels of every program for inflation (a giant hold-harmless procedure), and the adoption of generous aggregates in budget resolutions."[16] According to Fisher, the generous budget ceilings allowed members of Congress to justify amendments to increase appropriations by pointing out that the recommended higher spending would still be within the totals contained in the concurrent resolution.[17] Another budget scholar, Allen Schick, supports Fisher's contention, alluding to nearly one hundred interviews that he and his research associates held with members of Congress and their budget staff. During that time "no one expressed the view that the allocations in budget resolutions had been knowingly set below legislative expectations."[18]

Despite the passage of the Budget Act, budget deficits continued to grow throughout the ten-year period. Recognizing the deficit dilemma, the Congressional Joint Study Committee that designed the new process concluded that the "constant continuation of deficits plus their increasing size illustrates the need for Congress to obtain better control of the budget."[19]

The Budget Act also placed controls on **backdoor spending**. Agencies could no longer borrow funds or enter into contractual obligations without the necessary appropriation authority from Congress. The act placed no meaningful curbs on the growth of entitlement spending, nor did it eliminate continuing resolutions, in which Congress acts to continue a current year's spending at the previous year's levels (although continuing resolutions can also include selective increases—for example, a resolution could finance pay-plan adjustments for federal workers). Between the 1968 and 1975 fiscal years only two appropriations bills remained under a continuing resolution for the entire fiscal year, but that figure increased to twenty-seven in the ten years following the passage of the act.[20] Congress proved unable to act within the time lines required by the 1974 Budget Reform Act. The first budget resolution, required to be passed by May 15, was usually passed one to four months late.[21] The second budget resolution was passed so late that after 1981 it was abandoned altogether. In that year, although Congress realized that the fiscal 1982 deficit would exceed $90 billion (it actually reached $128 billion), it still set the second resolution at the same level as the first, calling for a deficit of only $48 billion.[22] That action provided the first clear sign that Congress would have great difficulty finding the political will to face the tough choices necessary to bring the deficit down.

Finally, the portion of the act that controls presidential impoundments has worked to a great extent as intended. Following its provisions, presidents have had to secure Congress's support for presidential initiatives to rescind appropriations authority and obtain legislation from Congress approving them. To thwart presidential proposals to defer spending, the act provided that only one House of Congress needed to object by resolution. The Supreme Court invalidated this provision in 1983, however, requiring that **deferrals** be approved by both houses.[23] Congress reacted by disapproving proposed presidential deferrals within the appropriations bills themselves.

Another critic of congressional budget reform attributes the act's failures to political grounds.[24] According to Aaron Wildavsky, the new congressional budgetary process highlighted and sharpened political differences in ways that limited Congress's ability to reach accommodations through the traditional routines of incremental budgeting and mutual partisan adjustment. The new politics of the budgetary process produced what Wildavsky labels "budgetary dissensus" within Congress, instead of the intended congressional consensus. In Wildavsky's view, the new politics were prompted in significant part by Congress's budgetary reforms.

The reforms forced Congress to make overarching policy choices early in the congressional phase of the budgetary process and decide on relative policy priorities as it fashioned the first concurrent resolution, building totals up from spending aggregates for discrete program categories. In order to decide how much to spend (and tax) overall, Congress had to determine how much should be spent for defense in relation to domestic affairs. Thus, Congress asked itself to make some basic policy choices before the traditional workings of the decentralized budgetary process had yielded them. Congress imposed a centralized budgetary process on people and institutions that had been accustomed to making choices in a decentralized political environment—a setting that thrived on ambiguity and compromise.

That traditional environment also provided a sense of stability to budget making. The budgetary base functioned as a decisional "given" of sorts, which was generally considered safe territory for budget participants. Instead of focusing on such matters as how much to spend on national defense in comparison to income security, health, or agriculture, for example, Congress made each spending decision without reference to the others, relying on the budgetary choices of member-specialists who acted on requested spending increases without any plan for congressional action. As Wildavsky describes it, general agreement on past budgetary decisions, combined with years of accumulated experience and specialization, allowed budget makers to be concerned with the relatively small increments to an existing base that give an agency its recognized fair share of the budget—a share that reflects many years of negotiations over the appropriate increments it can come to expect.

The Budget Act forced Congress to think explicitly in terms of relative policy tradeoffs and invited the budget committees to wade, early in the process, into the budget detail traditionally reserved for the spending committees. In order to arrive at recommended levels of spending for each of the functional areas of the budget, early judgments must be made on the big-ticket items in each area. Through assumptions about whether costly items are included in or excluded from budget resolutions, the budget committees are both making preliminary choices about the value and affordability of public programs and creating room (or constricting it) for the spending committees to appropriate funds in support of those programs. It is not surprising that the budget committees have become the arena where early congressional decisions are made regarding the major tradeoffs of public policy decisions that create expectations and constrain the choices of the other budget participants in Congress.

Nevertheless, the budget committees do not operate in isolation from the major forces influencing congressional decision making; they reflect them. Such forces, though, can often be conflicting. Some encourage integration and others encourage disintegration. Institutional rivalry between the presidency and Congress tends to unify the interests of Congress, as congressional actors pull together in mutual support of their institutional status and prerogatives. Faced with presidential incursions onto congressional turf, the legislators who passed the 1974 Act showed themselves willing to put aside their differences and support their institutional interests. The heightened partisan environment of the Reagan years, however, mitigated Congress's ability to put its distinctive stamp on national budgetary policy by making it more difficult for Congress to accommodate its own internal differences in shaping the first budget resolution.

The prominent place of budget making in congressional deliberations during the 1980s focused and centralized the legislative workload. As Congress became absorbed with continuing resolutions, the Democratic leadership was able to increase its influence over congressional decision making by using the budget committees as its "stalking horse." Congressional leaders, providing direction and keeping close tabs on the budget committees' actions, successfully used the budget resolution as an integrating and centralizing tool of policy making. The leadership's interest in budget resolutions as blueprints for policy direction not only furthered centralized power in Congress; it also contributed to heightened political partisanship.[25]

Recognizing the utility of these procedural tools, party leaders in Congress worked hard to line up their forces in support of their positions. They had learned that it was not good enough to attempt to win the votes at the appropriations or authorizing committee levels. The congressional plan itself had to be shaped from the beginning. The parties were quick to identify preferred budget scenarios, and voting on budget resolutions in the 1980s occurred largely along party lines.[26]

These expressions of partisanship could have been restrained had President Reagan demonstrated greater flexibility. He might have sent signals to Senate Republican leaders in Congress that he was willing to compromise on tax and spending matters and support their 1985 deficit reduction plan, which combined spending cuts, tax increases, and a social security freeze. Without the president's support, Republican leaders in Congress backed off, feeling dispirited about the prospects of reaching any compromise that would be acceptable to both the president and the Democrats. Frustration and immobility took over, and it appeared that the deficit would continue to grow without any restraint in the offing. The resulting inactivity in the face of a rapidly rising national budget deficit created a popularly perceived national crisis—one that public opinion would not allow to go unaddressed. The president's unbending posture, and Congress's unwillingness to get too far out in front of him on tax increases or reductions in entitlements, created a shared sense that something extraordinary had to be done. The process was leading to no apparent resolution. In desperation, Congress, led by members of the president's own party, passed what one member termed "a bad law whose time had come"—the Gramm–Rudman–Hollings Act.

The Balanced Budget and Emergency Deficit Control Act

According to one of its sponsors, Republican senator Warren Rudman of New Hampshire, Congress enacted the Balanced Budget and Emergency Deficit Control Act, with President Reagan's support, to "force a discipline into this Congress and this administration and succeeding administrations that is totally lacking."[27] The original act of 1985 (before it was amended in 1987) called for

Congress to reduce the national deficit by $36 billion in each of five consecutive years, bringing the budget into balance by the 1991 fiscal year. Since the legislation was presented as an amendment to a bill raising the national debt ceiling, the symbolism was inescapable: Congress held up the shield of the budget reduction legislation to deflect the inevitable criticism that would come from still another need to accommodate the Treasury Department's increased borrowing associated with the growing national deficit. With the president's blessing, Congress was saying that enough is enough, that something was being done to put the brakes on the soaring national debt.

Under the provisions of the act, if Congress is unable to pass a budget that brings the deficit to within $10 billion of the required target (except that no cushion was allowed for fiscal year 1991), automatic budget cuts would go into effect—apportioned equally across the board between defense and domestic discretionary spending—which collectively would bring spending into line with the targets. The legislation excluded several major entitlement programs from these reductions, the most significant being social security, Aid to Families with Dependent Children (AFDC), food stamps, Medicaid, and veterans' compensation. It placed limits on the cuts that could be made to other programs—most notably Medicare. The act also gave Congress a $10 billion cushion before the automatic spending cuts would be triggered. Once triggered, however, cuts were required to be apportioned so that the deficit would fall within the target, not the target plus $10 billion. With the automatic mechanism, the deficit would be reduced even in the face of congressional inaction or lack of political will.

The act also altered the budgetary timetable, pushing several key deadlines back and thus forcing Congress to face its difficult choices even earlier in the process than was required under the 1974 budget reform legislation (see Table 6.3). Major changes included moving the deadline for passage of the concurrent budget resolution back from May 15 to April 15, the deadline for all appropriations bills from the seventh day after Labor Day to June 30, and the deadline for the reconciliation bill from September 25 to June 15.

In spite of its intention to reschedule the budgetary process to force itself to complete action on the budget well before the start of the fiscal year, Congress was unable to meet its own timetable. (It came closest in 1988 and 1994, passing all appropriations bills before the beginning of the fiscal year.) This general inability to reach timely accord on a budget meeting the Gramm–Rudman–Hollings targets focused national attention on the act's automatic cut provisions. In its original form, the legislation gave the comptroller general the authority to determine whether the automatic cuts needed to be imposed. Using OMB and CBO projections of the deficit for the coming fiscal year and taking into account actions by Congress up to August 15, the General Accounting Office (GAO), headed by the comptroller general, was to report to the president by August 25 the amount of the cut and its required apportionment. On October 1, the president was to order sequestration of the apportioned amounts. The act, however, gave the president and Congress two weeks to work out an alternative deficit reduction plan. If they were unsuccessful, the act required the president to issue a final sequestration order by October 15, according him a mere ministerial role. Even after the president ordered sequestration, however, Congress could pass a reconciliation bill that would supersede that portion of the automatic cuts not yet implemented.

In July 1986, the U.S. Supreme Court ruled that making the president's decision-making authority subordinate to that of the GAO, an arm of Congress, represented a violation of the constitutional separation of powers provisions, which vest executive power in the president, not in the Congress. The court's decision read, in part, "By placing responsibility for execution in the hands of an officer who is subject to removal only by itself, Congress in effect has retained control over the executive function. The Constitution does not admit such intrusion."[28]

In response, in 1987 Congress amended the act to give the OMB exclusive responsibility for determining whether sequestration is necessary. The OMB baseline projections of revenues and spending cause a deficit projection to trigger the presidential sequestration order. The CBO continued to prepare and release its own independent projection, but it became irrelevant. Although Congress and others looked to it as a check on the OMB numbers, it held no legal standing. When the OMB determined that the deficit targets were not met, it used the agencies' projections of outlays to determine how big the across-the-board cuts needed to be, not the CBO's.

Ironically, Congress did not seem to mind that its own budget office had lost ground to the OMB, since the CBO historically projected higher deficits than the OMB. Use of the OMB estimates tended to require smaller automatic cuts, when they were imposed. Thus Congress and the president had a relatively more manageable task when faced with negotiating a compromise deficit reduction plan to obviate sequestration. Then chairman of the House Budget Committee, Democrat Leon Panetta of California, observed, "Politics has played against the CBO. If members have to choose between CBO's more realistic assumptions and OMB's more optimistic assumptions—[which] mean that you can achieve deficit reduction through optimism rather than through tough choices—there is an inclination to rely on OMB."[29]

Even with the less restrictive OMB estimates, the automatic cuts were expected to be so universally unacceptable that the president and Congress would be shocked into working together to produce a responsible budget and bring the deficit into line. Members of Congress and the media metaphorically characterized the automatic cuts as a sword, a loaded gun, a hammer, and a planned train wreck.[30] It was commonly assumed that neither the president nor Congress, neither Republicans nor Democrats would find such across-the-board cuts acceptable. Republicans and conservative Democrats would consider them destructive of national defense interests, while Democrats and liberal Republicans would find them inimical to social welfare interests, or so the supposition went. Nevertheless, there were signs already by late 1985 that

Congress as a whole was willing to pull back somewhat on real growth in defense spending. The fact that the act exempted the major social entitlement programs from the apportioned reductions tended to mollify the champions of social welfare programs.

Thus, despite the rhetoric, it is not entirely clear that Congress viewed the automatic cut mechanism as a calamity. In the face of tough political decisions as to whether to earmark reductions or raise taxes, the automatic cuts gave Congress an available escape hatch.

In allowing automatic cuts to take place, however, Congress realized that it ran the risk of a negative public reaction to its inability to make the difficult and responsible decisions its members had been elected to make. For many, a less threatening alternative proved alluring: changing the targets themselves (as illustrated in Table 6.4). Congress did this in September 1987, fashioning deficit reduction measures to make it appear that the Gramm–Rudman–Hollings targets were being met, even though favorable assumptions (revenue projections set unrealistically high and spending estimates pegged unrealistically low), accounting gimmicks (shifting expenditures backward and forward between fiscal years), and one-time revenue windfalls or savings (income from the sale of federal assets such as CONRAIL, government-owned loans and defaulted notes, and land) significantly contributed to the apparent (and quickly vanishing) success.

Democrat senator Howard Metzenbaum of Ohio, lumping all these tactics together, went beyond the widely used description of balancing the budget using "smoke and mirrors" to comment, "It is so much smoke you cannot see the mirror."[31] Henry J. Aaron, an economics professor at the Brookings Institution, asserted that Gramm–Rudman–Hollings legislation "has elevated to a sick passion the economically frivolous game of how to find tricks and dodges that will meet the targets for this year's deficit."[32]

This tactic of fashioning a package that claims to make the mandated target solely to forestall automatic cuts has proven to be transparent. Built on generous assumptions and advantageous adjustments, the budgeted level of deficit has seldom reflected reality by fiscal year's end.

The act's critics labeled it a failure. Even Ernest F. Hollings, a Democratic senator from South Carolina and one of the act's co-sponsors, later called it

Table 6.4 Deficit Targets and Estimates Compared to Actual Deficits, 1986–1993 (in $ billions)

	Fiscal Year							
	1986	1987	1988	1989	1990	1991	1992	1993
Original GRH 1985	171.9	144.0	108.0	72.0	36.0	0.0	—	—
Revised GRH 1987	—	—	144.0	136.0	100.0	64.0	28.0	0.0
Actual deficit	221.2	149.8	155.2	152.5	221.4	269.2	290.4	255.1

a "sham," suggesting that although it was intended as a "sword" it had been used as a "shield" to protect against the kinds of cuts that could bring the deficit down in reality.[33] Rudolph Penner, a former director of the Congressional Budget Office, saw both Congress and the White House playing the game of fictitious deficit reduction. Speaking of President George H. W. Bush's proposed budget for the 1990 fiscal year, which projected that the deficit would be within the act's requirements as of September 30, 1990, Penner lamented: "I couldn't have conceived in my wildest dreams how much cheating they'd engage in; I don't know that it's any worse than past years, but I'm more annoyed by it this year—just in the sheer number of gimmicks."[34]

Nevertheless, supporters of the act are fond of pointing out that the national deficit was still about $70 billion lower on September 30, 1989 than it had been on September 30, 1986. Senator Rudman of New Hampshire attributed that reduction directly to the act, suggesting that in its absence Congress would have lacked the collective political will to cut outlays as deeply as it did under the legislation; Rudman commented, "It is working exactly as I thought it would work. It's the only conceivable way that we have managed to cut the deficit, even with all the funny financing ... I never expected the bill to work with any great amount of precision. I always figured there would be the ways and means to try to get around sections of it."[35] But as the Congressional Quarterly noted, the $70 billion difference could largely be attributed to the combination of economic expansion and growing social security reserves. Under the unified budget concept, these are incorporated in calculating the size of the deficit.[36]

The Budget Enforcement Act of 1990 and the Omnibus Budget Reconciliation Act of 1993

Congress's passage of the 1990 Budget Enforcement Act, with the support of President Bush, not only temporarily took a bite out of the deficit; it also altered the direction that the Gramm–Rudman–Hollings legislation had set. Instead of establishing overall deficit reduction targets, the 1990 legislation re-conceptualized the way in which Congress would deal with the deficit. Discretionary spending's share of the deficit would be treated differently from entitlement spending's share. As introduced earlier, the act placed caps on budget authority and outlays for each of three categories of discretionary spending—defense, foreign aid, and domestic—for the fiscal years 1991 through 1993, collapsing them into a single cap thereafter. Spending in excess of the caps would be subject to sequestration. Although the separate caps permitted increased discretionary spending between 1991 and 1993, that spending slack was removed by the 1993 reconciliation act, as it froze discretionary spending through fiscal year 1998 at the level of fiscal year 1993 (see Box 6.4). Spending could be exempted from the cap only if both the president and Congress determined that added spending was for an emergency, such as a major military engagement or a natural disaster.

Box 6.4   Key Dates in Congressional Budget Reform

1974 Congressional Budget and Impoundment Control Act

- created congressional budget resolution
- created reconciliation process
- created House and Senate budget committees
- created the Congressional Budget Office
- put the federal government on an October 1–September 30 fiscal year

1985 The Balanced Budget and Emergency Deficit Control Act (Gramm–Rudman–Hollings Act)

- established deficit targets, decreased by $36 billion a year through the 1991 fiscal year, when the budget was to be balanced
- created sequestration, by which automatic cuts would go into effect, apportioned equally across the board between domestic and defense discretionary spending, if deficit targets were not reached
- altered the budgetary timetable established by the 1974 budget act, including moving the deadline for passage of the concurrent resolution back from May 15 to April 1, and the deadline for passage of the reconciliation bill from September 15 to June 15

1987 Amendment to the Balanced Budget and Emergency Deficit Control Act

- changed deficit targets for fiscal years 1988 through 1991, and pushed back the target years for a balanced budget until the 1993 fiscal year

1990 Budget Enforcement Act

- placed separate caps on budget authority and outlays for each of three categories of discretionary spending—defense, foreign aid, and domestic—for the 1991 through 1993 fiscal years, with the separate caps collapsed into one for the 1994 and 1995 fiscal years
- put entitlement spending on a "pay-as-you-go" (PAYGO) basis, requiring that any increase in the deficit due to expansion of entitlements or revenue legislation be offset by direct spending or revenue legislation, or by a sequester

- gave the Office of Management and Budget the authority to keep score regarding the amount of offset required
- exempted spending (as determined by both president and Congress) for the discretionary spending cap

1993 Omnibus Budget Reconciliation Act

- extended the Budget Enforcement Act through FY 1998
- established tighter spending caps that in effect froze discretionary budget authority and outlays at 1993 levels
- extended PAYGO and sequester provisions

1997 Balanced Budget Act

- extended the Budget Enforcement Act through FY 2002
- extended caps on discretionary budget authority and outlays through FY 2002, setting them at levels 10 percent less than required to maintain spending at projected rates of inflation
- extended PAYGO and sequestration provisions, but Congress allowed them to expire at the end of the 2002 fiscal year

2010 Statutory Pay-As-You-Go (PAYGO) Act

- reinstated PAYGO provisions, which trigger sequestration if not complied with

2011 Budget Control Act (BCA)

- placed caps on the level of discretionary appropriations for defense and non-defense programs, which trigger sequestration if not met

The act's pay-as-you-go provisions affecting entitlement spending required that any increase in the deficit caused by an expansion of entitlements or legislation that would reduce revenues, such as a tax cut, must be offset by commensurate constrictions of other entitlements or by revenue increases—effectively establishing a rule of deficit neutrality governing policy change. However, spending increases caused by the growth of eligible clientele under existing entitlement law would not be controlled by the act's provisions. Thus, economic downturns could still require higher entitlement spending to cover the increased number of Americans meeting established eligibility standards.

Balanced Budget Act of 1997

The 1997 Balanced Budget Act was highly important not only because of its bipartisan contribution to deficit reduction but also for the macro constraints it placed on budgeting in the years to follow. In the euphoria of deficit reduction, Congress extended and tightened caps on discretionary spending, setting them at levels 10 percent less than required to maintain spending at projected rates of inflation. Congress, in effect, tightened allowable spending limits at the very time that its deficit reduction measures, coupled with accelerating economic growth, were moving the federal budget from deficit to surplus.

Yet the caps could not withstand bipartisan pressures to increase both defense and domestic discretionary spending in an environment of rapid revenue growth. In revising the caps upward, Congress gave itself increased spending room—room that both the lame-duck Clinton administration and Congress proved eager to fill.

Allowing the Caps to Expire

Under federal law, the provisions of the Budget Enforcement Act of 1990 that created discretionary spending caps and pay-as-you-go (or PAYGO) requirements were scheduled to expire at the end of the 2002 fiscal year. Congress allowed them to do so. The demands for increased spending on homeland security and the war on terror, together with congressional Republicans' zeal for further tax relief, eroded majority support to continue constraints on Congress's ability to meet perceived needs for significantly increased discretionary spending, and for additional tax cuts.

It was not until the Budget Control Act of 2011 that caps on discretionary spending were once again established. A year earlier, Congress acted to rein in mandatory spending by passing the 2010 Statutory Pay-As-You-Go (PAYGO) Act, which required that any projected increases in the deficit resulting from the expansion of mandatory spending be offset (or paid for) by other changes to mandatory spending or taxes that reduce deficits by an equivalent amount.

The Budget Control Act of 2011

The Budget Control Act of 2011 re-imposed caps on defense and non-defense discretionary spending for each year through 2021. These caps were altered moderately in the **Bipartisan Budget Act of 2013**, which President Obama signed into law on December 26, 2013, following feverish work by the House and Senate to pass the legislation before Christmas.[37] It raised the Budget Control Act's sequestration caps for both defense and non-defense discretionary funding, hiking the overall caps by $63 billion, with the increase allocated evenly between the two. These changes capped discretionary spending at $1.012 trillion in FY 2014 and at $1.014 trillion in FY 2015. The Bipartisan

Budget Act also extended the caps through FY 2023, two years beyond the prior requirement.

Both Republicans and Democrats evidenced a willingness to compromise to avoid another government shutdown like the selective 16-day government shutdown that occurred in October, just two months earlier. The Republican-controlled House moved from its original overall cap of $967, as did the Democratic-controlled Senate move from its starting point of $1.055 trillion, together arriving at the compromise of $1.012 trillion.[38]

The Continuing Appropriations Resolution as Failsafe

One of the major objectives of congressional budgetary reform was to establish a deliberative process that would lead to passage of appropriations bills prior to the start of a new fiscal year. Meeting that objective would mean that federal agencies would know the funds they would have available during the coming year to devote to the programs that Congress charged them to deliver. It did not work out that way, however. From FY 1977 (the first year of implementation of the Budget Reform Act, and the start of a new October 1–September 30 fiscal year) through FY 2014, all appropriations bills were passed on time in just four fiscal years: 1977, 1989, 1995, and 1997. Overall, 164 continuing appropriations resolutions were enacted during the 1997–2014 period, and, each fiscal year contained approximately four continuing resolutions during that period.[39]

A **continuing appropriations resolution** takes the form, technically, of a joint resolution of Congress, not a bill. Yet, like a bill, it requires presidential approval to become law. It tends to be used as a stop-gap measure, providing continuing spending authority for a given period of time—a few days, weeks, months, or a good part of a year. Congress can pass some appropriations bills on time before the start of a new fiscal year while failing to pass others on time. For this latter group, Congress turns to the continuing appropriations resolution to continue spending authority. Congress can set the resolution to continue spending at its current level, or it has the option to increase or decrease the current amount. Without spending authority, however, agencies will ultimately have to cease their operations, at least after they have exploited the possibility of drawing upon available carry-forward funding.

The 2014 fiscal year provides a good illustration of how Congress uses the continuing appropriations resolution. Prior to the start of FY 2014, Congress failed to pass any of its twelve appropriations bills. To complicate matters, the House and Senate could not agree on the terms of a continuing budget resolution, with the most sensitive controversy centered on the House's attempts to use the continuing resolution to remove funding for provisions of the Patient Protection and Affordable Care Act most objectionable to the Republican majority. Congress's inability to fashion a resolution led to the

October shutdown, during which 800,000 federal employees were furloughed. Faced with widespread media condemnation and opinion polls showing the public's displeasure, Congress reached agreement on a continuing appropriations resolution providing spending authority at FY 2013 levels until January 15, 2014, temporarily setting aside partisan differences that would have gotten in the way of passage.

The continuing appropriations resolution also called for a conference of budget committee members from both chambers, led by Republican Representative Paul Ryan and Democratic Senator Patty Murray. From this effort emerged the compromises built into the Bipartisan Budget Act of 2013 (discussed above), which raised the caps on discretionary spending and provided appropriations authority through the remainder of the fiscal year.

But history repeated itself in an all-too-familiar reality, as Congress was once again unable to pass any of its appropriations bills prior to the new 2015 fiscal year's start and again resorted to continuing appropriations resolutions to extend spending authority through December 11, when Congress would be in its post-election, lame-duck session. The reality that Republicans would form the majority in the new session of Congress gave Democrats the incentive to negotiate with the GOP while Democrats still held a majority in the Senate, and before the number of seats they held in both chambers declined. Congressional leaders and the president wanted to see an omnibus appropriations bill, not a continuing appropriations resolution, enacted into law for the remainder of the fiscal year. Congressional leaders of both parties also wanted to avoid another government shutdown.

The stakes governing compromise, however, were high. Republicans wanted to use the negotiations as a means to weaken certain provisions of the Dodd-Frank Act, which heightened federal regulation of financial institutions and their practices, significantly including the trading of derivatives (most commonly collateralized mortgage obligations; see chapter 4) and strictly limiting proprietary trading (when banks make trades with their own financial resources instead of serving as financial agents of their depositors and investors, thereby creating potential conflict of interest). Republicans also complicated negotiations by including in the package a provision that would increase the limits on individual contributions to political parties. Another sticking point in negotiations centered on Republican angst over the president's recent executive orders to defer the deportation of nearly five million unauthorized immigrants. That anger led a coalition of Republicans pushing for sizable reductions in funding for the Department of Homeland Security. Democrats, for their part, put the bulk of their efforts into protecting the Patient Protection and Affordable Care Act from unacceptable amendments and avoiding cutbacks to Homeland Security's budget. Both parties supported increased funding for military operations against the so-called Islamic State.

The resulting Fiscal Year 2015 Omnibus Appropriations Act, signed into law by President Obama on December 16, 2014, included funding through the fiscal year's end for all appropriations except for homeland security, which was funded until February 27, 2015. This exception guaranteed continued bickering over the issue of immigration reform and the limits to be placed on executive action. The act's composition can be seen as a compromise, but one favoring Republican interests that extended beyond appropriations levels. Republicans prevailed in weakening key provisions of the Dodd-Frank Act (discussed above) and in securing increased limits on individual contributions to political parties. Democrats were able to keep Obamacare intact and avoid funding cuts for homeland security. And both parties took comfort in avoiding another short-term continuing resolution.[40]

Summary and Conclusions

Deliberations over the budget lie at the heart of national politics. The budget determines the extent to which resources will be transferred from the private sector to the public sector, and vice versa; indicates how much our national government is willing to spend on public purposes; sets substantive policy priorities within overall spending limits; and determines the amount that must be borrowed, along with available revenues, to finance the approved spending. In doing so, the federal budget provides a composite statement of the direction that the national government should take over the coming fiscal year and beyond.

For most of the past three decades the federal budget deficit was at the center of America's budgetary focus, with the exception of a brief period of surplus from 1998 to 2001. Large deficits captured the attention of presidents, Congress, the media, and the general public. Policy tradeoffs were viewed within the backdrop of the seemingly insurmountable deficit. Political commentators focused on the political implications of the deficit and on the intense partisan nature of budgetary politics. Economists concerned themselves with the macroeconomic effects of the deficit, including a mounting national debt. The general consensus was that the federal government was living beyond its means, financing overspending with debt and placing a financial burden on future generations to pay off that debt. Yet record revenue-producing economic growth and significant deficit reduction packages in 1993 and 1997 transformed the stubborn deficit pattern into a brief interlude of surplus.

The deficit, which had its roots in the 1981–2 national recession and the Reagan administration's agenda of major income tax cuts and significantly increased real defense spending, seemed to be rising almost uncontrollably during the 1980s and into the 1990s, despite attempts by Congress to institute reforms of the federal budgetary process. The Balanced Budget and Emergency Deficit Control Act, also known as the Gramm–Rudman–Hollings legislation, fell far short of achieving its goal of a balanced budget over six years. Although it failed for the most part to meet its annual deficit reduction targets, the federal budget deficit did fall moderately during the second half of the 1980s. It is difficult, however, to know how much of that improvement can be credited to the provisions of the Gramm–Rudman–Hollings legislation and how much can be attributed to an improving economy.

Clearly, the recession of the early 1990s greatly exacerbated the U.S. deficit dilemma and contributed significantly to President George H.W. Bush's electoral defeat. It reduced federal revenue collection well below expected levels and pushed up public assistance entitlement spending. By the time President Clinton took office in January 1993, the 1994 fiscal year deficit was projected to exceed $300 billion. This happened even though President Bush and the Democrat-led Congress reached accord on a major deficit-reduction package in October 1990—one that included budget cuts and tax increases. In fact, the recession's effects all but canceled out the projected deficit reduction associated with the Budget Enforcement Act.

While mitigating what would have been an even bigger deficit without the enactment of tax increases and spending cuts, the act's major contribution to deficit reduction came in the form of the procedural changes it introduced. Instead of establishing overall deficit reduction targets, the 1990 legislation re-conceptualized the way in which Congress would deal with the deficit. Discretionary spending's share would be treated differently from entitlement spending's share. Discretionary spending would be capped, with any excess spending subject to sequestration; entitlement spending was put on a pay-as-you-go basis. The so-called PAYGO provisions required that any increase in the deficit caused by legislation expanding entitlements or reducing federal revenue must be offset by reductions in other entitlements or increases in revenue. However, spending caused by the growth of eligible clientele would not be controlled. Thus, economic downturns could still require higher entitlement spending to cover the increased number of Americans meeting established eligibility standards.

The Omnibus Budget Reconciliation Act of 1993 extended these provisions through 1998 and tightened the cap on discretionary spending, effectively freezing discretionary budget authority and outlays at fiscal 1993 levels. The act also notably included $433 billion in deficit reduction over five years. No Republican in either chamber supported the Clinton-led package, reflecting the party's distaste for further tax increases. That package, along with an improving economy, reduced the federal budget deficit to $107.5 billion by the end of the 1996 fiscal year, well below earlier projected deficits in excess of $300 billion.

The Republicans, fresh from their decisive 1994 electoral victories that won them control of both the House and the Senate, committed themselves not only to further deficit reduction but also to balancing the federal budget by 2002. Congress's budget resolution and reconciliation legislation for the 1996 fiscal year pursued that tack, approving $664 billion in deficit reduction over seven years. Yet its approved legislation included sizable tax cuts and spending reductions that fell heavily on entitlement programs, most controversially on Medicare, Medicaid, and AFDC. President Clinton vetoed the congressionally approved reconciliation bill, setting off a protracted stalemate between the president and Congress—one that resulted in the intermittent shutdown of federal agencies and the furloughing of federal employees, along with the enactment of a series of continuing resolutions.

The Republican-led Congress seized the initiative to set America's budgetary and policy agenda in the mid-1990s, initially putting the president on the defensive and reversing the traditional order of national agenda setting. However, President Clinton painted the Republican majority as extreme, and successfully turned public opinion against partisan stalemate and in favor of compromise.

Increasingly strong economic growth and the widespread success of incumbents in the 1996 election created a setting conducive to political accommodation. In that light, both Clinton and Congress used the process of reconciliation to shape omnibus budget acts in 1997 and 1998 that helped pave the way for a growing budget surplus. Yet at the very time that revenue growth would permit increased spending, Congress extended and tightened its budget caps on spending.

By the 2000 budget session, both Congress and the president realized that the caps had become politically infeasible. The bipartisan pressures to increase spending beyond the caps became too intense. At President George W. Bush's urging, Congress passed large tax cuts in 2001 and 2003, totaling $1.7 trillion over ten years. The "war on terror" and the United States' military operations in Afghanistan and Iraq combined to significantly increase spending on homeland security and national defense. That increased spending, along with the forgone revenue associated with the tax cuts, once again set the federal budget deficit on an upward swing, reaching $413 billion at the end of the 2004 fiscal year. But accelerating economic growth subsequently generated a stream of revenue increases that dropped the budget deficit to $162 billion at the end of FY 2007, despite the rising cost of military involvement in Iraq and Afghanistan and ongoing revenue loss from the Bush tax cuts. But with economic growth slowing in FY 2008, and with interest costs associated with the federal debt projected to rise, the CBO projected a return to annual budget deficits exceeding $400 billion through FY 2010. The reality, however, proved even worse, as federal budget deficits averaged nearly $1.2 trillion between the 2009 and 2012 fiscal years, reflecting the economic impact of the Great Recession and the federal government's response to it.

Partisanship and the prevalence of partisan gridlock have characterized budget making over a good part of the past three decades. Budgetary reforms over the years have had three primary objectives: improving the use of the budget as a policy vehicle, controlling federal spending, and getting budgets enacted in advance of the coming fiscal year. As the discussion in this chapter has shown, success in meeting them has been mixed. Periodic use of PAYGO provisions to control mandatory spending and caps on discretionary spending have contributed to spending restraint. But use of the budget as a policy vehicle, particularly as an agent of advancing ideologically directed policy, has contributed to increasing episodes of partisan gridlock—and as gridlock rises, so does Congress's use of short-term continuing appropriations resolutions. Ironically, as continuing resolutions become more the norm, Congress becomes less able to use the budget as a tool of accomplishing policy objectives.

Notes

1 Allen Schick, The Federal Budget: Politics, Policy, Process (Washington, D.C.: Brookings Institution, 1995), 6.
2 Robert S. McIntyre, Inequality and the Federal Budget Deficit (Washington, D.C.: Citizens for Tax Justice, September 1991), 1–14; Alice M. Rivlin, Reviving the American Dream (Washington, D.C.: Brookings Institution, 1992), 71; Paul Krugman, The Age of Diminished Expectations (Cambridge, M.A.: MIT Press, 1994), 23–30.
3 Congressional Budget Office, Reducing Entitlement Spending (Washington, D.C.: Government Printing Office, September 1994).
4 This discussion of 1997 and 1998 is drawn from James J. Gosling, Politics and the American Economy (New York: Addison Wesley Longman, 2000), 14–16, and is included with permission of the publisher.
5 Daniel J. Parks, "Omnibus Spending Deal Clears as White House Settles for Less," CQ Weekly 58 (December 16, 2000): 2857–9.
6 Congressional Budget Office, The Budget and Economic Outlook: An Update (Washington, D.C.: Government Printing Office, September 2004), 5.
7 Congressional Budget Office, The Budget and Economic Outlook: An Update (Washington, D.C.: The Government Printing Office, September 2008), x.
8 Congressional Budget Office, The Budget and Economic Outlook: 2015–2015 (Washington, D.C.: The Government Printing Office, January 2015), 2, 27.
9 Aaron Wildavsky, The Politics of the Budgetary Process (Boston: Little, Brown, 1964), 58; Richard F. Fenno Jr., The Power of the Purse: Appropriations Politics in Congress (Boston: Little, Brown, 1966), chaps. 4, 5, 10; Ira Sharkansky, The Politics of Taxing and Spending (New York: Bobbs-Merrill, 1969), 42–49.
10 Office of Management and Budget, Budget of the United States Government, Fiscal Years 1961 and 1975.
11 United States Senate, Committee on the Budget, Congressional Budget Reform (Washington, D.C.: Government Printing Office, 1976), 8.
12 Howard E. Shuman, Politics and the Budget, 2nd ed. (Englewood Cliffs, N.J.: Prentice Hall, 1989), 221.
13 Louis Fisher, "The Budget Act of 1974: Reflections after Ten Years," paper presented at the annual meeting of the Midwest Political Science Association, Chicago, April 19, 1985.
14 Ibid.
15 Office of Management and Budget, Budget of the United States Government, Fiscal Years 1977 and 1986.
16 Fisher, "Budget Act," 12.
17 Ibid.
18 Allen Schick, Congress and Money (Washington, D.C.: Urban Institute Press, 1980), 313.
19 United States House of Representatives, 93rd Congress, 1st sess., House Report no. 147 (1973), 1.
20 Fisher, "Budget Act," 22.

21 Shuman, Politics and the Budget, 274.
22 Ibid., 275.
23 United States Supreme Court, INS v. Chadha, 103, 2764 (1983).
24 Aaron Wildavsky, The New Politics of the Budgetary Process, 2nd ed. (New York: HarperCollins, 1992), 224–71.
25 Roger H. Davidson, "The New Centralization on Capitol Hill," paper presented at the annual meeting of the Southern Political Science Association, Charlotte, North Carolina, November 5–7, 1988, 15–17.
26 James A. Thurber, "The Consequences of Budget Reform for Congressional-Presidential Relations," Annals of the American Academy of Political and Social Sciences 499 (September 1988): 101–13.
27 Jackie Calmes, "Gramm–Rudman–Hollings: Has Its Time Passed?" Congressional Quarterly Weekly Report 47, no. 41 (October 14, 1989): 2685.
28 United States Supreme Court, Bowsher v. Synar et al., July 7, 1986.
29 Ibid.
30 Calmes, "Gramm–Rudman–Hollings," 2685.
31 Elizabeth Wehr, "Summit Deal Fails to Forestall Automatic Cuts," Congressional Quarterly Weekly Report 45, no. 47 (November 21, 1987): 2862.
32 Calmes, "Gramm–Rudman–Hollings," 2685.
33 Ibid., 2684.
34 Jackie Calmes, "Congress Is Already Hedging on Deficit Reduction Plan," Congressional Quarterly Weekly Report 47, no. 29 (July 22, 1989): 1839.
35 Calmes, "Gramm–Rudman–Hollings," 2685.
36 Ibid., 2684.
37 Center on Budget and Policy Priorities, Policy Basics: Introduction to the Federal Budget Process, Updated September 10, 2014, 6–7.
38 Lori Montgomery, "Senate Passes Bipartisan Budget Agreement," The Washington Post, December 18, 2013, 1.
39 Jessica Tollestrup, "Duration of Continuing Resolutions in Recent Years," Congressional Research Service, April 28, 2011, 3–4; GAO Highlights, Budget Issues: Effects of Budget Uncertainty From Continuing Resolutions on Agency Operations, March 13, 2013, Figure 1.
40 Ashley Parker and Robert Pear, "Battle Over Spending Measure Shifts to the Senate," The New York Times, December 12, 2014, www.nytimes.com/2014/12/13/us/battle-over-spending-measure-shifts-to-the-senate.html?r=0

Chapter 7

Budgeting in the States

The American states provide a comparative laboratory for the study of public budgeting. Just as any comparative political analysis seeks to generalize about political behavior and to account for deviations, the study of state budgeting seeks to describe and explain the political behavior of state budget makers. Ideally, we hope to develop theories that explain the budgetary outcomes we get among the states. Those theories are most powerful if they can explain outcomes regardless of the state in question—a tall order given the great diversity of the American states.

The states are diverse in many ways. The dates of their admission to the union span three centuries. Their residents settled in several distinctive waves of immigration and migration, bringing with them different social, cultural, religious, and political heritages. State economies are built on different bases, yielding disparate levels of personal income and faring differently as national economic conditions change. States differ politically as well, even though they share an institutional structure very similar to that of the national government. The formal powers of the governor, although patterned after those of the president, are not uniform among the states. Gubernatorial powers to organize the executive branch of government, appoint agency officials, veto legislative acts, release and transfer appropriated funds, and exercise control over state financial management vary from state to state. On the legislative side, although the legislature has the authority to approve the budget in all fifty states, its authority to oversee execution of the budget varies among the states. In addition, state constitutions and statutes variously limit the extent to which state legislatures can authorize taxing and spending.

Structural differences in state budget making not only influence budgetary politics among the states but also render generalizations tenuous. For example, although governors and legislatures in eighteen states focus their deliberations on a single budget bill, the number of budget bills under consideration in the remaining states ranges from two to five hundred (found in Arkansas).[1] Similarly, there are differences among the states in what can be included within a budget bill. Some states limit it to appropriations; others permit expressions of legislative intent to accompany appropriations; still others allow statutory language to be created or changed within the budget bill itself.

The structure and size of legislative budget committees vary among the states. Some states employ joint budget committees, while others have separate committees in each chamber. Some committees have responsibility for both revenue and appropriations bills; others have sole responsibility for one or the other.

Differences can be found in the number, type, and level of personnel engaged in budget development, analysis, and control. Differences also exist among the states in the breadth of functional responsibilities performed by budget staffs and in the resources staff members have at their disposal to carry out those responsibilities.

The political implications of all these variations are discussed later in this chapter. At this point, it is important to note that although prevailing patterns in state budgeting can be identified, generalizations are frequently in need of qualification and caveat.

The Distinguishing Features of State Budgeting

Despite the great diversity that marks state budgeting, it still possesses several key distinguishing features.

The State Budget as Policy Vehicle

The budget serves as a policy vehicle at all levels of government; it establishes tangible resource commitments for a coming fiscal year or biennium and, in doing so, lays out spending priorities. Thus it can be used by chief executives and legislatures, within funding and other constraints, to continue and to reinforce existing priorities; alternatively, it can be used to change them. In this sense, the budget can serve as a vehicle to advance a given policy agenda.

A distinguishing feature of budgeting in the states is the significant extent to which the budget is used as a vehicle for policy change and new substantive policy proposals.[2] Under normal conditions, governors and state legislatures have much greater flexibility to use the budget as a policy vehicle than do their counterparts at the federal and local levels. Constitutions or statutes in many states permit substantive language to be included within a budget bill itself. Such language, depending on the state, can create new statutory sections, repeal existing ones, or make changes in others. Twenty-seven states permit appropriations bills to be used in this way. Maine, New York, Ohio, Pennsylvania, and Wisconsin provide policy makers with the greatest flexibility to include substantive policy within the budget. Twenty other states—prominently including California, Maryland, Michigan, Texas, and Washington—permit the legislature to include conditions on spending or expressions of legislative intent in appropriations acts. Expressions of legislative intent can be found in a budget bill itself or in associated letters of intent or committee reports. At the other extreme, the constitutions of Colorado, Illinois, and New Hampshire go so far as to proscribe any substantive language from being included in the budget.[3]

On the whole, the states give governors and legislatures far greater flexibility than their counterparts have received at the federal and local levels. As was noted in the previous chapter, the administration of President Ronald Reagan, in its honeymoon period, was able to use the U.S. Congress's own reconciliation process to change statutory authorizations and thereby reduce potential spending; but such an experience, to such an extent, has not been repeated since at the federal level. Substantive policy continues to be enacted at the federal level largely through the authorization process, falling under the auspices of the substantive standing committees, not those of the spending committees. At the local level, budget bills tend to be restricted to appropriations alone.

Governors have become particularly adept at using the budget as the primary vehicle with which to pursue their policy agendas. From an executive perspective, the practice of including substantive language in the budget has many advantages. First, depending on the extent of the governor's item-veto authority in a given state, it allows the governor to use his or her item-veto power either to delete funding for a particular line item or an entire appropriation or to delete language accompanying the appropriation itself, language in footnotes specifying legislative intent, or proviso or contingency language setting limits on how an appropriation is to be used. Forty-four states give their governor item-veto authority, with the exceptions being Indiana, Nevada, New Hampshire, North Carolina, Rhode Island, and Vermont. The availability of the item-veto also gives the governor a credible bargaining chip in gubernatorial–legislative negotiations over the budget's composition.

Second, it is easier for a governor to work with the legislative leadership in managing the more contained budgetary process. The legislative process with substantive bills tends to be more fragmented. Third, a governor has greater opportunity to offer and entertain compromises when a number of major policy items are up for consideration at the same time.

A study of budgetary policy making in fourteen states reached conclusions consistent with this reasoning. The study found that institutionally strong governors with liberal item-veto powers are most likely to advance their major policy initiatives through the budget.[4]

The legislature may include policy in the budget for some of the same reasons. The budgetary process restricts the number of legislative actors positioned to influence the budget's composition. The appropriations, budget, or fiscal committees—variously named—exercise the real legislative decision-making authority over the budget and the policy in it, serving as the committee of record that puts together the version of the budget that goes to the entire legislature for consideration. The substantive standing committees in most states play no official decision-making role in the budgetary process, although they may hold hearings on their policy-related portions of the budget and make non-binding recommendations to the appropriations committees.

After the budget committees report out a budget bill that bears their distinctive stamp, typically one developed in concert with legislative leaders (particularly those of the majority party), the rank-and-file members get their crack at the budget in partisan caucuses that meet before and during legislative deliberation on the chamber floor. In the majority caucus, legislative leaders usually try to generate support for the budget committee's recommendation. They often try to make the case that the budget committee's version already represents the interests of their party.

Individual members, however, advocate amendments to the committee bill and attempt to generate support for them. "Straw votes" are often taken to gauge support for the budget committee's version and for proposed amendments to it. In this setting, the chamber's leadership calculates what concessions are necessary to put together sufficient support to pass a budget acceptable to a sizable portion of the majority-party members. Party leaders want to garner enough support to guarantee passage of that version without any support of the minority party; however, to foster a good relationship with the minority party, the majority party will frequently solicit support from minority-party members, even if it amounts only to the support of a few. That support usually carries a price tag—guaranteed concessions that some agreed-to minority-party amendments will be adopted on the chamber floor.

After the legislature passes the budget, the governor uses the item-veto to bring the budget into line with his or her policy agenda. Research has shown that governors employ the item-veto primarily as a tool of partisan advantage and policy making rather than one of fiscal restraint. Governors use it to undo legislative changes and return budget items to the forms originally recommended in the executive budget.[5]

Stability and Change in Gubernatorial Policy Agenda

The governor's policy agenda and fiscal strategy focus the public debate on the budget. The agenda identifies policy problems and opportunities, puts forth preferred options, and prompts opponents to take issue with the governor's recommendations to demonstrate that the governor's policy objectives are misplaced, that others are more important, or that other means better accomplish the governor's objectives.

Gubernatorial policy agendas are identifiable, and they can be compared over time and across states. They exhibit patterns of stability and change, consistently according high priority to certain policy areas year after year while other policy areas rise and fall in priority over time, either cyclically or in response to special circumstances.[6]

Over the past four decades, primary and secondary education consistently stood at the top of gubernatorial policy agendas. Primary and secondary education provides a vivid example of the way policy makers can give strong sustained support to a policy area even though the rationale underlying that support may change. Governors appear to have directed their educational policy initiatives at different definitions of "the problem." Most gubernatorial initiatives of the 1970s, which had major budgetary implications, were advanced to further equal educational opportunity in its several manifestations.

During the 1970s, prompted by court orders in a few states, governors called for equalization of state aid to local school districts. Equalization was viewed as a means toward equal educational opportunity to ensure that each school district in a state is guaranteed a minimum level of financial support for each student regardless of its residents' ability to pay. Under equalization, districts falling below that guaranteed level receive the highest state aid; districts that exceed the guarantee receive no aid. State law may also require them to send some of their own property tax revenues back to the state office of education for reallocation to poorer districts.

In the 1980s, governors turned their attention to issues of educational accountability. Perhaps as a by-product of the large increases in state aid to education characteristic of the 1970s, governors increasingly questioned what taxpayers were getting for their investment. Educational outcomes, performance, and accountability became the watchwords of the day. The steep increases in equalized state aid gave way to budgetary support for competency examinations for teachers, statewide testing of students, merit pay for teachers, and state aid for local quality-improvement programs.

Attention in the 1990s and 2000s centered on student learning outcomes. That focus tended to include three dimensions: (1) the need to identify what students should know and be able to do at different stages of their education; (2) ways of assessing their achievements and progress; and (3) the development of tailored educational plans for each student responsive to that student's needs. This concern about learning outcomes and quality also took a more radical turn in the 1990s, as governors in several states initiated reforms that moved outside of the traditional educational system. Seeking to foster greater decentralization and flexibility, reform legislation carried a deregulatory thrust, as several state legislatures gave school districts increased discretion to determine how levels of student learning can best be achieved. It also permitted teachers to create schools governed by special charters in place of most state laws and regulations governing school districts. These "charter schools" had to describe the governance structure of the school and specify the educational outcomes sought and how they would be measured. By 2014, forty-three states had charter school legislation on the books and 2.5 million students attended nearly 6,500 charter schools across the nation. Charter school enrollment had risen by 225 percent since 2004.[7]

This focus on the bottom line of performance and outcome prompted governors in a number of states to rethink the traditional tenets of educational finance. Should initiatives be taken to reward districts with the most schools achieving or exceeding their learning outcome objectives, or should states aid the successful schools directly, bypassing districts? Such redirection could well have significant implications for the established policy of basing state aid on enrollments, costs, and equalization.

Governors in Florida, Ohio, and Wisconsin successfully pursued still more radical reform as they championed school voucher programs through their legislatures. Unlike charter schools, which are part of the public school system, voucher programs provide financial assistance to needy parents who wish to opt out of public schools and send their children to private schools. The Ohio and Wisconsin programs targeted needy families in their two biggest cities, Cleveland and Milwaukee, respectively. In 1999 Florida became the first state to enact a statewide voucher program, although the Florida Supreme Court later ruled it in violation of the state constitution. Instead of basing eligibility on family income, as in Cleveland and Milwaukee, the Florida program used school performance as its eligibility screen. Students in especially low-performing public schools—schools receiving an F grade for two years in a four-year period—could use state-funded vouchers to attend any private school, including religious ones.

On another front, the issue of inequality in educational finance reappeared in the late 1980s but took a different turn in the years to follow. In addition to the issue of closing the inequality gap, policy makers' attention turned to the issue of the very adequacy of funding to meet state guarantees of a quality education. Unlike the 1970s, when governors took the initiative to use school aid to help equalize the financial ability of districts across a state to support primary and secondary education, the later impetus for continued attention to equalization came from the courts. Between 1989 and 2007, state courts in fifteen states found educational funding inadequate to meet state constitutional guarantees of a quality public education.[8] Working with their legislative counterparts, governors frequently took the lead in coming up with sizable increases in appropriations in response to the judicial rulings, with the tab exceeding $100 million in Kentucky, Montana, New Jersey, Ohio, Tennessee, and Texas.

Economic development began to compete with primary and secondary education for top place on gubernatorial policy agendas during the decade of the 1980s. The recession of 1981–2 focused attention on the need for industrial development and job creation. By the late 1980s, economic development was often the unifying theme around which governors fashioned their budget messages. Governors were quick to show the contributions their budget recommendations for education, transportation, and taxation would make to economic development. The early 1990s recession found governors a bit more circumspect about the benefits of state investment in economic development. That heightened scrutiny extended to both promotional efforts and state-provided tax and loan concessions. Moreover, the recession cut into state tax revenues and compelled increased social welfare spending, creating a budgetary squeeze that prompted governors to reduce the costs of state administrative operations, including economic development promotion.

Welfare is a third area in which gubernatorial interest had traditionally remained high. As with primary and secondary education, however, the focus has changed significantly over that period. During the 1970s, governors supported state funding to match formula-based increases in federal funding and to pay the state share for liberalized optional social services for the needy. In contrast, the pendulum of gubernatorial support swung to cost control and welfare reform in the 1980s and 1990s, as governors called for tighter eligibility requirements, mandatory work and job training programs, and experiments that tied benefits to the school attendance of welfare recipients' children.

Governors were quick to seize the opportunities to experiment with welfare reform that congressional passage of the Family Support Act of 1988 afforded them. These experiments provided a comparative laboratory that paved the way for federal welfare reform. The Personal Responsibility and Work Opportunity Act, which was passed by Congress and signed into law by President Bill Clinton in 1996, eliminated the Aid to Families with Dependent Children program, replacing it with a new block grant program to the states labeled Temporary Assistance for Needy Families (TANF). In doing so, Congress stripped welfare of its entitlement status. The new legislation also imposed a maximum five-year limit on benefits for each recipient and established toughened work requirements as a condition of aid.

With these changes in place, and with the economy enjoying strong growth, caseloads fell dramatically, from a peak of 5.1 million families on welfare in 1994 to about 2 million in 2003—a reduction of 61 percent. It is unclear, however, what portion of this drop can be attributed to welfare reform initiatives and what part is a product of record employment growth. This decline in caseload has not only taken pressure off state budgets, but also enabled state budget makers to reallocate unspent welfare funds. The federal welfare reform legislation gave states the flexibility to transfer up to 30 percent of the new block grant funds to child care, and up to 10 percent to other social services. With these changes, welfare's prominence on the gubernatorial agenda receded.

In contrast, Medicaid has continued to put pressure on state budgets. With state spending on Medicaid rising three times faster than general inflation, gubernatorial initiatives have focused on cost containment. Measures commonly endorsed by governors include freezing or reducing payments to providers, increasing recipients' co-payments, and reducing benefits outside of required core services.

The federal Patient Protection and Affordable Care Act (ACA) of 2010, commonly referred to as Obamacare, expanded eligibility for Medicaid to those with incomes up to 133 percent of the federal poverty level. The U.S. Supreme Court, however, ruled the mandated expansion unconstitutional, leaving to the states the decision of whether they would implement the expansion. As an enticement for states to participate, the federal government would fully fund the costs of expansion through 2016. Thereafter it would cover 90 percent of the costs. Governors exercised considerable influence on state legislators' choices about whether to support the expansion. By early November 2014, governors in twenty-seven states had signed legislation authorizing expansion, extending Medicaid coverage to 7.5 million residents in those states, and reducing the number of insured by 40 percent. Governors in the non-adopting states, typically Republicans, worry about the costs to be picked up by the states once the federal government's financial participation drops to 90 percent. Yet several of them are also conflicted over missing the opportunity to lower the number of their state's uninsured, and to do it with sizable federal financial assistance.[9]

The State Budget's Policy Core

Although the relative priorities in gubernatorial policy agendas may change from year to year or biennium to biennium, certain areas of the budget always elicit the attention of governors and other budget makers regardless of whether they have been singled out for major policy or budgetary change. They remain significant because of their sizable claim on state resources, as their continuing costs alone comprise a substantial portion of the approved state budget.

These areas characteristically include school aid, Medicaid, state revenue sharing, public colleges and universities, welfare payments in the TANF program, community social service aid, state correctional institutions, and property tax credits. Collectively, these eight areas are likely to account for 70 to 85 percent of a state budget. This means that everything else falls within the remaining 15 percent to 30 percent.

This factor has major implications for state budget making. Decisions in these areas set the tenor of the budget as a whole. For example, if spending is to be restrained overall, budget makers must make difficult choices to control spending in these areas, which are often politically sensitive. When budget cuts become necessary, these eight areas cannot be held immune from reductions. At the same time, the greatest pressures to increase spending will come from these very policy areas. Cost-to-continue increases (to compensate for such factors as inflation and caseload growth) alone will put considerable pressure on any strategy of budgetary restraint. Pressures for increased state aid to school districts and local governments—for property tax relief, for higher university faculty salaries in order to keep or make them competitive in the educational marketplace, and for new prisons to accommodate rising inmate populations—all compete for any growth in state revenues.

Governors making recommendations and legislatures reacting to those recommendations and considering alternatives will of necessity devote the lion's share of their attention to these policy areas, regardless of budgetary strategy. Budget staffs in both the executive and legislative branches will need to ensure that the budgetary agenda is structured in such a way that policy makers face the pressing issues in these areas and make the associated difficult choices. Although policy makers tend to put off the most difficult decisions, they themselves know that these choices are necessary if they are to put a distinctive policy stamp on the budget, whether doing so entails budgetary restraint or increased financing of new policy initiatives.

Fiscal Responsibility

In contrast to the frequent use of deficit finance at the federal level, governors and legislatures have regularly made the tough political decisions necessary to balance state budgets (a requirement in all states except Vermont) during economically difficult years. They did so not by using "smoke and mirrors," but by raising taxes and cutting budgets when necessary. They also acted to decrease taxes when inordinate revenue surpluses accumulated, although the mounting surpluses of the late 1990s allowed budget makers in many states to cut taxes *while* sharply increasing spending. With an enlarged spending base, governors and legislatures again faced an economic downturn, leading to recession in 2001. Slow economic recovery shortly following the recession led to mounting budget shortfalls in the 2002 and 2003 fiscal years. As most state economies improved significantly in 2004, budget shortfalls narrowed, and a number of states transitioned to budget surplus.

The decades of the 1980s, 1990s, and 2000s must be viewed from the context of the late 1970s. In that earlier environment of rapidly growing revenues, rising budget surpluses, and increasing manifestations of taxpayer revolt, state legislatures—usually following their governors' recommendations—reduced personal income taxes in thirty-five states and sales taxes in nineteen between 1978 and 1980. During that period, only two states increased personal income tax and only six increased sales tax.[10]

The deteriorating economic conditions of 1981 prompted state budget makers to draw down their remaining surpluses in order to balance their 1982 fiscal year budgets. Only a few months into the fiscal year, however, it became apparent in most states that these dwindling balances would be insufficient to make revenues and expenditures meet. The recession quickly deepened and required both major budget surgery and tax increases to compensate. By the end of the 1982 fiscal year, legislatures in twenty-three states found it necessary to impose budget cuts after the budget had already been passed. Again during the 1983 fiscal year, but on a larger scale, legislatures were forced to approve midyear budget reductions in thirty-nine states in response to the deepening recession.[11] As a result, inflation-adjusted expenditures actually declined by nearly 2 percent among the states between the 1982 and 1984 fiscal years.[12]

On the tax side, the recession of the early 1980s created an environment that sharply contrasted with that of the late 1970s. Instead of cutting taxes, governors and legislatures were forced to increase them. Between 1981 and 1983, personal income tax was increased in twenty-eight states, and sales tax in thirty. General-purpose tax decreases were limited to three states, which benefited from sharply increasing oil and natural gas severance revenues that followed rising oil and natural gas prices nationwide.[13]

The post-recession period represented a mixed bag. While the heavily industrialized states of the Midwest were recovering from the recession, the farm belt states of the Midwest and the plains started to feel the effects of a downturn in the agricultural economy, as commodity and land prices dropped in 1985 and 1986. The energy-producing states (which had prospered a few years earlier) were hit even harder during this period. As oil prices dropped by nearly half during the 1986 fiscal year, policy makers in the energy-producing states found themselves faced with large shortfalls in oil-severance tax revenues at the very time when the industrial states of the Northeast and Midwest were gaining economic strength. As a result of this mixed picture, thirty-five states reduced general-purpose taxes between 1984 and 1986 while twenty-four increased them, making generalizations about state tax behavior during those years difficult.

Most states got a fiscal break in the 1988 fiscal year, when major federal tax reform enacted late in 1986 gave them a revenue windfall amounting to over $6 billion nationally. That windfall occurred because personal income tax systems in most states conform to the federal tax system. As tax reform changed the federal tax code—most notably by tightening up deductions and exemptions—the states benefited along with the federal government. Although this additional revenue would have flowed to the states without any legislative action, legislatures in thirty-one states acted to change their tax laws and return 81 percent of the windfall to the taxpayers. Only thirteen states kept all of the additional revenues.[14]

State policy makers also used this opportunity to reform their personal income tax systems by broadening tax bases, increasing personal exemptions and standard deductions, reducing the number of tax brackets, and lowering the tax rate.[15] In contrast, the 1989 and 1990 fiscal years were relatively uneventful for state tax policy, reflecting stable economic conditions in most states. Tax changes were largely confined to special purpose tax increases and minor adjustments in general-purpose taxes.

With the economy worsening in 1990, state legislatures were forced to raise taxes and cut expenditures for the 1991 fiscal year to keep their budgets in balance. During the 1990 legislative session, personal income tax was increased in eleven states; sales tax in seventeen. In contrast, six states lowered personal income tax and only two reduced sales tax.[16]

These actions proved to be a harbinger of even tougher choices ahead. As the recession deepened, many states faced budget deficits, forcing governors to recommend tax increases for the 1992 fiscal year and, to a lesser extent, for 1993. The biggest increases occurred in California, Connecticut, New Jersey, Ohio, and Pennsylvania, although significant increases could be found in Florida, Kansas, Maine, Maryland, and Washington. Smaller increases were approved in several other states.

Such increases were not without political consequences for the governors who recommended them: Ten governors—both Democrat and Republican—either lost their bids for reelection or chose not to run due to low popularity ratings associated with their support for tax increases.[17] One highly visible governor, Pete Wilson of California, survived reelection even after having recommended hikes in four state taxes—on income, sales, motor fuel, and cigarettes. However, his recommended tax increases were accompanied by a call for major budget cuts, presenting what was portrayed as a balanced package of shared pain. Another prominent governor, New Jersey's Jim Florio, championed a $2.8 billion income tax hike to aid inner-city schools. His reelection effort was thwarted at the polls.

Just as had happened during the volatile 1980s, recession-driven tax increases left states with tax structures that produced solid revenue growth as the economy improved. In fact, the combination of higher tax rates and significantly improved economic activity not only turned budgetary bottom lines from red to black but also began to generate sizable surpluses by mid-decade. End-of-year balances for the 1995 fiscal year amounted to 5.9 percent of expenditures, the highest level since 1980, prompting governors to advance tax cuts—a politically welcome change from a few years earlier.[18]

Governors in twenty-eight states proposed tax reductions for the 1996 fiscal year, with most targeting the personal income tax. Governors proposed the biggest reductions, in descending order, in New York, New Jersey, North Carolina, Connecticut, California, Michigan, Arizona, and Virginia. Notably, Republican governors led the way in all but North Carolina.

Continued strong economic growth filled state treasuries throughout the 1990s, giving budget makers in most states the opportunity to cut taxes and increase spending above the rate of inflation. In fact, states cut taxes by almost $5 billion in fiscal year 1999, the fifth straight year of aggregate tax cuts among the states. Education, corrections, and Medicaid were the disproportionate beneficiaries of increased state spending.[19]

The recession of 2001, and the slow economic recovery that followed it in the near term, took its toll on state revenues, while putting pressure on social welfare spending. Nearly all states suffered budget shortfalls in the 2002 and 2003 fiscal years. Some shortfalls were staggering. Budget makers in California, for example, faced shortfalls of $8.5 billion in 2002, and almost $15.1 billion in 2003. To put these amounts in perspective, California's budget shortfalls constituted 11 percent of its general fund budget in 2002, and almost 20 percent in 2003. On a relative basis, Alaska's shortfalls were even larger, amounting to approximately a third of its general fund budget. All told, states confronted budget shortfalls that approached $50 billion in fiscal year 2003.[20]

States responded by using a combination of spending cuts and revenue increases, and they drew down or liquidated balances in their "rainy day" or tobacco settlement funds. California relied on $15 billion in new bond revenue to help close the large gap between appropriations and available revenue.

Fortunately, economic growth led to an improving state budget picture in 2004. Still, eighteen states were forced to reduce their enacted budgets for fiscal year 2004 and state expenditures grew by 2.8 percent in that year, slightly exceeding the rate of inflation.[21]

As economic growth continued at a brisk pace in 2005 and 2006, states were variously able to increase spending, cut taxes, and replenish their rainy day funds. The improved economic times encouraged budget makers to restore cuts made during the 2002 and 2003 down fiscal years and enact tax and fee reductions totaling $2.1 billion for FY 2007. Rainy day fund balances across the states soared, reaching a thirty-year high as a percentage of expenditures. Revenues continued to grow during the 2007 fiscal year, rising about 3 percent faster than in FY 2006, and revenues exceeded budget projections in thirty-eight states. Only one state, Wisconsin, was forced to reduce its enacted budget in midyear.[22]

Economic prosperity, however, was soon to wane. The popping of the housing bubble and the growing fiscal precariousness of the nation's financial institutions conspired to slow economic growth, reduce state tax revenues, and push up state social welfare spending. Those states in which the housing markets have been hardest hit experienced the largest revenue shortfalls. The Florida legislature was forced to make $1.5 billion in cuts *after* the FY 2008 budget was enacted into law, California's post-budget cuts totaled almost $850 million, and Arizona's amounted to $312 million. In all, thirteen states reduced their enacted fiscal 2008 budgets by $5.2 billion.[23]

State general fund revenues fell beyond the 2008 fiscal year, dropping from $680 billion in FY 2008 to a low of $610 billion in FY 2010. State spending correspondingly fell from $687 billion in FY 2008 to $623 billion in FY 2010, creating the greatest budgetary challenge for the states since the Great Depression. Although the national recession officially ended in July 2009, state fiscal fortunes did not improve until the 2011 fiscal year, since state revenue collections tend to lag behind national economic recovery. The states closed FY 2010 with an aggregate revenue shortfall of $13 billion, in spite of legislatures approving $23.9 billion in increased taxes and fees in that year. State legislators, typically with their governor's support, had to tap carry-forward balances in rainy day funds to fill in the revenue shortfalls.

Benefited by moderate economic growth, state general fund revenues and spending continued their climb out of the deep trough of 2010, with general fund revenues rising to $726 billion and essentially covering enacted spending. Moreover, the nation's governors' revenue estimates for FY 2015 projected further revenue growth of $23 billion nationally, sufficient to finance their recommended increased spending, of which governors called for the lion's share to go to K-12 education and Medicaid.[24]

Box 7.1 highlights California's descent into deep budget deficits and its near-miraculous fiscal transformation under the unconventional leadership of Governor Jerry Brown.

Box 7.1 The California Comeback

Upon assuming office after his electoral victory in November 2010, Governor Jerry Brown inherited a $25 billion revenue shortfall projected to exist at the end of the 2011–12 fiscal year. Several factors contributed to that deep budget hole, most notably including the following:

1   A large structural imbalance between spending and revenues left unclosed in recent previous budgets;
2   The termination of federal stimulus funding made available to states by the American Recovery and Reinvestment Act of 2009;
3   The expiration on December 31, 2010 of temporary tax increases approved in February 2009, including an across-the-board rate increase of a quarter of 1 percentage point to the personal income tax, along with a 1 percentage point increase in the sales tax.

To help close the gap between spending and revenues, Governor Brown first requested that the legislature place a five-year extension of the temporary tax increases on the ballot in a June 2011 special election. The legislature refused. The governor then requested that the legislature pass legislation extending the temporary increases: five years for the sales tax, and four years for the income tax. The legislature again refused.

Faced with the reality of a gaping hole in revenues and budget cuts that would be required if that hole were not filled, Governor Brown took his case directly to the voters in the November 2012 election, making use of California's direct initiative process, through which propositions can be qualified and placed on the ballot by obtaining the required number of signatures by California residents. Following the governor's lead, voters approved two measures: Proposition 30 and Proposition 39.

Proposition 30 is the most widely consequential of the two, raising tax rates for both the sales tax and the personal income tax. The narrower Proposition 39 raised corporate taxes to finance improvements in energy efficiency, as well as to reduce the budget deficit. The Legislative Analyst's Office (LAO) projected that Proposition 30 would increase state revenues by $8.5 billion in its first year of application, and then grow with expected improvement in the economy. The LAO estimated that Proposition 39 would generate $500 million in its first year, and $1 billion in each year thereafter.

Proposition 30, entitled Temporary Taxes to Fund Education, merits special attention. It substantially increased taxes in an era of elected officials' political wariness of tax increases. The initiative raised the statewide sales tax rate by a quarter of 1 percentage point, from 7.25 percent to 7.50 percent, effective through December 31, 2016. It also increased personal income taxes for single taxpayers earning over $250,000, and for married filers earning over $500,000, effective through the end of 2018, raising California's top personal income tax rate to 13.3 percent, the highest of any state.

Just as notable as a governor championing tax increases in a national political climate of fiscal austerity, was Governor Brown's ability to rally support for them. His success rests in significant part on the way he framed the issues of need and consequence. His campaign to expand revenues as a necessary element of deficit reduction was pursued within a backdrop of the $12.5 billion of spending reductions included as part of his first budget submitted to the legislature. Following his lead, the legislature approved $11 billion in cuts. Of that amount, social welfare and health programs absorbed $5.5 billion of the cut. And although elementary and secondary education was largely protected from deep cuts, higher education took a $1.2 billion hit.

This disproportionate reliance on budget cuts still fell short of the governor's deficit reduction goals. In fact, the state's budget deficit grew moderately during the 2011–12 fiscal year, as revenues fell short of estimates and costs grew faster than expected. This reality prompted Governor Brown to take his case for revenue expansion directly to the people, as discussed above. Failure to approve the proposed tax increases in the November 2012 election would, argued the governor, necessitate deep cuts in education spending. No longer would it be possible to shield schools from the brunt of budget reductions. These cuts, branded as "trigger cuts," carried the message that failure to pass Proposition 30 would directly trigger $5.4 billion in cuts to schools and community colleges, even though no linked consequence was authorized by state law.

Since voters approved Proposition 30, California's budget climate has improved markedly. Strong economic growth has filled state treasuries. Governor Brown's budget for the 2015–16 projected that California would end the year with $3.4 billion in revenue surplus, compared to the large budget deficits confronting him early in his first term. What a contrasting picture! California experienced a budgetary transformation, commonly characterized as a "California comeback." A greatly improved state economy, with its associated surge in income tax and sales tax revenues, has put California's budget on sound footing, at least for now. Yet will it remain that way? The combination of expiring temporary tax increases and a future deteriorating economy could throw California's budget back into deficit, returning the public debate once again to budget cuts and tax increases.

Note: this box draws upon several publications of California's Legislative Analyst's Office, including several issues of its *Overview of the Governor's Budget*, along with several issues of its *Just the Facts*, summarizing and analyzing major features of California's state budget.

Developing the Executive Budget

By their very nature, budgets force action. The state budgetary process forces operating agencies to assess their programmatic and financial needs and set priorities in making their requests. But state agencies characteristically have tunnel vision; in setting agendas they look foremost to their own needs and opportunities and go after the resources necessary to finance them. They are not expected to reconcile their needs and wants with those of other state agencies. State agency heads may, and frequently do, establish relative priorities for their agencies, but those priorities are bounded by each agency's mission and programmatic authority. A director of highways, for example, may assign one priority to new highway development and construction and another to the maintenance of existing highways; it would be highly unusual for that same director (in public, at least) to assign relative priority to new highway construction in relation to quality-enhancement programs in primary and secondary education, expanded work release for prison inmates, additional student financial aid, or higher welfare benefits. That becomes the governor's job.

By submitting an executive budget to the legislature, the governor sets the fiscal and policy agenda for the state. He or she reconciles competing demands for state fiscal resources and recommends which public programs should be valued more highly than others, at least for the coming fiscal year or biennium. Beyond setting programmatic priorities, a governor also must show how all are to be financed. If the level of projected revenues from existing law appears to fall short of covering costs, the governor must cut back on his or her designs, suggest budget reallocations, or recommend revenue increases.

Governors bring their own values and experiences to the task of budget development. Several governors are political insiders who have served as legislative leaders or major state officials. About half of the governors have previously served in the state legislature, with one-third of them in leadership positions.[25] Others come to office as outsiders, from successful careers in the private sector, often running against the professional political establishment. The insiders have considerable experience with the politics of the state budgetary process, and they know how it works. They have closely observed other governors using the process to accomplish their political and policy ends, and they come to office realizing that it is their turn to get what they want done. Outsiders may lack the same appreciation of how the process works and how it can be used, but they nevertheless bring to office a sense of where the state needs to go and what policy directions are necessary to get it there, even if those policies center on restraining government activism and reducing its penetration into private life.

Although the governor sets the direction and tone for executive budget development and deliberation by the legislature, he or she personally initiates only a few of the many recommendations that become identified with the governor in the executive budget.[26] Gubernatorial budget initiatives come from many sources; they may be prompted by agency requests, the preferences of friendly legislative leaders, recommendations of commissions or task forces, successful initiatives of neighboring or bellwether states, recommendations of national organizations, advice from close political or policy staff members, or, most significant, guidelines from the state budget office.

State budget offices play several important roles in the process of developing the executive budget. First, they act as a governor's liaison with agencies for both budget development and execution. Second, they prepare guidelines and instructions that direct agency budget preparation. Those guidelines lay out a governor's overall approach to the budget and highlight the governor's major policy priorities. In addition, state budget offices in thirty-nine states place upper limits on funding targets as part of their guidance to state agencies.[27] Though these limits are not legally binding, both governors and state budget offices expect agencies to take them seriously. Cabinet agency heads, whom governors appoint and retain, feel particular pressure to stay within the targets. In contrast, both elected officials and those serving at the pleasure of boards or commissions often feel less compulsion to observe a governor's targets. The third job of state budget offices is to analyze the thousands of pages of budget requests and make recommendations about them to the governor. Finally, analysts may be encouraged in some states to conduct policy studies and develop budget initiatives independent of agency requests.

State budget offices are organized differently in different states. In ten states they are part of the governor's office. In another ten states the budget office constitutes a separate, freestanding executive agency, and in another thirty states the budget office is part of an executive agency such as a department of administration, finance, or management/planning and budget.[28] Unlike the budget director, budget analysts are most often hired and employed within a civil service system; thirty-one state budget offices operate within a civil service or merit code.[29]

State budget offices vary in size, role orientation, and the sophistication of their staffs. The largest number of budget analysts can be found in New York (245), California (114), Florida (51), and Washington (36). At the other extreme lie West Virginia (3), North Dakota (4), South Dakota (6), and Mississippi (5). The average number of analysts, for comparative reference, is twenty-four.[30]

Although the size of a budget office conditions the roles it is able to play in the state budgetary process, that size is also a function of the roles it is expected to play. The offices tend to play the most active policy roles. They not only condition and react to agency requests but also provide significant policy leadership to the process of executive budget development. Working under the guidance of the state budget director and team leaders, analysts (in teams organized along functional policy lines—for example, human resources and education) identify policy issues, outline alternative policy and budgetary approaches, and make recommendations. These policy analyses may be carried out in cooperation with state agencies or they may be conducted independently, particularly in cases in which the governor holds a policy position on a major issue at variance with that of a rival in the executive branch.

No close observer of state budgeting would write off the state budget office as an insignificant part of executive budget formulation, but few empirical studies have been made of the influence of state budget offices on gubernatorial decision making. One such study indicates that the state budget office does make a difference, both in influencing gubernatorial choice and in shaping a state budget's content. That study examined Wisconsin state budgeting and found that the governor agreed with the state budget office's recommendation 96 percent of the time.[31] It also shows that the state budget office significantly shaped the most important part of the approved budget, contributing about one-third of the approved budget items of major policy significance and high cost and 39 percent of those affecting local units of government.[32]

A comparative study of budgeting in Iowa, Minnesota, and Wisconsin provides further evidence that state budget offices make a difference.[33] Budget analysts and team leaders estimated the extent to which their recommendations shape both the official state budget office's recommendations to the governor and the governor's recommendations to the legislature. The study concluded that their influence appears to be strikingly high. Ten of the thirteen team leaders across the three states noted that the state budget office's official recommendations to the governor reflect their teams' recommendations about 90 percent of the time. Analysts, whose recommendations face review and possible change by their team leader and budget director, also rated their influence as high; fifteen of the analysts who had gone through at least one budget cycle estimated that their budget office superiors accepted 80 percent or more of their recommendations and another six put the figure between 70 and 79 percent, while only one estimated that concurrence was only 50 percent. A follow-up study of the three states undertaken ten years later found rates of concurrence remaining high, averaging 83 percent among the three states and ranging from 75 percent in Iowa to 84 percent in Wisconsin.[34]

What happens once the governor's office reviews the recommendations? Team leaders and analysts saw their influence remain high, pointing to a drop-off in agreement of only 10 percent to 15 percent. They attributed the difference largely to different perspectives on political feasibility. Though self-appraisal of influence is subject to the distinct possibility of "aggrandized assessment," since individuals generally tend to exaggerate their own accomplishments, two factors corroborate the validity of these assessments.

First, team leaders' independent appraisals of their teams' influence paralleled those of their analysts; and second, agency heads tended to concur in those assessments.

A study of decision making and influence in the Kansas state budget office reinforces the direction of the findings cited above. Budget analysts were perceived to have influence in large part because they developed recommendations that flowed from a shared sense of how the governor defined problems and set priorities. In other words, they had a good intuitive sense of what the governor's position might be on a particular request. Consistent with this reasoning, recently hired analysts appeared to be somewhat less successful in eliciting gubernatorial agreement with their recommendations than were the more experienced analysts. Perhaps it takes a period of learning before analysts get a good sense of the criteria a governor uses to evaluate alternatives and make choices.[35]

Studies of state budgeting in Georgia, Illinois, and Missouri provide further evidence of the influence of the state budget office on gubernatorial decision making.[36]

The Legislature and Budget Development

As a rule, the legislature plays a marginal role at best in the process of executive budget development. Governors generally view this phase of the budgetary process as one of clear executive prerogative. They see it as their opportunity to set spending priorities that respond to their states' needs as they view them. From the vantage point of a governor, the legislature's opportunity to shape the budget comes after it is introduced into the legislature. Wisconsin Governor Tommy Thompson summed this sentiment up by quipping: "It's the executive budget bill, not the legislature's budget bill."[37] That sentiment captures the approach followed in other states with strong executive budgets, including Illinois, Michigan, Minnesota, New Jersey, New York, Pennsylvania, and Washington.

On occasion, a governor gives the legislature a role in executive budget development. Governor Ned McWherter of Tennessee routinely welcomed the counsel of legislative leaders, and Governor Gerald Baliles of Virginia allowed key legislators to share their wish lists with him while the executive budget was being formulated.[38] Even when legislative leaders are permitted to participate, however, there is still a clear distinction between executive budget development and legislative review. The budget, without question, is the governor's; although a governor may invite legislative involvement, it is on his or her terms.

That distinction becomes blurred in a few states. In Arkansas, Mississippi, North Carolina, South Carolina, and Texas the legislature is intimately involved; in those states, the legislative branch shares responsibility with the governor for formulating the executive budget. Thus, the legislature is in a position not only to approve the state budget, but also to shape it from the outset.

This sharing of power takes several forms. In North Carolina, a twelve-member advisory budget commission, consisting of four gubernatorial appointees, four senators, and four representatives, actually develops the executive budget, even though the governor transmits it to the legislature. The commission is staffed by the state budget office, but legislative leaders are not averse to seeking counsel from legislative fiscal aides. The commission operates through committees and receives budget requests directly from the state agencies, holding public hearings and making formal budget recommendations to the governor. It also may initiate budget proposals on its own, even in areas where no agency requests have been made.[39]

The governor's authority for executive budget development is weakened further in South Carolina. In addition to legislative leaders sitting on the State Budget Control Board, the governor's own power on the board is further diluted by the presence of two other independently elected officials from the executive branch: the state treasurer and the comptroller general.[40]

In Arkansas, Mississippi, and Texas, the executive budget faces strong competition from an alternative version developed by legislative leaders. Although the Arkansas budget office receives agency requests, analyzes them, and puts together an executive budget, that document is referred to the legislative council, which works under the watchful eye of the legislative leadership to prepare the official state budget for introduction into the legislature. In Mississippi and Texas, the state budget office prepares the governor's executive budget, but legislative budget committees formulate alternative versions. Both the governor and the committees present their own recommendations to the legislature. Inevitably, the legislative version serves as the benchmark for consideration by the legislature.[41]

As has been noted, the executive budget bears the governor's clear stamp in most states. The governor's recommendations are highlighted in the executive budget book, which accompanies the budget bill or bills introduced into the legislature. In addition to serving as a guide to what is included in the executive budget, the budget book also establishes gubernatorial intent. Constitutions or statutes in twenty-five states require that the budget book specifically include all agency requests along with the governor's recommendations.[42]

The governor's budget recommendations must be reduced to bill form for consideration by the legislature. At a minimum, the budget bill contains appropriations to fund the various programs of state government. As discussed earlier, depending on state law, the budget bill may also change statutory or session laws or place limitations on how appropriated funds can be used. The legislative leadership, as a customary courtesy to the governor, introduces the budget bill or bills into the legislature. The number of appropriations bills can affect legislative decision making and executive–legislative relations. Using a large number of appropriations bills tends to fragment legislative decision making and limit the legislature's ability to draft a comprehensive alternative to the executive budget.

Legislative Action on the Budget

Just as the governor is positioned to dominate the process of executive budget development, the legislature is constitutionally situated to dominate the process of budget review and enactment. The legislature is empowered to appropriate state funds, subject to gubernatorial veto. The governor can propose, but only the legislature can dispose, as the saying goes. Even if the governor objects to the legislature's action through use of the veto, the legislature can still do as it wants by overriding the governor's veto. Essentially, legislatures are empowered to do whatever they want to the state budget, as long as they have the votes.

The constitutions of two states limit the legislature's discretion somewhat. In Maryland, where the legislature faces the most stringent limitation, it cannot increase appropriation authority beyond the level recommended by the governor. In Nebraska, the legislature must have at least a three-fifths vote to increase spending above the governor's recommendation. In the other forty-eight states the legislature is limited only by politics in its ability to get the support of a majority of its members for passage and the extraordinary majority required for veto override.

Legislators attempt to use the budget to advance their own conceptions of public policy and spending priorities, reconciling their preferences with the need to represent their constituents. However, for the legislature to put its stamp on the budget, its leaders need to amass enough political support for its passage. In that process, the legislature as a whole makes concessions to individual legislators and groups of legislators in order to win their support.

Legislative leaders appoint their colleagues to appropriations, finance, or budget committees—variously named among the states—to improve the prospects of enacting a budget responsive to their collective interests. In significant part, an appropriations committee tends to be representative of the legislature as a whole, and thus able to reconcile diverse interests before the budget reaches the legislative floor for debate. Members are selected, in part, for their capacity to see beyond their own parochial interests and put them in the perspective of the larger "corporate partisan good." Fifteen states have joint appropriations committees, which tend to break down legislative parochialism even further and accommodate potential inter-chamber differences.[43]

Appropriations committees make use of subcommittees in thirty-four states.[44] Subcommittees are typically organized along functional policy lines, often paralleling the structure of the appropriations bills themselves. For example, a subcommittee on highways may consider the highways appropriations bill. Obviously, legislatures facing more than a hundred appropriations bills do not create a subcommittee to consider each one. Instead, a single subcommittee reviews several appropriations bills, usually functionally related. The number of subcommittees employed in the lower chambers among the states ranges from twenty in Massachusetts to three in Arizona, North Dakota, and Pennsylvania. In state senates, Maryland and Rhode Island are at the low end with three each, while Michigan tops the list with thirteen.[45]

A legislature's real budget work is done in these subcommittees. Appropriations committee chairpersons often consult with their party leadership to develop dollar allotments for the various subcommittees. Then it is up to them to apportion the sums among the agencies and programs within their jurisdictions.[46] Subcommittees hold hearings on the appropriations bills before them or on the functionally related parts of the budget bill that parallel their jurisdiction. Chairpersons usually invite state budget office and agency representatives to attend subcommittee hearings and respond to questions about the governor's budget recommendations. In the process, the subcommittee's chairperson or members may invite agency representatives to express any concerns they have about the way the governor treated them in the executive budget. Such an invitation can create a dilemma for cabinet agency heads, who must calculate how far they can go in pleading their case without incurring the boss's disfavor. Non-cabinet agency heads face less of a problem; some clearly welcome the opportunity to take on the governor in the public legislative arena. Upon completion of their deliberations, subcommittees vote on motions to amend the executive budget, and successful motions are referred to the full committee for action. Subcommittee votes give members an opportunity to size up how well motions are likely to fare at the hands of the full committee. Subcommittees, however, attempt to work out their differences before potentially divisive issues come before the full committee; and that effort, when successful, greatly enhances the likelihood of further success in the full committee.

Reciprocity is a key principle underlying the full committee's decision making. There is a clear expectation that members of each subcommittee will support the other subcommittees' recommendations. The making of subcommittee motions is often carefully orchestrated in advance, with the chairperson of one subcommittee seconding another chairperson's motion. Legislative fiscal staffs assist appropriations committees in their work. Fiscal staffs are organized into central service agencies in thirty-one states; they are assigned directly to the appropriations committees in the other states. Five state legislatures employ both central fiscal offices and appropriations committee staffs.[47]

The size of legislative fiscal staffs nearly doubled between 1975 and 1988, the last date for which data have been collected by the National Conference of State Legislatures.[48] Legislative fiscal staff offices averaged nearly fifteen professional members. The largest fiscal staffs could be found in New York and California, each having more than a hundred. Illinois, Michigan, and Texas have more than fifty. At the other end of the scale, Wyoming had only three analysts.[49]

In addition to summarizing executive budget recommendations, legislative fiscal staffs develop and offer alternatives to the governor's recommendations.

In some states, they provide recommendations for the appropriations committees' consideration. The California legislature's Office of the Legislative Analyst provides a prominent example of the latter approach. It presents a comprehensive package of recommended alternatives to the governor's budget along with an analysis of their fiscal effects.[50]

In most states, legislative fiscal staffs confine themselves to offering alternatives to the governor's recommendations without making recommendations per se. Fiscal offices present alternatives, however, in a way that often clearly conveys their preferences. Fiscal analysts also perform another important function: They keep a running tally of the fiscal effects of legislative adjustments to the executive budget. That way legislative leaders know the collective costs or savings associated with their changes to the budget.

After an appropriations committee reports the amended budget to the chamber where it was first introduced, legislative fiscal staff's involvement in budget deliberations generally declines. Legislative leaders may still call upon fiscal staff members to prepare brief analyses and fiscal notes on the major and most serious amendments, but the emphasis at this stage of the process is more on the politics of coalition building and less on policy analysis.

Executive–Legislative Influence in State Budgeting

Few empirical comparative studies of the relative influence of the executive and legislative branches on state budget outcomes can be found. Ira Sharkansky's classic study of influence and budgetary decision making in nineteen states demonstrates that a legislature generally follows the governor's recommendation instead of an agency's request. Agencies that requested the largest increases received proportionally the greatest cuts from governors, but realized the largest relative increases over their base budget levels. Sharkansky found governors trimming agency requests by about 14 percent on average, while legislatures cut them back by 13 percent. Therefore, although state legislatures usually followed their governors' leads, they allowed a little more budget growth than governors.[51]

Using data from eleven states, Gary Moncrief and Joel Thompson replicated Sharkansky's methodology but added an additional independent variable, the partisan balance between the governor and the legislature. Their results confirm Sharkansky's findings in the aggregate but, controlling for partisanship, they show even closer patterns of agreement when the governor and legislative majority represent the same party, and lower levels of agreement when they are drawn from opposing parties.[52]

Nearly a decade later, Thompson analyzed budget data collected from 671 agencies in eighteen states. The overall patterns remain consistent: agencies continued to request significant increases; governors continued to cut them back; and legislatures continued to appropriate approximately what the governors recommended, although they allowed relatively larger increases than the governors. The average percentage increases also exceeded the levels found during the period examined by Sharkansky.[53] A significant portion of that additional growth could be attributed to inflation, since the period from 1978 to 1980 covered by Thompson's data was one of much greater inflation than the period from 1965 to 1967, which was the source of Sharkansky's data.

In another multistate study, Glenn Abney and Thomas Lauth asked executive and legislative budget officers in thirty-seven states who has the greatest impact on budget making: the governor or the legislature? Of the respondents, 61 percent pointed to the governor, while 39 percent saw the legislature as the dominant institution. The researchers found that the governor tended to have the upper hand where the state budget office plays an active policy development role for the governor, in contrast to a more comptroller-like role found in other states. A policy-oriented budget office gives the governor an important resource in setting a state's policy agenda and representing that agenda before the legislature.[54]

In a related study of thirteen states conducted by scholars closely familiar with the budgetary processes of those states, Edward Clynch and Thomas Lauth classified the states in terms of gubernatorial and legislative influence over the budget. Three states—California, Illinois, and Ohio—were categorized as executive-dominant states. Connecticut, Georgia, Idaho, Kentucky, and Minnesota were classified as states in which the governor occupies a central position in the budgetary process but works with legislatures that have the capability to make independent judgments and effectively challenge executive budget initiatives and assumptions. Florida, Mississippi, Texas, and Utah were classified as legislative-dominant states. South Carolina was judged to be unique, with the executive and legislative branches participating in budget formulation through a budget control board, but the legislative members having the upper hand.[55]

Several studies of budgeting in a single state also suggest that a state legislature does not just "rubber stamp" the governor's budget recommendations. Legislatures have come to exercise independence from governors in shaping state budgets. A governor, assisted by the state budget office, continues to set the state's budget and policy agenda, but the legislature puts its own distinctive stamp on the final budget product.

A study of Wisconsin state budgeting found that the legislature contributed one-quarter of the items included in the budget as finally enacted into law while the executive branch contributed three-quarters. Nevertheless, the legislature contributed more than half of the most important part of the budget items judged to be of major policy significance and relatively high fiscal effect; the Joint Committee on Finance contributed 38 percent; and amendments from the floor added another 18 percent.[56] This picture of legislative influence contrasts with that drawn by researchers twelve years earlier, who found the Wisconsin legislature regularly accepting the governor's recommendation.[57]

A study of budgeting in the state of New York shows the legislature as an active participant in state budget making. It changed more than three-quarters of the budget items for nineteen departments over a six-year period. Approximately one-third of the items were characterized as having undergone "moderate" as opposed to "minor" change.[58]

Studies of budgeting in Georgia suggest that its legislature's influence has also increased in recent years. Although the legislature still appears to follow the governor's lead in reducing agency requests, it has exhibited independence from the governor in estimating the costs to continue the current budget, consistently placing them lower than the governor's estimate. The estimate of continuation is a significant element in the politics of Georgia budgeting because it determines how much of the projected available revenue is "reserved" to cover those costs and is therefore unavailable to finance new spending initiatives. Consistently lower estimates, made during the legislative phase of budget deliberations, give the legislature some additional spending room of its own.[59]

Another study found the North Carolina legislature generally going along with the governor's recommendation for 99 percent of the budget; for the other 1 percent, however, the legislature deviates sharply from the governor's lead. That 1 percent, $36.8 million in 1984, was dispensed by the Democratic leadership as special "pork barrel" appropriations. Its allocation does not follow gubernatorial priorities; nor does it follow comprehensive legislative policy alternatives. Instead, it provides funding to loyalists from the majority party that have cooperated with the leadership and whose vote for budget passage is vital to legislative leaders. The governor's role in the process appears to be minimal at best; as the author notes, "None of the legislators interviewed suggested that the governor had any influence in the process."[60] The governor of North Carolina has no item-veto authority and therefore cannot use, or even threaten to use, this power to eliminate the most obnoxious "slices of pork." But perhaps the governor is willing to accept the special interest items as a tradeoff for the legislature's support of the executive budget.

Another single-state study found the legislature in Ohio upping the governor's spending ante, increasing spending to reflect legislative priorities that were not included or adequately funded in the executive budget.[61]

In response to these single-state studies that show increased legislative influence in state budget making, Glenn Abney and Thomas Lauth returned in the mid-1990s to the comparative research they conducted in the early 1980s. Their earlier surveys of chief executive and legislative budget officials in the states found that although the governor remained dominant over the legislature in the appropriations process, the governor's dominance was not as pronounced as previous studies had suggested. Their research leads them to conclude that legislatures have almost pulled even with governors in shaping the budget, bringing about the end of executive dominance in the appropriations process. In explaining this shift, the authors point to the inroads that legislatures have made in controlling the appropriations agenda and to court action that has weakened governors' use of the item-veto.[62]

Doug Goodman's study of thirteen western states also provides evidence for increased influence exercised by legislatures. Using surveys of perceived influence of budgetary participants administered early in the first decade of the twenty-first century, Goodman concludes that legislatures have increased their influence over budgetary outcomes, driven in significant part by a growing independence of legislative agenda setting.[63]

Other factors also help to account for the resurgence of legislatures in state budgeting. First, as discussed earlier, legislatures are far better staffed today than they were more than two decades ago—the era in which students of state budgeting wrote about disproportionate gubernatorial influence in the state budgetary process. Second, legislators have much better information today as a basis for choices than they did in the 1960s and early 1970s. Systematic budget data are available on legislative information systems, and staff members are able to model a state's various aid formulas and illustrate the redistributive effects of proposed changes. Third, legislatures have developed their own revenue-estimating models and freed themselves from reliance on the executive branch. They therefore have greater flexibility to set spending levels for legislative action levels that usually differ, generally on the high side, from those permitted by the executive branch's estimates of revenue availability. Legislative staffs in twenty-eight states prepare state revenue estimates or revise those prepared by the executive branch.[64]

Besides acquiring heightened influence in shaping state revenue budgets, legislatures have over the past decade inserted themselves into the receipt and allocation of federal funds, long an executive prerogative. Federal appropriations traditionally entered state budgets as non-binding estimates of federal funds expected by each agency. If the federal funds received exceeded the estimate, the state budget office acted on behalf of the governor to give the agency authority to spend up to the amount actually received. In the early 1980s, legislatures began to rein in the discretion the executive branch had long enjoyed.

In the 1981 legislative session alone, almost half the state legislatures passed laws increasing their oversight of federal funds.[65] By 2008, forty-six state legislatures had given themselves the authority to appropriate federal funds. The legislatures in thirty states authorized state agencies to spend federal funds received during the fiscal year without the legislature appropriating specific amounts.[66]

Legislatures took these steps for three primary reasons: first, to advance their own priorities for the use of federal funds; second, to control the need for them to appropriate state funds to replace those used by state agencies to match federal funding; and third, to limit future demands for state funding when federal funding has terminated.

The governors of several states have challenged their legislatures' newly acquired authority over federal funds, arguing that state constitutions give them, as chief executive officers, authority over intergovernmental funds. The first major test case occurred in Pennsylvania, where the legislature gave itself the statutory authority to make binding sum-certain appropriations of federal funds. In response to the governor's petition for hearing, the state supreme court upheld a lower court's ruling that the law was not in violation of the state constitution. The U.S. Supreme Court refused to review the case, letting stand the state court's decision in *Shapp v. Sloan*. Subsequent decisions in Kansas, Montana, and New York have supported the legislative position, but state courts have supported the governors' in Arizona, Colorado, Massachusetts, and New Mexico.

Summary and Conclusions

The states provide a laboratory for the comparative study of public budgeting. State budgeting reflects the diversity of the states, and that diversity encompasses differences in political culture, institutional structure, the formal powers of the governor and the legislature, and staff resources. In some states, there are also limitations on spending or revenue raising.

In spite of this diversity, three common features distinguish budgeting at the state level: the extent to which the budget is used as a vehicle of policy making, the high degree of fiscal responsibility demonstrated by governors and legislatures in acting on state budgets, and the political salience of state financial assistance to local units of government.

Governors tend to dominate the process of budget formulation. Assisted by state budget offices, they condition and act upon state agency requests, establish priorities among competing claims on state resources, and selectively pursue initiatives independent of state agencies. In doing so, governors set state policy and budgetary agendas.

The organization of state budget offices varies. They come in all sizes and place different priorities on the several roles they play in budget development and control. Although every state budget office assists the governor in executive budget development and subsequent execution of the legislatively approved budget, some offices play a more active role in policy development, while others tend to emphasize budget control.

As a rule, the legislature plays a marginal role in executive budget development. Governors may invite legislative leaders to communicate their top priorities while the executive budget is still being formulated, but such legislative participation is at the governor's behest and on his or her terms.

Just as the governor typically has the upper hand in developing the executive budget, the legislature is constitutionally positioned to dominate the process of budget review and enactment. Only the legislature can appropriate public funds, subject to the governor's objection through the veto. Even if a governor vetoes the legislature's actions, the legislature can override that veto. Essentially, legislatures have the power, within constitutional limits, to do whatever they want with a state budget, as long as the votes exist.

The legislature's real budget work is usually done in subcommittees, which appropriations committees in all but six states make use of. Often they receive spending allotments from the chairperson of the full appropriations committee, and it is up to them to apportion those sums among the agencies and programs within their jurisdiction. After holding hearings at which agency and state budget office representatives defend their requests and recommendations, subcommittees act on motions to amend the executive budget. Approved motions then go to the full committee for final action. Committee decision making is characteristically marked by inter-subcommittee reciprocity; there is a clear expectation that members of each subcommittee will support the others' recommendations.

Legislative fiscal staffs assist appropriations committees in their deliberations. They summarize executive budget recommendations, identify alternatives for the legislature's consideration, make budget recommendations in some states, and keep track of approved legislative amendments.

State legislatures are increasing their influence in the state budgetary process. They not only have increased fiscal staffs, independent revenue-estimating capabilities, and better information systems to make them more formidable competitors in the traditional arena of state budgeting but also have inserted themselves in the receipt and allocation of federal funds—an area of long-standing executive prerogative.

Notes

1 National Conference of State Legislatures, Legislative Budget Procedures: Appropriations Bills and the Budget Document, http://204.131.235.67/programs/fiscal/lbptabls/lbpc3t2.htm
2 National Conference of State Legislatures, A Comparison of Wisconsin's Budget Procedures to Other States: Selected Issues (Denver, C.O.: National Conference of State Legislatures, 1984), 7–9; Sydney Duncombe and Richard Kinney, "Agency Budget Success: How It Is Defined by Budget Officials in Five Western States," Public Budgeting and Finance 7, no. 2 (summer 1987): 24–37; Dennis L. Dresang and James J. Gosling, Politics, Policy and Management in the American States (New York: Longman, 1989), 156–69; Alan Rosenthal, Governors and Legislatures: Contending Powers (Washington, D.C.: Congressional Quarterly Press, 1990), 131–62; James J. Gosling, "Patterns of Stability and Change in Gubernatorial Policy Agendas," State and Local Government Review (winter 1991): 3–12; Thomas P. Lauth, "State Budgeting: Current Conditions and Future Trends," International Journal of Public Administration 15, no. 5 (1992): 1067–96; Robert D. Lee, "The Use of Executive Guidance in State Budget Preparation," Public Budgeting and Finance 12, no. 3 (fall 1992): 19–31.
3 National Conference of State Legislatures, Legislative Budget Procedures: A Guide to Appropriations and Budget Processes in the States, Commonwealths and Territories (Denver, C.O.: National Conference of State Legislatures, 1998), 3–7 through 3–9.

4 Gosling, "Patterns of Stability," 3–12.
5 James J. Gosling, "Patterns of Influence and Choice in the Wisconsin Budgetary Process," Legislative Studies Quarterly 10 (November 1985): 457–82; Glenn Abney and Thomas P. Lauth, "The Line-Item-Veto in the States," Public Administration Review 45 (January–February 1985): 372–77; James J. Gosling, "Wisconsin Item-Veto Lessons," Public Administration Review 46 (July–August 1986): 292–300; Pat Thompson and Steven R. Boyd, "Use of the Item Veto in Texas," State and Local Government Review 26 (winter 1994): 38–45; Catherine C. Reese, "The Line-Item Veto in Practice in Ten Southern States," Public Administration Review 57 (November–December 1997): 510–16.
6 E.B. Herzik, "Governors and Issues: A Typology of Concerns," State Government 54 (fall 1983): 58–64; E.B. Herzik, "Gubernatorial Policy Agendas and Policymaking," paper presented to the annual meeting of the Western Social Science Association, Albuquerque, New Mexico, 1989; Gosling, "Patterns of Stability," 3–14; Thad L. Beyle, "Enhancing Executive Leadership in the States," State and Local Government Review 27 (winter 1995): 18–35.
7 The Center for Education Reform, www.edreform.com/2014/12/school-choice-education-by-the-numbers
8 Sarah A. Hill, "The Impact of State Supreme Court Decisions on Public School Finance," Journal of Law, Economics, and Organization, Advance Access, February 17, 2014, 12.
9 Robert Pear, "How Has the Expansion of Medicaid Fared?," New York Times, www.nytimes.com/interactive/2014/10/27/us/is-the-affordable-care-act-working.html#/medicaid
10 John Shannon and Robert J. Kleine, "Characteristics of a 'Balanced' State-Local Tax System," in State Government, ed. Thad L. Beyle (Washington, D.C.: Congressional Quarterly Press, 1986), 159.
11 National Association of State Budget Officers, Fiscal Survey of the States, 1981–82 (Washington, D.C.: National Association of State Budget Officers, 1982); Fiscal Survey of the States, December 1982 Update (Washington, D.C.: National Association of State Budget Officers, 1982).
12 National Association of State Budget Officers, Fiscal Survey of the States, 1985 (Washington, D.C.: National Association of State Budget Officers, 1985), 7.
13 Shannon and Kleine, "Characteristics," 159.
14 Steven D. Gold, Corina L. Eckl, and Martha A. Fabricius, "State Budget Actions in 1988," Legislative Finance Paper no. 64 (Denver, C.O.: National Conference of State Legislatures, 1988), 64.
15 National Association of State Budget Officers, Fiscal Survey of the States, October 1988 (Washington, D.C.: National Association of State Budget Officers, 1988), 11–13.
16 Corina L. Eckl, Anthony M. Hutchinson, and Ronald K. Snell, "State Budget and Tax Actions," Legislative Finance Paper no. 74 (Denver, C.O.: National Conference of State Legislatures, 1990), 20–1.
17 Stephen Moore and Dean Stansel, A Fiscal Policy Report Card on America's Governors: 1994 (Washington, D.C.: CATO Institute, 1994), 7.
18 State Legislatures 21 (October–November 1995): 9.
19 Corina Eckl, "Can It Get Any Better than This?," Governing 25 (October–November 1999): 14.
20 National Association of Legislative Fiscal Officers, Survey of National Association of Legislative Fiscal Officers (Denver: National Conference of State Legislatures, October 2002), table 1.
21 National Association of State Budget Officers, Fiscal Survey of the States (Washington, D.C.: National Association of State Budget Officers, April 2004), ix.

22 National Association of State Budget Officers, Fiscal Survey of the States (Washington, D.C.: National Association of State Budget Officers, December 2006), vii–viii; National Association of State Budget Officers, Fiscal Survey of the States (Washington, D.C.: National Association of State Budget Officers, December 2007), viii–ix, 1).

23 National Association of State Budget Officers, Fiscal Survey of the States (Washington, D.C.: National Association of State Budget Officers, June 2008), 1–2.

24 National Association of State Budget Officers, Fiscal Survey of the States (Washington, D.C.: National Association of State Budget Officers, June 2014), 1–5.

25 "Governors of the States and Territories," Washington Alert (Washington, D.C.: Congressional Quarterly, June 8, 1995).

26 Gosling, "Patterns of Influence and Choice," 468–9; Rosenthal, Governors and Legislators, 98; Kurt Thurmeier, "Toward a Theory of Microbudgeting: Debunking Budget Mythology," paper presented at the annual meeting of the Association of Budgeting and Financial Management, Washington, D.C., October 1993.

27 National Association of State Budget Officers, Budget Processes in the States (Washington, D.C.: National Association of State Budget Officers, Summer 2008), 30.

28 Ibid., 8.

29 Ibid., 5.

30 Ibid.

31 Gosling, "Patterns of Influence and Choice," 474–5.

32 Ibid., 470–2.

33 James J. Gosling, "The State Budget Office and Policy Making," Public Budgeting and Finance 7 (spring 1987): 51–68.

34 Ibid., 53–4; Kurt Thurmaier and James J. Gosling, "The Shifting Roles of State Budget Offices in the Midwest: Gosling Revisited," Public Budgeting and Finance 17 (winter 1997): 68.

35 Thurmaier, "Toward a Theory of Microbudgeting."

36 Thomas P. Lauth, "Roles and Perspectives of the Executive and Legislative Budget Offices in Georgia," paper presented at the annual meeting of the Southern Political Science Association, Charlotte, North Carolina, 1987; Kenneth Oldfield, "A Comparative Analysis of Executive Budget Analysts in Illinois and Missouri," paper presented at the annual meeting of the American Society for Public Administration, Anaheim, California, 1986; Michael D. Connelly, "Budgeting and Policy Analysts in Missouri," Ph.D. dissertation, University of Missouri-Columbia, 1981.

37 Rosenthal, Governors and Legislatures, 138.

38 Ibid., 137–8.

39 Charles K. Coe, "The Roles and Perspectives of the Executive/Legislative Budget Offices in North Carolina," paper presented at the annual meeting of the Southern Political Science Association, Charlotte, North Carolina, 1987.

40 Marcia Lynn Whicker, "Legislative Budgeting in South Carolina," State and Local Government Review 18 (spring 1986): 65–70; Cole Blease Graham Jr., "The Roles and Perspectives of the Executive/Legislative Hybrid Budget Office in South Carolina," paper presented at the annual meeting of the Southern Political Science Association, Charlotte, North Carolina, 1987.

41 Edward J. Clynch, "Budgeting in Mississippi: Are Two Budgets Better than One?," State and Local Government Review 18 (spring 1986): 49–55; Alan Rosenthal, Legislative Life (New York: HarperCollins, 1981), 287.

42 National Association of State Budget Officers, Budget Processes in the United States (Washington, D.C.: National Association of State Budget Officers, Summer 2008), 30.

43 National Conference of State Legislatures, Legislative Budget Procedures, 1998, 5–7 through 5–9.

44 Ibid., 5–11 through 5–13.

45 Ibid.

46 Rosenthal, Governors and Legislatures, 144.

47 National Conference of State Legislatures, Legislative Budget Procedures, 1998, 8–5 through 8–8.

48 The information for 1975 was provided by the National Conference of State Legislatures, Denver; the 1988 information is from National Conference of State Legislatures, Legislative Budget Procedures in the Fifty States (Denver: National Conference of State Legislatures, 1988), 130.

49 Ibid.

50 Legislative Analyst's Office, Analysis of the 2000–2001 Budget Bill (Sacramento, C.A.: Legislative Analyst's Office, February 17, 2000).

51 Ira Sharkansky, "Agency Requests, Gubernatorial Support, and Budget Success in State Legislatures," American Political Science Review 62 (December 1968): 1220–31.

52 Gary Moncrief and Joel A. Thompson, "Partisanship and Purse Strings: A Research Note on Sharkansky," Western Political Science Quarterly 33 (September 1980): 336–40.

53 Joel A. Thompson, "Agency Request, Gubernatorial Support, and Budget Success in State Legislatures Revisited," Journal of Politics 49 (August 1987): 756–79.

54 Glenn Abney and Thomas P. Lauth, "Perceptions of the Impact of Governors and Legislatures in the State Appropriations Process," Western Political Quarterly 40, no. 2 (June 1987): 335–42.

55 Edward J. Clynch and Thomas P. Lauth, eds., Governors, Legislatures and Budgets: Diversity across the American States (Westport, C.N.: Greenwood, 1991).

56 Gosling, "Patterns of Influence and Choice," 468–70.

57 Ira Sharkansky and Augustus B. Thurnbull III, "Budget-Making in Georgia and Wisconsin: A Test of a Model," Midwest Journal of Political Science 13 (November 1969): 631–45; George D. Edwards III and Ira Sharkansky, "Executive and Legislative Budgeting: Decision Routines for Agency Totals and Individual Programs in Two States," in Perspectives on Public Policy Making, ed. W. B. Gwyn and George C. Edwards III (New Orleans: Tulane University Press, 1975), 167–78.

58 Eagleton Institute of Politics, Rutgers University, "The Role of the New York Legislature in the Budget Process," August 22, 1977, cited in Rosenthal, Legislative Life, 301–2.

59 Thomas P. Lauth, "The Executive Budget in Georgia," State and Local Government Review 18 (spring 1986): 56–64; Thomas P. Lauth, "Exploring the Budgetary Base in Georgia," Public Budgeting and Finance 7 (winter 1987): 7282.

60 Joel A. Thompson, "Bringing Home the Bacon: The Politics of Pork Barrel in the North Carolina Legislature," Legislative Studies Quarterly 11 (February 1986): 91–108.

61 Richard Sheridan, State Budgeting in Ohio (Columbus, O.H.: Ohio Legislative Budget Office, 1978).

62 Glenn Abney and Thomas P. Lauth, "The End of Executive Dominance in State Appropriations," Public Administration Review 58 (September–October 1998): 388–93.

63 Doug Goodman, "Determinants of Perceived Gubernatorial Budgetary Influence among State Executive Budget Analysts and Legislative Fiscal Analysts," Political Science Quarterly 60, No. 1 (2007): 53–54.

64 National Association of State Budget Offices, Budget Processes in the States (Washington, D.C.: National Association of State Budget Officers (Summer 2008), 22.
65 Ibid.; William Pound, "The State Legislatures," in The Book of the States, 1982–83 (Lexington, K.Y.: Council of State Governments, 1982), 184.
66 National Association of State Budget Officers, Budget Processes in the States (Washington, D.C.: National Association of State Budget Officers, Summer 2008), 3, 51.

Chapter 8

Budgeting in Local Units of Government

The U.S. Constitution makes no reference to local units of government, which are legally creatures of the states, dependent on those states for their creation and continued existence. States must expressly enumerate the powers and rights of local governments, and the latter are without authority to act unless their actions fall within the powers granted to them by state constitution or statute.

Given this dependency, local units of government are subject to state constitutional or statutory requirements that they balance their budgets for each fiscal year, paralleling the same legal requirement for all state governments except Vermont. In theory, the requirement means that local governments must enact budgets that are in balance, including sufficient appropriated revenues to cover budgeted expenditures. In practice, the budget can get out of balance during the course of the fiscal year; in extreme cases, a deficit may result at the close of a fiscal year despite efforts to cut back on discretionary spending late in the year. When revenues fall significantly short of projections, local policy makers find it difficult to bring the budget into balance through spending reductions, since a high percentage of local budgets—particularly those of municipalities—goes to cover the salaries and fringe benefits of employees, who usually have civil service protection. Thus, program administrators have only marginal flexibility in reducing expenditures late in the fiscal year as an adjustment to revenue shortfalls. Faced with a deficit at year's end, budget makers must enact a budget for the coming fiscal year that not only eliminates the carried-forward deficit but also closes the new year in the black.

Because of the nature of local governmental budgets, local budgeting can most aptly be described as revenue budgeting. Expenditures must be approved at levels that fall within projected revenue availability. Few incentives, political or other, prompt local budget makers to enact budgets that appear to be in balance at time of passage but hold little promise of staying in balance through the close of the fiscal year. The political risks of running in the red are too high. Although a deficit calls into question the managerial competence of both the chief executive and the legislative body, most often it is the mayor or county executive, rather than the municipal council or county board, who bears the brunt of criticism.

Local policy makers have an incentive to build a politically acceptable surplus into the budget. A surplus provides contingency against revenues falling short of estimates. It also provides a cushion to protect against inflation when it turns out to be higher than expected, or against un-anticipated arbitration judgments or court awards. The surplus cannot be too big; however, if it is, it can become the object of criticism. Detractors can point to large surpluses as evidence of political irresponsibility and accuse local policy makers of excessive taxation. If elected officials can avoid such castigation, a general-fund operating surplus carried over into the next fiscal year will reduce revenue requirements for the new year and even make possible that politician's delight—a budget calling for no tax increases. Agency officials like to see some level of surplus because a surplus reduces the chances that they will be asked to make unforeseen spending reductions during the course of the fiscal year. A surplus also holds out the promise that sufficient revenues may be available for the coming fiscal year, so that agencies can lay claim to additional resources to augment existing programs or add new ones. Too large a surplus, however, means that additional untapped revenues were, in fact, available for increased support of agency programs in the current fiscal year—an undesirable situation from the agency's vantage point.

Despite these incentives for local budget makers to build an acceptable surplus into the budget, economic recessions have diminished or eliminated surpluses, with the greatest impact felt during the Great Recession of 2007–9. The major fiscal choices facing local politicians overall have been not how to use surpluses but how to find adequate revenues to continue present service levels while expenditures grow faster than revenues. State legislatures have also enacted laws that placed limits on local tax and expenditure increases. Where legislatures failed to act, citizens in several states took matters into their own hands, passing initiatives and popular referenda that set local tax and spending limits. To make matters worse for local policy makers, cuts in federal aid reduced revenues that had been used to supplement local funds. In addition, the states, for the most part, have chosen not to increase local aid sufficiently to fill the gap. The resulting challenge for local policy makers has been to find new revenues amid revenue-raising constraints while seeking to keep expenditure increases within the limits of revenue availability.

Although local units of government across the nation share common elements of the characteristic problem of local government finance, some have worse problems than others. Jurisdictions that have lost their tax base—as a result of lost employment and declining population—face greater pressures on the revenue side than those that have grown. Nationally, cities experience employment and population decline more than suburbs do. As productive people and jobs move from cities to suburbs, so do economic resources. The extent of that economic impact can be approximated by focusing on per capita income as a measure of the economic health of a community and as an indicator of its potential tax base. As reported by the U.S. House of Representatives' Ways and Means Committee, central cities had 15 percent of their residents living in poverty in 1978; by 1998, that percentage had risen to 19 percent, and it remained there in 2013.[1]

In contrast, growing jurisdictions have not only enjoyed expanding tax bases but also faced rising demands for the extension and expansion of government services. Their fiscal prospects are brighter, in comparison, because they can use the expanded revenue base to finance the growing services. Declining jurisdictions find it difficult to reduce service costs in proportion to reductions in population and employment. They are left with fixed overhead costs—most of them in personnel—that support declining levels of service. Accordingly, declining jurisdictions are more likely to see program expenditures rise faster per capita than are expanding jurisdictions, especially in the economically sensitive program areas of social welfare, public health, and community development. At the same time, governments in decline face the need to replace revenues forgone by a diminished tax base; but the very reality of tax base decline makes raising the needed revenues more difficult. Tax increases reduce the prospects of attracting economic development and the jobs that come with it, by creating a disincentive to growth that further exacerbates the problem.

Pearl Kramer, in her book *Crisis in Urban Public Finance*, employed a case-study approach to determine empirically the cause, manifestations, and relative degree of fiscal stress in thirty-eight large cities.[2] In attempting to describe and account for urban fiscal stress, she turned to Irene Rubin's model of urban migration,[3] a model that has three components. First, residents and jobs migrate from central cities to the suburbs, reducing the local tax base and leaving the cities populated by increasing percentages of persons more likely to be dependent on public assistance and social services. Second, in addition to this out-migration, a discernible pattern of in-migration brings the disadvantaged, often unemployed, minorities into the central cities in search of opportunities, thus placing still greater demands on the cities' limited resources for supporting educational, welfare, health, and job-training services. Third, interregional migration, characteristically from the "snowbelt" to the "sunbelt," is prompted by structural changes in the economy, particularly those occurring within the heavy manufacturing sector, which result in permanent loss of jobs and make an entire region less economically competitive.

Kramer's findings corroborate that social and economic changes, and their consequences, have occurred as suggested by Rubin's migration and tax base erosion model. Changes in industrial production processes were found to contribute to, and later reinforce, the migration of people and the movement of jobs out of the snowbelt and into the sunbelt, and from central cities to suburbs. The search for what was perceived as increased opportunity, whether within the city or in suburban areas, prompted differential patterns of growth and decline. The net effect has been to erode municipal tax bases in major northern industrial cities at the very time that they face added pressure on the expenditure side of the budget. These same factors have fueled rapid growth in the south and the west where, on the one hand, job growth has provided employment opportunities for many newly arrived residents but, on the other, the more recent influx of unskilled and often non-English-speaking immigrants has taxed the ability of local governments to meet their needs.

Whereas metropolitan areas of the west and south grew by 23 percent and 19 percent, respectively, during the 1970s, those of the Northeast actually lost population, and those of the Midwest increased by less than 3 percent. During the 1980s, the Midwest's population continued to remain relatively flat, still growing by slightly less than 3 percent. The Northeast reversed the preceding decade's population decline, growing by a modest 3 percent during the 1980s. In sharp contrast, the metropolitan areas of the west and south continued to grow at about the same fast pace of the 1970s as the west increased its population by 24 percent, compared to the south's 18 percent growth rate. All ten of the fastest growing areas during the 1970s and 1980s could be found in the west or south, while the ten areas of greatest population decline were in the Midwest and Northeast.[4]

The decade of the 1990s saw growth rates in both the Northeast and Midwest pick up their 1980s pace. The population in the Northeast grew by 5.5 percent between 1990 and 2000, almost doubling its 1980s rate of growth. The Midwest's population rose by 7.9 percent, 2.6 times its 1980s growth rate. Yet, just as in the 1970s and 1980s, both the west and the south grew much faster. Between 1990 and 2000, the west added 10.4 million residents, an increase of 19.7 percent. The more populous south added 14.8 million residents, an increase of 17.3 percent.[5]

The contrast becomes even sharper looking at the list of the fastest growing and fastest declining cities in the United States since 1970. As Table 8.1 shows, cities in Arizona, California, Nevada, and Texas top the growth list from 1970 to 2010. At the other extreme are the major industrial cities of the Northeast and Midwest—cities that are home to the manufacture of automobiles, steel, glass, chemicals, rubber, and heavy industrial machinery. Manufacturing jobs were lost as the demand for these products fell or was met by imported goods. With the loss of jobs, population declined; not only did displaced workers seek employment in more promising economic environs, but also the economic climate of the Northeast and Midwest attracted few job seekers. Cleveland, Detroit, and St. Louis lost about half of their population between 1970 and 2010, and Buffalo and Pittsburgh lost about four-tenths (see Table 8.2).

The drastic fiscal consequences of Detroit's massive population loss and the associated drop in city revenues, combined with the city's large geographical footprint and the built-in inefficiencies of providing municipal services to

Table 8.1   Percentage of Growth in the Population of Selected Cities and Metropolitan
Areas from 1970 to 2010

	City			Metropolitan area		
	1970	*2010*	*% Change*	*1970*	*2010*	*% Change*
Albuquerque, NM	245,000	545,852	122	316,000	887,077	180
Austin, TX	254,000	790,390	211	360,000	1,716,289	376
Bakersfield, CA	70,000	347,483	396	330,000	839,631	154
Colorado Springs, CO	136,000	416,427	206	236,000	645,613	173
Dallas, TX	844,000	1,197,816	41	2,352,000	6,426,214	173
El Paso, TX	322,000	649,121	101	359,000	804,123	123
Fresno, CA	166,000	494,665	197	413,000	930,450	125
Houston, TX	1,234,000	2,099,451	70	1,891,000	5,920,416	213
Las Vegas, NV	126,000	478,434	280	273,000	1,951,269	614
Modesto, CA	62,000	201,165	224	195,000	514,453	163
Phoenix, AZ	584,000	1,445,632	147	971,000	4,192,887	331
Sacramento, CA	257,000	466,488	81	848,000	2,149,127	153
San Antonio, TX	654,000	1,327,407	102	888,000	2,142,508	141
San Diego, CA	697,000	1,307,402	87	1,358,000	3,095,313	127
Stockton, CA	110,000	291,707	165	291,000	685,306	135
Tucson, AZ	263,000	520,116	97	352,000	980,263	178

Source: Bureau of the Census, U.S. Department of Commerce. Population data for 1970 is
reported in rounded form.

Table 8.2   Percentage Decline in the Population of Selected Cities from 1970 to 2010

City	*1970*	*2010*	*Percent change*
Baltimore, MD	905,000	620,961	−31
Buffalo, NY	463,000	261,325	−43
Chicago, IL	3,369,000	2,695,598	−19
Cleveland, OH	751,000	396,815	−47
Detroit, MI	1,514,000	951,270	−52
Milwaukee, WI	717,000	594,833	−17
Newark, NJ	382,000	277,140	−27
Philadelphia, PA	1,949,000	1,526,006	−21
Pittsburgh, PA	520,000	305,704	−41
St. Louis, MO	622,000	319,294	−48

Source: Bureau of the Census, U.S. Department of Commerce.

neighborhoods with a large number of abandoned or blighted houses and buildings, contributed to Detroit's filing for Chapter 9 Bankruptcy protection on July
18, 2013. Moreover, the city's fiscal plight was made worse by its generous
pension and health benefit plans for city workers (see Box 8.1 for an expanded
discussion of Detroit's fiscal crisis).

Box 8.1   Detroit's Bankruptcy

On March 1, 2013 Michigan Governor Rick Snyder declared Detroit in a financial emergency. Nearly two weeks later, the governor appointed bankruptcy lawyer Kevyn Orr as emergency manager of the City of Detroit. Orr was charged with analyzing the city's fiscal position and preparing a financial and operating plan of remediation. The evidence of severe financial distress was indisputable. Detroit had an unrestricted budget deficit of $327 million at the end of the 2012 fiscal year, which was expected to grow by another $60 million in FY 2013. It had negative cash flow of $116 million in FY 2012, and borrowed $80 million from Bank of America to avoid running out of cash. Yet even with that temporary infusion of cash, Detroit still had a $162 million negative cash position as of April 26, 2013, about a month prior to the issuance of Orr's report. To get by in the short run, the city deferred payments on its financial obligations, including contributions to employee pensions, and borrowed from other previously restricted funds. As of April 26, 2013, the city's general fund had deferrals and fund-transfer obligations totaling $226 million. Beyond its operating budget woes, Detroit faced $18 billion in debt and unfunded liabilities. Pension and health care liabilities alone amounted to $9.5 billion of the total. On July 18, 2013, Detroit filed for Chapter 9 Bankruptcy.

Detroit's fiscal crisis had been in the making for some time. Its causes were readily recognized. They include:

- Population Loss
  Detroit's population declined from 951,000 in 2000 to under 700,000 in 2013, continuing its historic downhill slide. In comparison, Detroit's residents totaled nearly 1.9 million in 1950.
- Large Service Footprint
  Detroit's city limits cover 139 square miles, requiring the delivery of municipal services in a geographic area larger than Boston, Manhattan, and San Francisco combined. A declining population widely distributed within a large service area is a recipe for inefficiency and the higher costs that accompany it. Add 78,000 vacant structures, many only suitable for demolition, and operating costs rise.
- High Unemployment
  Unemployment stood at about 18 percent at the time of the emergency manager's report.
- Falling Property and Income Tax Revenues
  Population decline and falling property values depressed property tax revenues, and low and declining per capita income depressed local income tax revenues. Consider, too, the connection of population

loss and ability to pay. Generally, those leaving Detroit have had significantly higher incomes than have those remaining as residents.

Detroit emerged from bankruptcy protection on December 10, 2014, following the bankruptcy judge's approval of the city's plan of adjustment, a plan that emerged after seventeen months of negotiation and political accommodation. The pain of remediation was widely shared. Pensioners took a 4.5 percent cut in benefits and loss of cost-of-living increases. Both present workers and retirees found their health benefits reduced. Private foundations contributed $466 million, and the Detroit Institute of Arts added $155 million. The Michigan Legislature approved another $195 million in support, and the federal government released $300 million of funds from existing federal programs for which Detroit had already been eligible.

In addition to eliminating the unrestricted budget deficit and restoring adequate cash flow, the plan increased funding of long-neglected city services, and included the hiring of new police officers. It also provided resources for the city to demolish dangerous, vacant structures; restore street lighting on darkened streets; and clean up blight.

To reduce debt and long-term liabilities, the plan included successfully negotiated reductions of debt principal in loans made to the city, and in the city's financial obligations to holders of its bonds. Cuts in pension and health-care benefits reduced the city's long-term liabilities.

Sources: City of Detroit, Office of Emergency Manager Kevyn D. Orr, Financial and Operating Plan, May 12, 2013; Nathan Bomey, "Detroit Bankruptcy: A Master Time Line," Detroit Free Press, November 8, 2014.

Suburban Phoenix provides a dramatic example of metropolitan growth. Although the population of Phoenix increased by 147 percent between 1970 and 2010, adding over 861,000 residents, its greater metropolitan area grew by 331 percent, adding almost 3 million residents. During that same period, Las Vegas grew by 280 percent, while its metropolitan area grew by a staggering 614 percent, adding 1.7 million residents. The Dallas–Fort Worth area added 4.1 million residents between 1970 and 2010.

California, too, experienced its share of population growth, its greatest in and around once small and midsized cities. Simply look at the cities and metropolitan areas of Bakersfield, Fresno, Modesto, Sacramento, and Stockton for evidence. Outside the west, Florida has seen the largest population growth, and it has been widespread and predominantly suburban. The largest population increases have occurred in the Miami–Ft. Lauderdale–Hollywood area, the Tampa–Clearwater–St. Petersburg area, and the West Palm Beach–Boca Raton–Delray Beach area. Yet the Ft. Myers–Cape Coral and the Ft. Pierce areas have witnessed the fastest growth.

Patterns of Taxing and Spending

As was illustrated in chapter 5, local government expenditures have risen dramatically since World War II in both current and constant dollars, reaching their height in the mid-1970s. In contrast, own-source, constant-dollar local expenditures declined sharply during the latter half of the 1970s, to a point where 1979 per capita spending even fell below the 1969 level. If spending from intergovernmental aids is included in the picture, local government expenditures continued to rise throughout the 1970s, reaching new peaks at the decade's close in both actual- and constant-dollar spending. Thus growth in federal and state aid compensated more than enough for the decline in constant-dollar local expenditures funded from own-source revenues. However, that situation too was soon to change as a result of the administration of President Ronald Reagan's federal aid policy. Total local spending actually declined in constant-dollar terms between 1979 and 1983 before rising again in subsequent years. Its later rise was not a product of a resurgence in federal and state aid; rather, it largely reflected an increased reliance on local revenues themselves.

As Table 8.3 illustrates, federal aid made up 10 percent of total local general revenues in 1978, its highest percentage ever. By 2012, it stood at 4.3 percent. State aid, in comparison, reached its highest share to date in 1980, at 35 percent of total local general revenues, but fell to 28.7 percent in 2012 as states,

Table 8.3 Percentage of Local Revenues by Governmental Source, Selected Fiscal Years, 1902–2012

Fiscal year	Amount (in $ millions)	From own sources	From state	From federal government
1902	854	93.4	6.1	0.5
1913	1,637	94.1	5.6	0.4
1922	3,866	91.7	8.1	0.2
1932	5,690	85.7	14.1	0.2
1940	6,939	72.2	23.8	4.0
1950	14,014	68.4	30.1	1.5
1960	33,027	69.4	28.8	1.8
1970	80,916	63.5	33.3	3.2
1978	194,783	56.8	33.2	10.0
1980	232,453	55.9	35.0	9.1
1982	281,045	58.5	33.9	7.6
1987	410,347	61.9	33.3	4.7
1990	512,322	62.8	33.6	3.6
1992	573,584	62.3	34.2	3.5
1997	747,030	61.6	34.6	3.8
2001	955,428	60.7	35.6	3.7
2006	1,243,748	61.7	33.9	4.4
2012	1,652,935	67.0	28.7	4.3

Source: Bureau of the Census, U.S. Department of Commerce, 2012 Census of Governments: Finance – Surveys of State and Local Governments, December 16, 2014.

still feeling the fiscal pinch of the Great Recession, reduced aid to local governments as they met their own budgetary challenges. In contrast, local government own-source revenues, while falling as a share of total revenues throughout the 1960s and 1970s, increased throughout the 1980s, remaining relatively constant until state legislatures were forced to add tax increases to budget cutting as a means to balance budgets during the Great Recession and its near-term aftermath.

Not all local units of government were forced to become more self-reliant. The dependency of school districts increased significantly from the early 1970s through the early 1990s as states expanded general school aid, often in the name of local property tax relief or in response to court orders directing increased state support to fiscally disadvantaged school districts. For their own-source revenue, school districts remained heavily reliant on the property tax.

Cities and counties, in contrast, were forced to find additional locally generated revenues to offset declining intergovernmental aid. Table 8.4 provides evidence that for most of the period they did not find those revenues in property tax. As a percentage of municipal and county own-source tax revenue,

Table 8.4   Percentage of Local Tax Revenues by Major Source and Type of Government, Selected Fiscal Years, 1957–2006

Fiscal year	Property taxes	Sales and gross receipts taxes	Individual and corporate income taxes	All other taxes
Cities				
1957	72.7	15.8	3.1	8.4
1967	70.0	15.7	7.8	6.6
1972	64.3	18.8	11.1	5.9
1977	60.0	22.3	11.9	5.9
1982	52.6	27.5	13.4	6.5
1987	49.1	28.2	14.6	8.1
1992	52.6	26.8	13.4	7.2
1997	55.0	24.8	12.8	7.4
2001	52.9	26.3	12.8	8.0
2006e	54.7	23.5	13.1	8.7
Counties				
1957	93.7	2.8	0.0	3.6
1967	92.1	4.5	0.3	3.1
1972	85.6	8.9	1.9	3.6
1977	81.2	12.4	2.4	3.9
1982	77.3	16.0	2.9	3.8
1987	73.5	18.8	2.7	5.0
1992	74.3	18.5	2.8	4.4
1997	69.4	22.3	3.3	5.0
2001	68.3	22.7	4.5	4.5
2006e	66.5	23.3	4.9	5.3

(Continued)

Table 8.4 (Continued)

Fiscal year	Property taxes	Sales and gross receipts taxes	Individual and corporate income taxes	All other taxes
School districts				
1957	98.6	0.1	0.2	1.2
1967	98.4	0.2	0.7	0.8
1972	98.1	0.4	0.7	0.9
1977	97.5	0.9	0.7	1.0
1982	96.8	1.2	0.9	1.1
1987	97.4	0.9	0.8	0.8
1992	97.4	0.9	0.9	0.8
1997	96.9	1.1	0.9	1.1
2001	96.0	2.3	0.9	0.8
2006e	95.1	2.1	1.4	1.4
Special districts				
1957	100.0	0.0	0.0	0.0
1967	100.0	0.0	0.0	0.0
1972	94.9	5.1	0.0	0.0
1977	91.2	7.6	0.0	1.1
1982	78.9	19.4	0.0	1.7
1987	72.4	24.0	0.0	3.6
1992	67.6	29.3	0.0	3.1
1997	76.5	16.9	0.0	6.6
2001	68.0	26.9	0.0	5.1
2006e	57.8	33.5	0.0	8.7

e = estimate

Sources: 2001 Census of Governments, State and Local Government Finances (Washington, D.C.: Bureau of the Census, U.S. Department of Commerce, 2003), Tables 2 and 3; 1997 Census of Governments, State and Local Government Finances, Table 2; Significant Features of Historical Federalism, 1994, ed. 2 (Washington, D.C.: Advisory Commission on Intergovernmental Relations, 1994), 70–1; Significant Features of Historical Federalism, 1989, ed. 2, 67.

property taxes fell in the 1970s and the 1980s. Although the property tax share has remained fairly constant for cities over the past two decades, it continued to slide for counties. To compensate, cities and counties found additional general revenue through both sales and income taxes and other revenue sources, such as user fees.

Not all cities and counties, however, have the option of levying income or sales taxes. Those not given the authority by their states have found themselves between the proverbial rock and a hard place of taxpayer opposition to property tax increases and the need to become more reliant on local revenue. Figure 8.1 shows the states that have extended the income tax or sales tax options to their local governments. Five states (Alabama, California, Missouri, New York, and Ohio) permit local governments to use both sales tax and income tax. Within those states, only seven cities levy both—Birmingham, Alabama; Los Angeles and San Francisco, California; Kansas City and St. Louis, Missouri; and

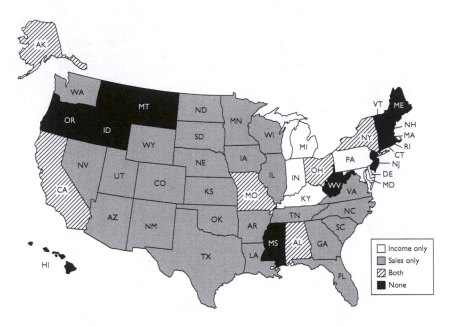

Figure 8.1   States in which Cities or Counties Levy Income or Sales Tax.

Source: Bureau of the Census, U.S. Department of Commerce.

New York City and Yonkers, New York. Ohio limits income tax to cities and sales tax to counties.[6]

Though local income taxes provide only 3.9 percent of local own-source tax revenue nationally, their relative share in the states permitting their use ranges from 1.5 percent in Alabama to 30.6 percent in Ohio.[7] As Table 8.5 illustrates, local income taxes provide a sizable share of own-source revenues for many major cities in the eastern part of the nation. This heavy reliance on income tax not only shifts a significant tax burden away from property tax; it also shifts part of the tax burden to nonresidents, who work but do not live in the taxing jurisdiction. All of the cities listed apply the local income tax to nonresidents and residents alike, most commonly at the same tax rate, although Detroit and Philadelphia tax nonresidents at a lower rate.

The rationale for taxing the income of those who work in a jurisdiction but do not live there is that such persons, who usually live in adjoining suburban communities, use the services of the major metropolitan jurisdiction in which they work. Their sheer numbers, concentrated in discrete areas, place added demands on such government services as police and fire protection, sewage treatment, and sanitation. Moreover, their daily commuting adds wear to local streets and raises the aggregate costs of public transit subsidies. Nonresidents also frequent major cities for cultural and recreational activities, visiting museums, parks, athletic

Table 8.5 Major Cities Reliant on the Income Tax, Fiscal Year, 1999

City	Population (1996 est.)	Income tax as percentage of own-source tax revenue
Toledo, Ohio	317,606	75.0
Cleveland, Ohio	498,246	75.0
Columbus, Ohio	657,053	64.8
Philadelphia, P.A.	1,478,002	59.0
Kansas City, M.O.	441,259	40.0
Washington, D.C.	543,213	33.0
St. Louis, M.O.	351,565	33.0
Detroit, M.I.	1,000,272	29.2
New York City	7,380,906	24.0

Source: Bureau of the Census, Statistical Abstract of the United States, 1999 (Washington, D.C.: U.S. Department of Commerce, 1999), 1415; municipality telephone survey December 2000.

facilities, and the like. Reliance on the property tax places the financial obligation to support such services exclusively on the shoulders of property owners, who disproportionately are residents of the locality.

In comparison to property tax, most local income tax rates are low. Assuming that the potential annual income yield on real property subject to income tax is only 5 percent, the effective property tax rate, on average, can be estimated conservatively to be about three times that of the typical local income tax rate. However, if the potential income earnings of the property are estimated at 10 percent, a figure used by the Advisory Council on Intergovernmental Relations (ACIR), the differential grows to about sixfold.[8]

Local sales taxes, to a lesser extent, also shift some of the tax burden from residents to nonresidents, while simultaneously providing property tax relief. Customers and patrons drawn from surrounding bedroom communities to retail businesses and to the entertainment offered by major metropolitan centers support those city and county governments by paying sales taxes on their purchases. Compared to the local income tax, the local sales tax is more broadly employed nationally.

Sales taxes average only 16 percent of all local tax revenue nationally, but comprise 24 percent of municipal tax revenue and 23 percent of county tax revenue. The difference can be attributed to the considerably lower use of a sales tax by school districts and other special taxing districts. Across the country, Oklahoma municipalities rely most heavily on the general sales tax, deriving about three-quarters of their local tax revenue from it. Municipalities in Alabama, Arizona, Colorado, New Mexico, and South Dakota also receive at least 50 percent of their tax revenue from sales tax. Among counties nationally, those of Missouri and New York are most dependent on sales tax.[9]

In a few states—Alabama, Louisiana, Missouri, and New Mexico—both municipalities and counties make relatively heavy use of sales tax, creating a potential problem of same-tax overlap, wherein the taxing decisions of one jurisdiction act to constrain, and potentially crowd out, the taxing discretion of the overlapped jurisdiction. Where overlap occurs, local officials need to be sensitive to the overall tax bite their combined actions will place on their common electorate, and they occasionally map out cooperative tax-increase strategies based on their respective needs and use of other revenue sources.

In some states the coordinating mechanism is formal. In Utah, for example, a county tax applies only outside city limits. In California and Washington, the existence of a municipal tax lowers the tax of the county where the municipality is located. Moreover, the taxing decisions of the other jurisdictions can affect a jurisdiction's bond ratings, since bond markets take into account the aggregate local tax burden of all general taxing jurisdictions with coterminous or overlapped boundaries.

In their search for additional local revenues, cities and counties also have turned increasingly to user fees (or fees for services received), which constitute another significant element of revenue diversification. User fees are applied to such diverse services as garbage collection, admission to public educational and recreational facilities (museums, zoos, and golf courses), boat launching privileges, and even ambulance services. All user fees are premised on the "payment for benefits received" principle that those who receive a direct benefit from a service should pay for it.

Revenues from user fees charged by local governments grew almost six-fold over the twenty years between 1977 and 1997, a period of especially fast growth in the use of user fees, increasing from approximately $27 billion to over $175 billion, and far outstripping the overall growth in local tax revenues. Local units of government raised 62 cents in user charges for every dollar of taxes in 1997, compared to 37 cents for every dollar in 1977.[10]

This growth in user fees is not surprising given the results of the 1987 ACIR survey that asked a sample of local voters to indicate which of a number of revenue-raising alternatives they would prefer to see implemented to help meet costs and improve services. The responses were as follows:

- User charges for specific service, 33 percent
- Local sales taxes, 20 percent
- No new taxes at all, 17 percent
- Local income taxes, 9 percent
- Local property taxes, 9 percent
- Don't know/no answer, 12 percent[11]

The respondents clearly preferred user fees to any other form of additional local taxation. Property taxes and local income taxes were least favored—a viewpoint that began in the preceding decade as local property taxpayers rebelled against rising property assessments, calling for property tax limits and relief, and as federal taxpayers signaled their discontent with the federal income tax by electing Reagan president.

Although many states have placed limitations on the growth of local property taxes and many others have increased programs of property tax relief, property tax still evokes strong negative feelings among taxpayers. Similarly, income tax, even with recent rate cuts and tax reform, appears to continue to attract little popular support as a revenue-raising mechanism.

The Roots of Changed Local Government Finance

Three forces converged in a relatively short period to change the patterns of local government finance. The first was the so-called taxpayer revolt of the late 1970s, which initially focused on the property tax, struck local units of government with its greatest force, then moved to the states and reached its pinnacle at the national level with Reagan's election to the presidency in 1980. Taxpayers served notice that they demanded tax and spending restraint. Responding to what it viewed as a popular mandate, the Reagan administration set out to reduce federal taxes and trim the growth in federal domestic spending. Cuts in federal aid to localities and states comprised a significant part of the administration's strategy to curtail domestic spending. This federal retrenchment, the second agent of change, came at the same time that local governments found themselves coping with the reduced tax revenues occasioned by citizen action or legislatively imposed limits on the property tax. The third force for change, a severe national recession from 2007 into 2009, reduced the rate of growth in local income and sales tax revenues at the very time that growth was most needed to offset declines in the property tax occasioned by the popping of the real estate bubble. Moreover, the Great Recession minimized the extent to which the states could increase financial aid to the fiscally hard-pressed local governments. State aid to local governments dropped in real-dollar terms during the recession, although it subsequently rose again as states recovered from the effects of economic downturn.

From a comparison of government spending, it is by no means obvious that local governments would be the first objects of the taxpayer revolt of the late 1970s. Between 1949 and 1978, local government spending grew at a lower annual rate than federal or state spending, both in actual dollars and as a percentage of gross national product.[12] In fact, in constant dollars, local spending even dropped during the 1970s as federal and state spending both rose, with state spending from own-source revenues rising the fastest, at a real rate of growth of 28 percent.[13] Nevertheless, the first target of the tax revolt was local government and the property tax in particular. California served as the setting for the first major campaign against the property tax.

The passage on June 6, 1978 of Proposition 13 by a 2:1 margin provided vivid testimony of the frustration that Californians felt over state and local spending, which had been growing faster than California's economy. Proposition 13 halted rising property taxes, which had been driven upward by steeply increased property values. These values and their corresponding assessments soared during the 1970s, especially in southern California, rising by 36 percent in Los Angeles County alone in the three years preceding Proposition 13.[14] The prospect of continuing increases was ominous in a state where property taxes were already 51 percent above the national average.[15]

One property taxpayer summarized the concerns of many southern Californians: as he described his dilemma, "I bought my house in 1974; in 1975 the house was worth $110,000. I was paying approximately $3,400 in property taxes, and as a result of Proposition 13 I paid $1,022. The house is now [1982] worth about $400,000. Without Proposition 13, I would be paying about $13,000 [in property taxes]."[16] This example is not at all atypical, so it is not surprising that the drive to put Proposition 13 on the ballot started in southern California.

Proposition 13 limited property tax rates in California to 1 percent of assessed valuation; rolled assessed values back to 1975–6 levels for properties that had not been transferred since then; limited annual increases in assessment to 2 percent (except when real estate changed hands); and prohibited new property taxes.[17] These provisions reduced property tax revenues in California by $6.6 billion in 1978–9, the first year after passage.[18]

Fueled by the notoriety of Proposition 13, the taxpayer revolt spread to other states. Within six months of the approval of Proposition 13, property tax limitation measures appeared on ballots in seventeen states and received voter approval in all but five. Between 1978 and 1982, thirty-four measures aimed at restraining local revenues or expenditures were enacted into law, with twenty-eight of them directed at the property tax.[19] As a prominent example, Massachusetts voters in November 1980 approved a local tax limitation initiative known as Proposition 2½.

Proposition 2½ required voter approval of proposed annual property tax increases in excess of 2.5 percent, regardless of the extent to which property values increased during the prior year. It also confined property tax levies to 2.5 percent of a jurisdiction's total taxable property value. This imposition of both a levy limit and a levy ceiling presented a dual approach to constraining the growth of property taxes raised by local governments. Although the levy ceiling remained inflexible, flexibility could be found in the levy limit, as long as voters were willing to approve annual levy increases in excess of 2.5 percent—increases that became possible because of increased property values.

Torn between a desire for property tax relief and preservation of public services, voters not uncommonly allowed annual property tax increases exceeding the 2.5 percent limitation. In fact, 60 percent of override referenda were successful in 1990. However, the success of referenda in ninety-eight communities added $58 million to the level of tax levies otherwise permitted by the levy limit. Even with this successful use of flexibility, the ceiling provision still provided a constant measure of limitation regardless of growth in assessed property values. Between 1981 and 1991, real-dollar tax levies declined by 5.1 percent—a percentage that would have been significantly higher without successful override referenda.[20] Proposition 2½ put the presumption on tax limitation; the voters selectively provided added tax latitude.

As a result of the changes affecting local public finance since the late 1970s, local governments, with the exception of school districts, have been forced to become more self-reliant just to continue existing levels of services, pursuing the following initiatives.

Efforts to Expand Revenues

Federal general revenue sharing (GRS) and grants-in-aid gave local governments some discretionary funds to initiate new programs and expand others; but with the demise of GRS and major reductions in federal grants, that latitude has been diminished. In response, municipalities and counties recommitted themselves to the basics, financing traditional core services out of general tax revenues and charging special fees for other services or for service levels that go beyond the service core. For example, although garbage collection is still widely regarded as a basic public service appropriately financed from local general revenues, some cities now collect only a fixed number of trash containers and charge to take any more or to remove special bulky items. In addition, user fees have been instituted for such services as leaf collection, the privilege of reserving books at public libraries, emergency ambulance rides, police and fire responses to false alarms due to faulty alarm systems, and fire inspections.

Moreover, growing regional and intercity competition for economic development has prompted localities to enter public–private partnerships intended to encourage business and industrial development within their boundaries. When successful, such development enlarges the local tax base through the increased taxes paid by new and expanded enterprises as well as those paid by residents drawn to newly created jobs. The developer reaps the profits returned by a successful business venture.

In the parlance of economics, local governments offer supply-side incentives to attract mobile industries to locate within their boundaries and to entice existing firms to expand there. These incentives are based on the theory that firms will make rational decisions to locate their operations in settings that reduce production costs and offer the promise of increasing the rate of return from their investments. Such incentives include offers of cheap or free land, capital subsidies, loan guarantees, tax abatements and exemptions, and relaxed regulations.

Beyond offering these traditional direct incentives to lure development, local governments have also turned to other mechanisms to expand their revenue base through economic development. Several major devices are discussed below.

Tax-Increment Financing

If successful, tax-increment financing (TIF) benefits both a municipality and private enterprise by allowing the municipality to earmark the increased property tax revenue resulting from a development project to pay off bonds used to finance certain elements of the project, which can include the acquisition and clearance of sites; the construction of public facilities such as roads, sidewalks, and storm sewers; and even the provision of landscaping. TIF is not characteristically used to finance the construction of private buildings or the purchase of equipment. Introduced in California in 1945, TIF did not spread widely to other states until the late 1970s, when the mechanism was rediscovered as a means of financing economic development that would both benefit private industry and ease the immediate financial burdens placed on municipalities by economic development projects. Municipalities have traditionally had to pay for improvements associated with new industrial or commercial development within their boundaries. If those ventures proved successful, however, other local jurisdictions, such as counties and school districts, shared the benefits of the broadened tax base, even though they bore none of the additional costs. With TIF, other local general purpose-taxing jurisdictions had to share the costs.

Under TIF laws, municipalities are authorized under certain conditions to create a tax-increment financing district. Frequently these conditions include requirements that a certain percentage of the district be "blighted" or in need of renovation and that the district be zoned appropriately for industrial or commercial use. State law also may limit the percentage of a municipality's total taxable property value that can be designated as a TIF district. In addition, state laws generally proscribe the creation of a TIF district when development would have occurred without it.

Once a municipality creates a TIF district, it is necessary to calculate the value of all property within the district at the time of its creation. That value, called the tax increment base value, remains constant for the duration of the project. If the project proves successful, property value will increase; the portion of taxes collected on the increased value is known as the tax increment. All tax increments are placed in a special fund, and its proceeds can be used only to finance the project. When the bonds are paid off, the TIF district is dissolved. That period can be lengthy for the most costly projects; some states permit bond indebtedness to last as long as thirty years.

Regardless of the period of indebtedness, once the agreed-upon improvements are made the developer comes into the "ready" site to build, remodel, or make any further improvements deemed fit, consistent with the locally approved development plan. The developer gets a suitable site—complete with public improvements—and the municipality has found a means of financing the very improvements that attracted the private investor. Further, if the enterprise proves successful, both the municipality and the other local jurisdictions benefiting from the expanded tax base brought about by the project realize additional tax revenues that would not otherwise have materialized.

The only losers—most often temporary losers, at that—are the county, school district, and any other general taxing jurisdictions for which tax revenues beyond the tax increment base value are deferred. Nevertheless, if the development project is successful, the longer-term gain in tax revenues will exceed the amount forgone. Even during the period of the TIF district, the other local jurisdictions still receive property tax revenues at the base level. Although they forgo any growth above the base, without the improvements made possible by TIF, that growth would probably have been marginal at best.

Chicago and suburban Cook County have been avid creators of TIF districts. In 2012 they had 435 TIF districts in operation, generating $723 million in tax revenue. Through 2012, the city's TIF program alone has generated $5.5 billion in tax revenue.[21]

Equity Arrangements

Local governments have acted much less like partners in other instances. Particularly in rapidly expanding metropolitan areas, they have generally taken advantage of developers' zeal to profit from population growth and the promise of still greater expansion. Using their authority to issue building permits as leverage, local governments have increasingly encouraged developers into contributing toward, or supplying, such infrastructure as streets, sewers, sidewalks, traffic signals, parks, and fire stations. For example, to obtain the necessary permits to build Rancho Carmel, a large, upscale development east of San Diego, Shapell Industries had to finance about $85 million in improvements.[22] While this practice has been labeled by some as "the legal equivalent of extortion," others view it as a legitimate way of coping with local fiscal austerity.[23]

Equity arrangements represent a creative form of local "revenue enhancement." Their terms commonly stipulate that local governments receive a percentage of after-tax profits of developments within their jurisdictions. The rationale, of course, is that major new developments place a significantly increased burden on the necessary services provided by local governments.

Local governments have even become agents of private enterprise, entering into contracts to provide their customers with services for a fee. For example, such California cities as San Rafael and Mill Valley have become partners with Avco Financial Insurance and receive a share of insurance premium income for providing fire inspections of property belonging to Avco's clients.

Impact Fees

Local governments have also turned to another extractive mechanism to raise additional revenues from development—the charging of impact fees. Impact fees differ from permit-tied extractions. Impact fees are not taxes, but one-time charges on new development instituted to pay for the public facilities required to serve that development. The California and Florida legislatures, in the 1970s, were the first to authorize local governments to charge impact fees; by 2007, local governments in twenty-six states had that authority. In those states, 60 percent of cities with more than 25,000 residents use some form of impact fees.[24] Enabling legislation typically restricts the purposes for which impact fee revenue may be used. Commonly restricted uses include water and waste treatment facilities; storm water drainage and flood control operations; streets, curbs, and gutters; lighting; open space; and police and fire stations. State statutes tend not to allow impact fees to be used to finance ongoing operational expenses or to increase service levels for existing residents, and they usually require that municipalities demonstrate that the fees are commensurate with the infrastructure costs that development imposes on them.

Impact fees raise the cost of development, and studies have shown that developers pass the costs of impact fees on to commercial lessors and homebuyers. Yet substantial evidence exists that the imposition of impact fees typically does not deter development. Market demand appears to be the key. Where demand is strong and development sites are deemed desirable, impact fees do not appear to bias locational choices significantly.[25]

Payments in Lieu of Taxes

Local governments, particularly municipalities, are saddled with providing services to properties exempt from the property tax. Since tax-exempt status is usually determined by state government statute, most city governments have little discretion over the amount of their property value that is tax-exempt. Although the benefits of exempt institutions, such as universities and hospitals, accrue to a large geographic area, taxpayers of the host community bear the cost of exemption. With the value of tax-exempt real estate growing significantly across the nation, local governments are seeing the value of their forgone revenue rising. In Florida and Rhode Island, for instance, the assessed value of tax-exempt properties rose threefold between 1984 and 1994. Faced with this dilemma, a large number of municipalities are fighting back by adopting payments in lieu of taxes (PILOTs).

Some PILOTs originate from state laws. An example comes from Wisconsin, where the state legislature enacted a program of state payments for municipal services to state-owned property. This formula-driven program authorizes state appropriations to municipalities to help defray the costs they incur in providing myriad services to state-owned properties, such as prisons, universities, and hospitals. Another statutory authorization allows municipalities to exact payments from local special purpose districts, such as water treatment and solid waste recycling facilities.

Where statutory authority does not exist, local governments are pressuring nonprofit organizations to chip in to cover the cost of services they use. City officials have turned up their efforts to attract voluntary contributions from nonprofits, often relying on aggressive public relations campaigns to shame prominent tax-exempt entities to contribute to the costs of city services they enjoy. The experience of Philadelphia is instructive here. The city adopted this approach in the mid-1990s, asking for financial support equal to 40 percent of the property tax an organization would owe were it not tax-exempt. The program has been surprisingly successful. Many of the city's 300 largest non-profits have gone along with it, including Philadelphia's forty hospitals. The program raised over $6 million in its first year alone.[26] The major users of PILOT programs at the end of the 2000s included Boston, generating $5.7 million in payments, and New Haven, Connecticut, grossing $7.5 million. Another municipality, Bristol, Rhode Island, is especially noteworthy, as its program collects $2.1 million out of a budget of only $44 million, amounting to almost 5 percent of city revenue.[27] Des Moines instituted a TIF program but turned to the legislature to enact a state law mandating the payment of PILOTs instead of relying on voluntary contributions. Given the sizable impact on several large nonprofits, the proposal failed, even though city officials developed a payment formula and city council members made courtesy calls to encourage support from nonprofit organizations.[28]

Faced with rising costs and revenue constraints, other municipalities are likely to join the effort to exact financial support from nonprofit organizations. Cities prize the jobs and services to their residents that nonprofits provide, but they have become increasingly resistant to the uncompensated, growing demands these organizations make on municipal services.

Franchise Fees

The communications revolution sweeping across America offers local governments another prospect of finding additional revenues. Already utility and cable companies pay more than $2 billion annually in franchise fees to local governments, comprising up to one-fifth of the many municipalities' general operating funds.[29] The biggest winners include major cities in Texas and Illinois. For instance, Houston received $184 million in franchise fees in 2007, and Dallas got $125 million.[30]

Local governments typically base franchise fees on a percentage of a company's gross receipts for services sold within their borders, in exchange for utilities' use of public rights of way. However, not all states give their local governments the authority to assess franchise fees.

With the rapid expansion of fiber-optic networks and the new personal communication services, local governments having the authority to impose franchise fees are well positioned to increase their revenues significantly. Those lacking the authority have an even greater incentive to acquire it.

Efforts to Control Expenditures

Initiatives to balance the budget have not been limited to innovative ways of finding new revenues; local officials have also turned their imaginations to ways of reducing expenditure growth while preserving, or even expanding, the quantity and quality of public services. Traditionally, local governments have expanded public services through increases in the public work force, thus pushing salary and fringe benefit costs up and building greater rigidity into the base-level budget. The higher the percentage of costs devoted to salaries, the less the ability of a jurisdiction to reduce expenditures in times of fiscal austerity, particularly in jurisdictions subject to civil service regulations and collective bargaining agreements. New approaches have focused on ways to provide and expand essential public services in a way that falls outside the bureaucracy. Two such efforts receiving growing national attention are privatization and volunteerism.

Privatization

Privatization, as the label implies, involves government contracting with the private sector for services that have traditionally been provided by government itself. Though state and local governments have long relied on contracting to meet their legal, architectural, engineering, and heavy construction needs, municipalities and counties in the 1980s and 1990s increasingly turned to the private sector to deliver other services such as garbage and refuse collection, water treatment, buildings and grounds maintenance, street maintenance, security, and golf course management and maintenance. In the area of water and wastewater services, for example, of the 60 percent of systems owned by local governments, the dollar value of contracts with private operators grew by 84 percent during the 1990s. By 2001, nearly 1,100 local governments had outsourced the operation of water systems and 1,300 had done the same with wastewater systems.[31]

Yet the private sector's involvement has not stopped there; it has extended into the human service area, as private, for-profit enterprises have received contracts to operate halfway houses and jails and to provide probation, alcohol and drug rehabilitation, and family counseling services. Local governments have also contracted for computer, accounting, and public relations services.

A survey sponsored by the International City Management Association, Touche Ross and Company (a major consulting firm), and the Privatization Council (a nonprofit advocacy body for privatization) found that 37 percent of the cities and counties responding contract for solid waste collection, 36 percent for tree trimming and planting, and 80 percent for vehicle towing and storage. In the human services area, 34 percent contract for drug and alcohol rehabilitation programs, 34 percent for mental health and retardation programs, and 43 percent for homeless shelters. In addition, for administrative support,

55 percent contract for legal services, 33 percent for labor relations services, and 17 percent for data processing services.[32]

This heightened interest in privatization on the part of local officials appears to be grounded in three standards: economy, budgetary flexibility, and service quality. Supporters of privatization argue that private sector contracts can result in lower-cost public services without any sacrifice in quality. In fact, the argument is often made that private provision increases quality because the providers know that if the quality is not satisfactory, the governmental jurisdiction can turn to other providers. Competition not only acts as a guarantor of quality, but also functions to keep the costs of services down. Fixed-term contracts give public officials the flexibility to renegotiate contract terms or to choose to discontinue contracts upon their expiration. All three standards, however, assume the existence of competition. The absence of competition entails dependence, and with dependence can come inescapable cost increases.

There is little broadly comparative research to support a conclusion that privatization has cut the costs of public services among American governments, improved their quality, or provided increased budgetary flexibility. Supporters of privatization turn to case studies and anecdotal evidence suggesting that private sector contracts have produced cost savings, typically attributed to reduced personnel costs. Because the growth of privatization is a comparatively recent phenomenon, it offers a limited history on which to base valid generalizations. Assessments of quality tend to be even more impressionistic. Nonetheless, case experience grew significantly throughout the 1980s and 1990s, and continues into the twenty-first century.

Proposition 13 provided the impetus for California communities to expand their use of private vendor contracts. Their motivation has been largely economic, as reduced tax revenues have prompted local officials to search out ways to cut expenditures. Los Angeles County contracts, to various degrees, for park maintenance, security, medical testing, hospital food services, trash removal, and some public defender services.[33] Several municipalities near San Diego have also turned to contracting. One such community, Imperial Beach, had forty-seven contracts with private companies, nonprofit organizations, and other area governments.[34] In northern California, the city of Lafayette, near Oakland, contracts for most of its public works and engineering services, street repair and cleaning, traffic signal installation and maintenance, tree trimming, and parking operations. Savings of up to 25 percent associated with contracts for service have been claimed for cities such as Lafayette.[35] The city of Fairfield, also in northern California, turned to private firefighters when its unionized public firefighters refused to accept changes in job descriptions and schedules.[36]

San Diego County decided in 1999 to privatize its entire computer and telecommunications operations, at a contracted cost of $644 million over seven years. County administrators formed an alliance—led by Computer Science

Corp, Pacific Bell, and Lucent Technologies—to take over the county's information technology operations. The alliance quickly promised to provide the county with new desktop computers (which will be replaced every three years), along with new phones, phone switches and routers, computer networks, and in-ground fiber-optic cable connections. Not only did county officials expect to get improved service from the move; they also saw it as a way to stop the revolving door of information technology employees leaving county service for more attractive jobs in the private sector.[37]

A number of large counties have privatized all or part of their welfare systems. Maricopa County, Arizona (in which Phoenix is located) and Milwaukee County, Wisconsin, have privatized their entire welfare operations, even permitting contract workers to make eligibility determinations—the only counties to do so. Orange County, California relies on private sector contract employees to make 60 percent of the program's job placements.[38]

In addition to jurisdiction-specific case studies, one recent multi-city study deserves attention. Using a sample of twenty medium-size cities (population ranging from 10,000 to 250,000) for each of eight public services provided widely in the metropolitan Los Angeles area, Eileen Berenyi and Barbara Stevens compared contracted services to services delivered directly by municipal employees in terms of costs and quality. For each service—refuse collection, street resurfacing, street cleaning, traffic signal maintenance, tree trimming, turf maintenance, janitorial services, and payroll services—the cities were divided into two groups, one half providing the service using one or more private firms under contract and the other half using municipal workers. Within each category, the researchers selected a representative sample of ten cities, by size and median family income, holding service level and scale of operation constant. They found that on the average, municipal-delivered services were "54 percent more costly than the same services provided by private contractors, with scale, service level, and service condition."[39] Moreover, they found no difference in the quality of service provided.

In offering an explanation for their findings, the authors point to structural differences between the private contractors and the municipal agencies. They consistently found that private contractors used fewer layers of management between the director of the service and the line workers. The contractors also had management and personnel policies that contributed to lower-cost operations, and they were able to exercise greater discretion in the deployment of more technically advanced and efficient equipment. Municipal managers complained that they were frequently unable to exercise discretion regarding equipment use because its maintenance was the responsibility of another department.[40]

A number of local governments have invited their own public agencies to compete with private industries for the delivery of public services. Phoenix fosters competitions in thirteen service areas, most prominently including garbage collection, landfill operations, landscape maintenance, and billing services. Using bidding, city officials selected private competitive companies thirty-four times, and public agencies twenty-two times. The city has accepted low bids from private providers for such traditional public services as trash collection, security, bus transportation, and building maintenance. In order to ensure service continuity and to have available backup, however, Phoenix limits contracting to 50 percent of any service. According to city auditors, competitive bidding has yielded over $27 million in savings since its inception, with 84 percent of that savings being realized in public works operations.[41] Cleveland offers another example of head-to-head competition, but one in which the city workers won. Responding to the growing costs of public works. Cleveland let contracts for catch basin cleaning to a private vendor. Later, the union representing municipal workers offered a proposal of its own that significantly undercut the private firm's price. The city public works department got the job back, and the city no longer seeks private bids for that service. Indianapolis put its golf courses up for bid, and their sewer billing has gone private. City workers, however, have won contracts for filling potholes and sealing pavement cracks.[42]

Michigan's local governments make widespread use of outsourced contracting. Nearly two-thirds contract out at least one service, and the most commonly outsourced services or operations include legal (86 percent), engineering (51 percent), waste removal/recycling (45 percent), property assessing (43 percent), and inspections (42 percent). Moreover, responding to a survey conducted in 2014 by the University of Michigan's Center for Local, State, and Urban Policy, a sizable majority of officials in jurisdictions engaged in contracting stated that they were somewhat or very satisfied overall with their experiences. [43]

Volunteerism

Besides relying more heavily on the private sector for delivery of public services, local governments are increasingly asking residents to volunteer their own time toward enhancing the quality or quantity of services they receive. Such citizen involvement can come in both the design and the delivery of city services. As one academic observed, "The co-production process is based upon the recognition that public services are the joint product of the activities of both citizens and government officials."[44]

Citizen volunteerism is deeply embedded in the fabric of local government. Local residents have long served on planning commissions, zoning boards, and school boards, to mention just a few. Beyond this tradition of citizen involvement in local decision making—wherein local agencies benefit from broad community input into decisions and residents learn firsthand about government policy making and how they can shape it—local governments are increasingly turning to volunteers to help maintain, and even expand, essential services. The scope of those activities has transcended the traditional arenas of volunteer fire departments and ambulance drivers.

Citizens can contribute their efforts individually or in groups. Individually, they can take on such simple tasks as picking up litter on their streets or separating items for trash collection. The concept of co-production is most useful, however, when it is applied to collective citizen action. For example, citizens form neighborhood watch groups in an effort to reduce crime or band together to remove graffiti, clean city parks, and serve in police reserve units and fire department auxiliaries.

Expanding the use of citizen volunteers requires an organized commitment toward that end by local government managers. Local governments themselves can be the organizing locus, or they can work with nonprofit organizations such as the United Way, the Urban League, local churches, or neighborhood associations, which solicit and organize volunteers.

In a budget address to the Detroit City Council, former mayor Coleman Young put that city's residents on notice that "for the near future we will have to get used to doing things for our city that we have come to expect our city to do for us."[45] As a critical observer put it, "Ask not what your city can do for you—it's broke."[46]

Public services provided voluntarily by residents extend the quantity of service within a local jurisdiction and make an economic contribution to the community as well. For example, if neighborhood residents fail to remove graffiti from public structures, the work will either go undone or be done at city expense. Thus, localities that organize collective citizen volunteer efforts do so in part as a means to ease the pressure on an already overtaxed public budget. Although local government officials recognize that citizen volunteerism contributes only a marginal portion of all local public services, they have demonstrated increasing interest in nurturing broadened citizen involvement. That growing interest has, in good part, been motivated by the new fiscal realities facing local governments today.

Mandates Pushing Expenditures Up

As municipal and county officials increasingly turn to privatization and co-production to reduce expenditures and balance their budgets, federal and state mandates continue to exert pressure on local governmental spending. Mandates have been characterized as "requirements for expenditures beyond what a locality would otherwise have spent."[47] These requirements can be either programmatic (e.g., certain service standards must be met) or procedural (e.g., record keeping and reporting must meet certain specifications), and they can be imposed by direct order or as a condition of financial aid. For both federal and state mandates, the vast majority have been procedural rather than programmatic, although the states are somewhat less inclined than the federal government to use programmatic mandates. State mandates also are most likely to take the form of direct orders (96 percent), whereas federal mandates tend to be conditions of federal aid (82 percent).[48]

Federal mandates of state and local expenditures, and state mandates of local expenditures, were important issues in state and local politics during the late 1970s and the early 1980s. In 1978, a highly publicized study by the Advisory Council on Intergovernmental Relations documented the breadth and depth of the state mandates that increase operating costs for local governments. The study found that states on the average imposed thirty-five mandates on their local governments, a number that includes only those requirements used most widely among the states.[49]

The study generated publicity, triggered debates within national and state associations of local units of government and in state legislatures, and prompted a flurry of political activity in many states. State legislators debated how to address the state mandate problem and citizens' groups (supported by elected local officials and local government interest associations) worked hard to get mandate-relief propositions on the ballots of those states permitting initiatives or popular referenda.

Several citizen initiative campaigns proved successful. California voters approved Proposition 4 in 1979, directing the state to reimburse local governments for all costs attributable to state mandates. Michigan passed a constitutional amendment in 1979 similarly requiring full state reimbursement for any newly mandated activity or service. Using the direct initiative again, the Massachusetts legislature followed suit in 1980, statutorily requiring reimbursement for all state mandates increasing a local government's personnel costs unless the law is enacted by a two-thirds majority or is accepted by the affected jurisdictions. New Hampshire voters approved an amendment in 1984 similar to the provision enacted in Massachusetts, requiring either full reimbursement or local approval of the mandate. Also in 1984, the voters of New Mexico added a new twist by amending their state's constitution to require either full reimbursement of mandated costs or state approval of a new revenue source from which to finance the increased expenditures. In all, fourteen states either restrict the authority of state governments to issue mandates or provide state reimbursement to cover the newly required expenditures.[50]

California voters in 2004 modified the mandate provisions approved in 1979, by passing Proposition 1A in 2004. This later use of the direct initiative required the state to suspend or repeal mandates that are not fully funded by the legislature.

Unfortunately, except in California, there is no systematic report on the amount of reimbursement actually paid by states to localities. California's record, however, suggests that state reimbursements to local governments have failed to meet the increased costs occasioned by state mandates. For FY 2008 California had amassed over $900 million of unpaid claims, after the legislature paid a mere $66 million for the 2006 and 2007 fiscal years. Governor Schwarzenegger's budget request for FY 2008 contained no funding for mandated cost reimbursement.[51] The real value of state constitutional amendments has been to reduce significantly the incidence of new mandates rather than to release a torrent of cash flowing from state treasuries to local coffers.[52]

At the national level, two bills were introduced in the U.S. Congress in the late 1980s to address federal mandates placed on state and local governments. One would require federal reimbursement for all mandates costing at least $25 million nationally. The other would allow a "point of order" to be raised during floor debate on any bill that would impose more than $50 million in aggregate increased annual costs on state and local governments. Neither bill was enacted. Concern over reducing the national deficit has dampened congressional interest in reimbursement. However, Congress did act in 1995 to place procedural hurdles in the way of mandate legislation. The Unfunded Mandates Reform Act of 1995, initiated as part of the House GOP's "Contract with America," prohibits consideration of any mandate costing states or local governments more than $50 million in the aggregate unless the Congressional Budget Office has provided an analysis that identified the direct costs and benefits to state or local governments subject to the mandate. The legislation gives Congress the option to override this restriction by majority vote. The restriction does not apply at all if Congress creates an entitlement (either raising taxes to pay for it or making offsetting reductions in other entitlements) or appropriates funding to cover the costs of compliance.

Though the reform act fails to require federal reimbursement of the mandated costs borne by state and local governments, it does make it more difficult and visible for Congress to impose new regulations on state and local governments without corresponding funding. Nevertheless, existing mandates still impose significant costs on local governments.

A 1991 study done by the City of Chicago, in conjunction with faculty members of Roosevelt University, put the costs of complying with federal mandates at $191 million annually, or 8.3 percent of the city's own-source revenues. Another study of the costs of federal mandates in a smaller municipality, Lewiston, Maine, put the 1992 price tag at $1.6 million, or about 3 percent of its annual budget. In addition, however, the study estimated that it would cost almost $8 million for the city to comply with all of the federal mandates proposed for the following year, taking an amount equal to 14 percent of the city's budget.[53]

The Enduring Features of Local Budgeting

Municipalities and counties have, on the whole, been forced to become more self-reliant today than they were a decade ago. Local policy makers have found new revenue sources and ways of reducing the growth of expenditures, and they have been inventive in accomplishing both. The expansion of non-property tax revenue sources, the pursuit of greater public–private ventures to promote economic growth and expand local tax bases, the encouragement of volunteerism, and the efforts of local governments to accommodate unfunded federal and state mandates have obscured the enduring features of local budgeting.

Executives dominate local budgeting in populous urban counties and cities. Although only 25 percent of all counties have chief executives, these counties account for about 75 percent of the population served by counties nationally.[54]

There are two forms of executive government at the county level: a popularly elected county executive or a county administrator appointed by the county board. Both exercise responsibility for developing a county budget that is subsequently reviewed and acted upon by the county board. Of the two, however, only the elected county executive can veto the budgetary decisions of the county board—politically a highly significant difference.

In most major cities, the mayor is responsible for developing a budget for consideration and action by the city council. Some cities have city managers, appointed by the city council and serving at its pleasure. In that case it is the city manager who develops the budget proposal. Unlike his appointed counterpart at the county level, the city manager is not empowered to veto legislative actions.

Regardless of the form of executive government, the chief executive often conditions budget development by issuing budgetary policy guidelines for agencies to use in developing their requests. These conditions are usually advanced in the form of constraints, and are characteristically tied to projections of revenue availability. Chief executives may set ceilings for agency requests or ask agency heads to present alternative budget levels for review by budget staff. The chief executive's guidance may highlight the administration's priorities for the coming fiscal period and urge agency heads to reflect those priorities, where applicable, in their requests.

Professional budget staffs provide assistance to the chief executive in budget preparation and control. Staff services include making revenue estimates, analyzing agency requests, recommending budget actions, preparing the executive budget documents, and monitoring agency expenditures vis-à-vis the legislatively approved budget. Budget offices in larger jurisdictions, regardless of the type of local government, tend to perform all these functions. Budget staffs in smaller jurisdictions generally play a much more limited analytical role and concentrate more on budget control.[55]

Local governments rely on their own staffs to formulate revenue and expenditure estimates. Only 16 percent of local governments responding to a national survey of local budget practices indicated that they use consultants in these areas. Even where they are used, local officials describe the consultants' role as minor.[56] In addition to local officials' informed judgments, the largest jurisdictions are more likely to employ econometric models or other modeling methods in the revenue-estimating process. Such tools typically are the province of the executive budget staff.

The legislative branch dominates budgeting in the less populous rural counties. In counties with populations under 25,000, the budget is typically prepared by an executive committee of the board (usually called the board of supervisors or the board of commissioners) with assistance from an elected county clerk. The board thus performs both the traditional executive function of budget development as well as the legislative function of budget approval. The clerk's role is usually limited to providing technical assistance, but long-serving clerks can exercise significant influence based on their accumulated knowledge and expertise. In other counties, it is the elected county clerk or the county auditor who develops the budget, independent of board involvement. However, the board exercises sole authority for final budget action, typically performing that role with only modest or no staff support. When staff support is absent or weak, the potential influence of the clerk or auditor on budget outcomes is enhanced. In both of the above cases, neither the clerk nor the auditor possesses veto authority over the board's actions.[57]

In contrast, in executive budget systems found in populous cities and urban counties, it is uncommon for legislative bodies to offer major budgetary alternatives to a chief executive's recommendations. If they propose to increase spending, they are then required to show how to accommodate those increases, either by raising taxes or by cutting back the chief executive's recommendations in other areas. The former is not an attractive alternative to legislative bodies, since public expectations about the required level of taxes are usually set by the chief executive. Consequently, when local legislative bodies do alter the executive budget, they are inclined to make selective cuts in executive proposals and, if they propose new or increased spending, to fund it through reallocation. In some municipalities, councils are even prohibited from increasing the mayor's recommended spending amounts. It is not surprising that research has consistently shown that it is the chief executive's recommendation that regularly shapes the legislatively approved budget.[58]

Regardless of the form of local budgeting, both cuts in federal aid and continued political pressure on the property tax have kept local budget makers attentive to holding the line on spending. Their primary budgetary challenge continues to be that of meeting the revenue constraint, despite the fact that localities have had some success in stretching those constraints through the addition of new revenue sources. Ideally, as always, local budgeters would prefer to create a surplus; toward that end they continue to estimate revenues conservatively, knowing that any over-realized revenues are likely to remain outside agency operating budgets for the course of the fiscal year. The revenue constraint makes it easier for budget reviewers to cut the requests of executive agencies. "The money is just not available" is an easy and convenient retort to would-be spenders. The revenue constraint also tends to promote budgetary choices that are aprogrammatic, inviting decisions made in terms of needed percentage reductions, as budget makers consider incremental departures from budgeted base-spending levels that are in line with available revenues.

The structure of local government budgets promotes incremental budget decisions. A large share of both municipal and county budgets—typically more than three-quarters—is devoted to salaries and fringe benefits, reflecting the service-intensive nature of local government. Unlike state governments, where a significant portion of the budget is devoted to providing financial aid to other governments or to individuals directly, nearly all of each local government budget supports day-to-day government operations.

Programmatically, municipalities and counties provide several services common to both, including law enforcement, highway and street construction and maintenance, park development and maintenance, and welfare (with overlap particularly found in the so-called "general relief" area). There are also service differences. Municipalities are usually responsible for garbage and trash collection, fire protection, libraries, building inspection and permits, public housing, and environmental health. Some municipalities—primarily towns—may provide few services directly, electing instead to contract for those services with larger contiguous municipalities or with counties. Counties have administrative responsibility for public assistance programs, such as Temporary Assistance for Needy Families, supplemental security income, and food stamps; social services; institutions providing care for the aged, mentally ill, and those in need of medical care who cannot afford it; and the courts (although some municipal courts still exist across the country).

Within the enduring reality of tight budgets and revenue constraint, local officials have devoted their efforts toward expanding the resource pie. The recent growth in public–private endeavors toward this end has acted to strengthen the local chief executive's influence over budgetary and financial matters. More than ever, it is to the chief executive that city councils, county boards, and civic and business leaders turn for leadership in the current political environment. The basic incentives influencing local budgetary choice are still operative and are unlikely to change in the foreseeable future. State financial assistance will probably not return to the growth levels of the 1970s; nor can federal aid realistically be expected to return to its peak in the late 1970s. Local governments will be forced to become even more self-reliant. For municipalities and counties, the fiscal future appears to lie with efforts to expand the revenue base. Unless the aggregate economic pie can be enlarged, however, such local efforts will either fail or succeed at the expense of competing local jurisdictions. Taxpayer distaste for tax increases will continue to force local governments to seek new ways of expanding revenues and slowing expenditure growth. That very pressure will constrain local governments' ability, in the short run, to offer all the incentives that they believe necessary to foster economic development within their borders. The resource constraint, then, will indeed continue to be the central feature of local budgetary politics.

Summary and Conclusions

The U.S. Constitution makes no reference to local units of government. As legal creatures of the states, state constitutions and statutory law govern their organizational structure and operational powers. States also delimit the tax instruments that local government may use to finance their authorized programmatic operations. Heavily reliant on property tax, local governments face greater revenue constraints than do states, which use sales and income taxes as their major revenue producers. Local governments, therefore, have sought to become more self-reliant and to find new sources of revenue beyond the property tax. Local budgeting can best be characterized as revenue budgeting. Faced with balanced-budget requirements, the revenue constraint conditions the decision making and politics of local budgeting.

In their efforts to expand revenues, local governments, where permitted by state law, have turned increasingly to local income tax and sales tax as sources of badly needed additional revenue, and all local governments have come to rely more heavily on user fees. Municipalities and counties, beyond adopting and expanding particular revenue instruments, have also pursued competitive strategies aimed at encouraging economic development within their borders, whether the expansion of existing enterprises or the location of new plants and facilities. In doing so, they have employed supply-side incentives as lures. Municipalities and counties, when given the authority by their state, have also used revenue-expanding devices of TIF, franchise fees, equity sharing with private enterprise, impact fees on new developments, and payments in lieu of taxes (from tax-exempt property, such as public universities and hospitals, and religious institutions).

In addition to expanding their revenue bases, local governments have turned to imaginative ways of reducing the cost of government operations while preserving, or even expanding, the quantity and quality of public services. Two approaches receiving growing national attention are privatization and co-production. Privatization involves local governments contracting with the private sector to provide services that these governments have traditionally provided for themselves. Co-production initiatives make use of citizen volunteers in both the design and direct delivery of services.

As legal creatures of the states, local governments are fiscally vulnerable to mandates imposed by state governments. Mandates can be either programmatic (e.g., service requirements that must be met) or procedural (e.g., required processes and record keeping and reporting), and they can be imposed by direct order or as a condition of financial aid. In either case, they bring costs that must be borne.

Under this overlay of self-help and broadened public–private ventures lie the enduring features of local budgeting: executive dominance in budget making and budget control, the need to meet the revenue constraint in the short run and stretch it in the long run, and the political desirability of creating a surplus.

Notes

1 Thomas Gabe, Poverty in the United States: 2013 (Washington, D.C.: Congressional Research Service), 10; United States House of Representatives, Committee on Ways

and Means, 2000 Green Book: Background Material and Data on Programs within the Jurisdiction of the Committee on Ways and Means, Table H-8, 1293.

2 Pearl M. Kramer, Crisis in Urban Public Finance (New York: Praeger, 1983).

3 Irene S. Rubin, Running in the Red: The Political Dimensions of Urban Fiscal Stress (Albany: State University of New York Press, 1982).

4 U.S. Bureau of the Census, Statistical Abstract of the United States, 1995 (Washington, D.C.: Bureau of the Census, U.S. Department of Commerce, 1995), 39; U.S. Bureau of the Census, Statistical Abstract of the United States, 1987 (Washington, D.C.: Bureau of the Census, U.S. Department of Commerce, 1987), 25.

5 U.S. Bureau of the Census, Resident Population of the Fifty States, www.census.gov/population/cen2000/tab05.pdf, table 5.

6 U.S. Advisory Council on Intergovernmental Relations, Local Revenue Diversification: Local Income Taxes, SR-10 (Washington, D.C.: U.S. Advisory Council on Intergovernmental Relations, 1988), 3.

7 U.S. Bureau of the Census, Statistical Abstract 1995, 300; U.S. Advisory Council on Intergovernmental Relations, Significant Features of Fiscal Federalism, 1994 ed., book 2 (Washington, D.C.: U.S. Advisory Council on Intergovernmental Relations, 1994), 200–36.

8 U.S. Advisory Council on Intergovernmental Relations, Local Revenue Diversification: Local Income Taxes, 30.

9 U.S. Bureau of the Census, Local Government Finances by Type of Government and State: 2012, www.census.gov/govs/local; U.S. Bureau of the Census, 1997 Census of Governments, vol. 4, Government Finances (Washington, D.C.: Bureau of the Census, U.S. Department of Commerce, December 2000), 2.

10 Tax Foundation, Facts and Figures on Government Finance, 33rd ed. (Washington, D.C.: Tax Foundation, 1999), 251–2.

11 Penelope Lemov, "User Fees, Once the Answer to City Budget Prayers, May Have Reached Their Peak," Governing 2 (March 1989): 24.

12 U.S. Advisory Council on Intergovernmental Relations, Significant Features of Fiscal Federalism, 1988 ed., book 2, 22.

13 Ibid.

14 Figures provided by Ned Daugherty, Office of Research and Development, Department of Statistics, Assessment Division, Los Angeles County, June 1989.

15 Jack Citrin, "Introduction: The Legacy of Proposition 13," in California and the American Tax Revolt, ed. Terry Schwadron (Berkeley and Los Angeles: University of California Press, 1984), 9.

16 Ibid., 18.

17 Ibid., 7.

18 Ibid.

19 Ibid., 11.

20 Dennis Hale, "Proposition 2 1/2—A Decade Later: The Ambiguous Legacy of Tax Reform in Massachusetts," State and Local Government Review 25, no. 2 (spring 1993): 117–29.

21 Progress Illinois, "Cook County Property Tax Bills to Provide More TIF Transparency But More Changes Are Needed," July 12, 2013, www.progressillinois.com; The 2013 TIF Revenue Report: Executive Summary (Chicago: Office of County Clerk David Orr), www.cookcountyclerk.com/tsd/tifs/pages/tifreports.aspx

22 Paul Richter, "How Local Government Responded," in Schwadron, ed., California and the American Tax Revolt, 107–8.

23 Ibid.

24 Duncan Associates, Impactfees.com, www.impactfees.com/faq/general.php

25 National Association of Homebuilders, Impact Fee Handbook (Washington, D.C.: Homebuilder Press, 1997), 13; Alan Altshuler and Jose Gomez-Ibanez, Regulation for Revenue: The Political Economy of Land Use Exactions (Washington, D.C.: Brookings Institution, 1992), 102.

26 Penelope Lemov, "Tin Cup Taxation," Governing 9 (October 1995): 26.

27 Ibid.

28 Daphne A. Kenyon and Adam H. Langley, Payment in Lieu of Taxes: Balancing Municipal and Nonprofit Interests (Cambridge, M.A.: Lincoln Institute of Land Policy, 2010), 22.

29 George S. Ford and Thomas M. Koutsky, "Franchise Fee Revenues After Video Competition: The 'Common Dividend for Local Governments'," Phoenix Center Policy Bulletin No. 12, November 2005: 1.

30 Bill Peacock, "Cities Profit from Excess Fees," GoSanAngelo, www.gosanangelo. com/news/jun/17/cities-profit-from-excess-fees

31 Geoffrey F. Segal, "Navigating the Politics of Water Privatization: The Battles of New Orleans, Atlanta, and Stockton," Annual Privatization Report 2003, www.rppi.org

32 International City Management Association, Service Delivery in the Nineties: Alternative Approaches for Local Governments (Washington D.C.: 1989), xii–xiii.

33 Ibid., 50.

34 Philip E. Fixler and Robert W. Poole Jr., "The Privatization Revolution," Policy Review (summer 1986): 68.

35 Ibid.

36 Thomas B. Darr, "Pondering Privatization May Be Good for Your Government," Governing 1 (November 1987): 42.

37 Ellen Perlman, "Taking Tech Private," Governing 13 (May 2000): 20.

38 "The Welfare Bonanza," Governing 13 (January 2000), 16.

39 Eileen Brettler Berenyi and Barbara I. Stevens, "Does Privatization Work? A Study of the Delivery of Eight Local Services," State and Local Government Review 20 (winter 1988): 19.

40 Ibid., 16–19.

41 "Summary of Presentation Made by Ronald Iensen," in Privatization in a Federal System: An Executive Summary, ed. William T. Gormley (Madison, W.I.: Robert M. La Follette Institute of Public Affairs, 1988), 8.

42 Stephen Goldsmith, "Bringing Competition to City Services," Cato Policy Report 15, no. 1 (January–February 1993): 6.

43 Thomas Ivacko and Debra Horner, "Most Michigan Local Officials Are Satisfied with their Privatized Services, but Few Seek to Expand Further," Michigan Public Policy Survey (Ann Arbor, M.I.: The Center for Local, State, and Urban Policy, University of Michigan, November 2014), 1.

44 Elaine B. Sharp, "Toward a New Understanding of Urban Services and Citizen Participation: The Coproduction Concept," Midwest Review of Public Administration 14 (June 1980): 110.

45 Coleman Young, quoted in Jeffrey L. Brudney and Robert E. England, "Toward a Definition of the Coproduction Process," Public Administration Review 43 (January–February 1983): 59.

46 Kirk Cheyfitz, "Self-Service: The City that Governs Least Governs Best," New Republic, November 15, 1980, p. 14.

47 Marcia Whicker Taror, "State Mandated Located Expenditures: Are They Panacea or Plague?," National Civic Review 69 (September 1980): 440.

48 Max Neiman and Catherine Lovell, "Federal and State Mandating," Administration and Society 14 (November 1982): 356–7.

49 Joseph F. Zimmerman, State Mandating of Local Expenditures (Washington, D.C.: U.S. Advisory Council on Intergovernmental Relations, 1978).

50 U.S. General Accounting Office, Legislative Mandates: State Experiences Offer Insights for Federal Action, Document no. HRD-88–75 (Washington, D.C.: U.S. General Accounting Office, September 1988), 30–1.

51 California Legislative Analyst's Office, Analysis of the 2008-2009 Budget Bill: General Government, www.lao.ca.gov/analysis_2008/general_govt/gen_anl08018. aspx

52 John F. Zimmerman, "The State Mandate Problem," State and Local Government Review 19 (spring 1987): 81–2.

53 Philip M. Dearborn, "Assessing Mandate Effects on State and Local Governments," Intergovernmental Perspective 20, no. 3 (summer–fall 1994): 25–6.

54 Herbert Duncombe and Florence Heffron, "Legislative Budgeting," in Handbook on Public Budgeting and Financial Management, ed. Jack Rabin and Thomas Lynch (New York: Marcel Dekker, 1983), 447–8.

55 Daniel E. O'Toole and James Marshall, "Budgeting Practices in Local Government: The State of the Art," Government Finance Review 3 (October 1987): 12.

56 Ibid., 13.

57 Sydney Duncombe, William Duncombe, and Richard Kinney, "Factors Influencing the Politics and Process of County Government Budgeting," State and Local Government Review 24, no. 1 (winter 1992): 19–27.

58 Thomas I. Anton, Budgeting in Three Illinois Cities (Urbana, I.L.: Institute of Government and Public Affairs, 1964); John P. Crecine, Governmental Problem Solving: A Computer Simulation of Municipal Budgeting (Chicago, I.L.: Rand-McNally, 1969); Arnold I. Meltsner, The Politics of City Revenue (Berkeley and Los Angeles: University of California Press, 1971); Paul Peterson, City Limits (Chicago: University of Chicago Press, 1981); Daniel R. Mullins and Michael A. Pagano, "Local Budgeting and Finance: 25 Years of Development," Public Budgeting and Finance 25, Issue 4 (December 2005): 3–45.

Chapter 9

Fiscal Federalism and Intergovernmental Fiscal Relations

State governments operate within a federal system. The U.S. Constitution and subsequent interpretations by the federal courts establish the basis for the legal relationship between the federal government and the states. The Constitution does not place the federal government over the states; it allocates power between the two, enumerating the respective authority of each and providing a framework under which the national government and the states can exercise non-enumerated prerogatives. It is the application of that framework of non-enumerated powers that has been frequently tested in the U.S. Supreme Court over time. Although the Tenth Amendment to the Constitution provides that "any powers not explicitly delegated to the United States by the Constitution, nor prohibited by it to the states, are reserved to the states respectively," the Framers of the Constitution created a tension in Article 1 between the federal government and the states by giving Congress the authority to "make all laws which shall be necessary and proper for carrying into execution the foregoing [enumerated] powers," thus shifting the initiative to the federal government to interpret what constitutes necessary and proper federal initiative. Article 1 further gives the federal government the authority to "provide for the common defense and general welfare," creating an even broader latitude for it to justify federal action based on its furtherance of the general welfare.

The Constitution makes no reference to local units of government. They are creatures of the states, operating under provisions established by state law for their creation and operating authority, and are the recipients of financial aid provided by the states, as well as by the federal government when such federal aid is authorized or not prohibited by the states. Thus state and federal aid to local governments represents another important element of public budgeting.

Federal and state intergovernmental aid takes a number of forms. **Categorical grants** are restricted to narrowly defined purposes. For instance, federal aid to the states in support of the Medicaid program must be used for that purpose alone, and cannot, for example, be used to maintain highways or bridges. Similarly, federal highway aid to the states must be used in support of highway construction and maintenance. **Block grants** broaden the purposes for which grants can be used, giving flexibility to states and local governments to fund their distinctive spending priorities within a functional area of policy. As a case in point, the federal Title XX social services block grant to states allows state policy makers to allocate funds for a wide array of purposes consistent with the objectives of this authorizing legislation, including protecting children from abuse and neglect, preventing teen pregnancies, providing child care services for poor and low-income working mothers, serving meals to the needy elderly, and counseling victims of sexual assaults, to name just a few.

Both the federal government and the states also make use of **formula grants**, for which an approved formula serves as the basis for allocating funds to eligible recipients, whether that takes the form of allocating federal funds to metropolitan transit systems or allocating state funds to school districts. In order to change respective allocations, the formula itself must be altered. The politics of formula grants turn on attempts to modify the formula to magnify the size of the grant.

Federal–state relations have taken a number of turns since the Constitution's ratification in 1788, but the overall direction of presidential and congressional action has been toward broader intervention by the federal partner in affairs traditionally the domain of the states. The states, too, have increasingly acted to condition local governments' spending priorities, using both their regulatory authority and fiscal carrots to compel and entice policy choice in line with the states' priorities.

The New Deal and Cooperative Federalism

The Great Depression of the 1930s precipitated increased federal involvement in the affairs of the states. Until then, the federal government had played an almost negligible role in domestic policy making. The states exercised responsibility for education, social welfare, health, and criminal justice, receiving only minuscule financial assistance from the federal government in those pursuits. However, with national unemployment topping 20 percent, heightened demands for government assistance prompted the states to turn to the federal government for help. President Franklin Delano Roosevelt, a Democrat, and the Democrat-controlled Congress responded with a raft of national initiatives to turn the economy around and help the states assist those most hurt by the deep economic and social dislocations. At Roosevelt's urging, Congress approved emergency grants to assist the states in meeting the rising costs of unemployment compensation. It also created over twenty-five programs as part of New Deal legislation, including job-creating public works initiatives for adults and youths; matching federal funds in support of state emergency relief efforts; government loans to struggling financial institutions and railroads; and federal aid in support of state-administered social welfare programs assisting dependent children, the elderly, and farmers. As a measure of the greatly expanded federal financial commitment, federal grant-in-aid spending rose to $2.7 billion after the first five years of the New Deal, compared to the $193 million spent in 1932, the last year of the Republican administration of Herbert Hoover.

World War II completed the attempt to put Americans back to work—in military uniforms or in industries supporting the war effort. Increased taxes and the financing of federal debt provided the required resources. Even though the Allied Forces' victory allowed federal spending to drop by nearly half by 1950, the U.S. Treasury had amassed a base level of tax resources that was available to support domestic programs aimed at assisting state and local governments to educate and retrain returning veterans, renew urban areas, provide housing assistance, and expand the nation's highway system. This period of "cooperative federalism" gave way to a more prescriptive "centralized federalism" associated with the Great Society initiatives of President Lyndon B. Johnson.[1]

The Great Society and Centralized Federalism

For President Johnson, a truly great society was one that assured an adequate quality of life for all of its citizens, including the less fortunate. Congress responded to his lead by creating many new social programs to provide financial aid and medical assistance to the needy, construct low-cost housing, make available compensatory education to the underprivileged, support mass transit, and finance legal counsel for the poor. Instead of assisting the states to develop programs to meet their definitions of emerging domestic needs, the federal government articulated "national" policy goals and held out a greatly increased fiscal carrot to entice state participation, which often involved state administration. During the Johnson administration alone, Congress created over 209 new **federal grants-in-aid**, each with its own programmatic, administrative, and reporting requirements.[2] The federal government also increasingly turned to mandates to elicit state and local government compliance with statutory and regulatory requirements associated with these new programs. Mandates carry the threat of sanctions for noncompliance, which can entail the loss of federal funds or even the imposition of fines.

This new prescription was in part a reaction to state and local governments of the time. Most states were dominated by rural interests, which were not all that attentive to pressing urban issues. Governors such as George Wallace of Alabama, Lester Maddox of Georgia, and Orval Faubus of Arkansas personified and led state resistance to the recognition of the rights and needs of African Americans. Moreover, the gubernatorial and legislative institutions were relatively weak in the mid-1960s, preceding the significant institutional reforms of the 1970s, which saw an expansion of the powers of governors, the lengthening of legislative sessions, and increased staff support for both governors and legislatures.

The vast majority of Great Society programs significantly expanded the use of categorical grants to distribute federal funds to state and local governments.

Categorical grants can be used only for the narrow purposes established by Congress or promulgated in the federal administrative code. For example, categorical grants are made for such specific purposes as building bridges, providing medical care for the needy, and subsidizing mass transit; they cannot be diverted to any other use. In accepting the grant, state and local governments become obligated to comply with the grant's various requirements, which dictate the purposes to which the funds may be put as well as any conditions attached to their use.

Some of the largest categorical grants can be classified as **entitlements**: people who qualify for assistance have an entitlement, or legal right, to receive benefits. For entitlements, the federal treasury must pay the bill even if the cost of meeting all benefit claims exceeds expenditure estimates for the program. Prominent examples of entitlement programs created or greatly expanded during the Great Society years include Medicaid, Supplementary Security Income, and Aid to Families with Dependent Children (AFDC).

Most grants-in-aid require matching funds from state or local governments. State and local matching shares typically run from 10 percent to 50 percent, depending on the program, with the federal government providing the remainder. For some joint state and local programs, the state picks up the full nonfederal share, but for others the state passes a percentage of the matching costs on to the participating local governments.

Presidential administrations and Congresses in the years after the Johnson administration not only continued support for most of these programs but also significantly increased funding for them as well (see Table 9.1). They also added 134 new categorical grants-in-aid between 1969 and 1980, perpetuating centralized federalism.[3] As a result of these initiatives, state and local governments became even more dependent on federal revenues, and federal grants-in-aid rose as a percentage of state and local expenditures.

Despite this continuity, President Richard M. Nixon, a Republican, added a new twist to federal aid by introducing the block grant. Block grants can be used for a number of related purposes consistent with their authorization and carry fewer restrictions and regulations than do categorical grants. Congress approved three block grants during the Nixon administration: the now defunct Comprehensive Employment and Training Grant, which provided job training and public service employment; the Community Development Block Grant, tying together a number of preexisting urban development and renewal programs; and Title XX of the Social Security Act, which consolidated several social service programs into one block grant.

At President Nixon's recommendation, Congress also approved general revenue sharing in 1972, which provided funds, without strings, to state and local governments based on an allocation formula that took into account population, income, urbanization, and tax effort. State and local governments that did best under the formula included those with the largest populations—particularly

Table 9.1　Federal Grants-in-Aid to State and Local Governments, Selected Fiscal Years, 1940–2018

Fiscal year	Amount (in $ billions)
1940	0.9
1950	2.3
1960	7.0
1970	24.1
1975	49.8
1980	91.4
1985	105.9
1990	135.3
1995	225.0
2000	285.9
2003	388.5
2007	443.8
2009	538.0
2011	606.8
2013	546.2
2014e	607.2
2016e	649.7
2018e	668.2

e = estimate

Source: Office of Management and Budget, Budget of the United States Government, FY 2015, Historical Tables, Table 12.1.

those having the highest percentage of poor residents, which made the greatest relative effort in raising their own revenues.

Revenue sharing no longer exists today. Revenue sharing with state governments was ended during the administration of President Jimmy Carter, at a time when rising state **budget surpluses** prompted state legislatures to cut state income and sales taxes—a climate not suggestive of the need for untargeted federal financial assistance. Later, at President Ronald Reagan's urging, Congress eliminated revenue sharing for local governments as one of a number of measures to reduce the ballooning federal **budget deficit**. Yet even with the creation of block grants and general revenue sharing, categorical grants-in-aid still constituted nearly 80 percent of all federal aid by 1980.[4]

Ronald Reagan's New Federalism

The election of Ronald Reagan in 1980 marked a turning point in federal aid to state and local governments. For President Reagan and his administration, federal aid had gotten out of hand. The number of federal grant programs had grown to 534 by the start of Reagan's first year in office, at a cost of more than $91 billion.[5] President Reagan not only saw that growth as an inordinate drain on the federal treasury but also, more significantly, viewed it as a normatively inappropriate role for the federal government to play. For Reagan, domestic policy choices should be made at the state level, not the federal. As Reagan noted in his 1982 State of the Union address,

> Our citizens feel they have lost control of even the most basic decisions made about the essential services of government, such as schools, welfare, roads, and even garbage collection. They are right. A maze of interlocking jurisdictions and levels of government confronts the average citizen in trying to solve even the simplest of problems. They do not know where to turn for answers, who to hold accountable, who to praise, who to blame, who to vote for or against. The main reason for this is the overpowering growth of federal grants-in-aid programs during the past few decades.[6]

Following that reasoning, President Reagan sought to cut funding for federal aid to state and local governments and to reduce the number of categorical grants-in-aid. He had success in both areas. In contrast to annual real-dollar increases that averaged over 8 percent between 1960 and 1980, federal aid decreased by an annual real-dollar average of 1.4 percent between 1980 and 1988, falling by over 10 percent between 1980 and 1982 (see Figure 9.1).[7] Because programs aiding needy individuals were protected by benefit entitlements, direct grants to state and local governments bore by far the greatest share of the reductions. The Reagan administration also eliminated categorical grant programs and consolidated others into block grants. At Reagan's recommendation, Congress eliminated forty-three categorical grant programs and consolidated another seventy-seven into nine block grants, but at reduced levels of funding.[8]

President Reagan wanted to go beyond his own efforts to create new block grant programs. In the 1982 State of the Union address, he proposed a substantive sorting out of state and federal responsibilities. Having quickly acquired the tag of the "big swap," Reagan's proposal called for the federal government

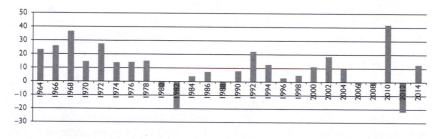

Figure 9.1   Biennial Percentage Change in Federal Grants-in-Aid to State and Local Governments, 1964–2014 (in constant FY 2005 dollars).

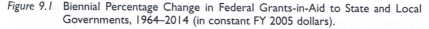

Source: Office of Management and Budget, Budget of the United States Government, FY 2015, Historical Tables, 257–8.

to turn over to the states sole responsibility for the nation's basic income maintenance programs, AFDC and food stamps. In exchange, the federal government would assume full responsibility for Medicaid. In addition, the president's package included fully turning back to the states sixty-one other grant-in-aid programs. In some cases, Reagan surmised, state officials might even decide that without federal support the programs were not of sufficient priority to be continued. The states would then assume total responsibility for administering and financing the programs they elected to continue. To assist them, Reagan called for a comparable amount of federal tax revenue to be returned to the states. Toward that end, a New Federalism Trust Fund would be created, providing a vehicle, during a transitional ten-year period, to help the states pay the costs of their newfound program responsibilities. After the transition, the states would assume full financial responsibility. Presumably they would use the transitional period as a time to enact the necessary state revenue increases, filling the gap left by the federal partner. To give them tax room, Reagan proposed a phased reduction of federal excise taxes, which the states were invited to reenact if they so chose.

However, the president's proposal, other than in the general sketch just discussed, contained little concrete elaboration—a fact that greatly bothered state policy makers. Precise amounts were not mentioned; nor was any sliding schedule provided for federal support over the ten-year period. The concept of program turnbacks met with general sympathy among state governors and legislators, but they shared great concern over how the transitional funding arrangement would work and how the states would ultimately pay the full bill. Top state administrators and affected interest groups promptly turned from a discussion of the relative conceptual and theoretical merits of the proposals to narrow assessments of how their programs would fare under the change. In the public welfare area, for example, interest groups, together with program-supportive administrators, expressed their concerns that devolution would result in lower benefit rates and stricter eligibility standards.[9]

Another significant issue in the debate over program and revenue devolution dealt with whether the federal government should play the role of "fiscal equalizer" within the federal system. In other words, is it appropriate for the federal government to step in and ease the disparities in fiscal capacity among the states? Fiscal capacity is a hypothetical measure of how much revenue a state could raise if it levied national average tax rates in relation to its tax base. Employing that measure, fiscal capacity among the states ranged at that time from 70 percent of the national average (Mississippi) to 250 percent (Alaska). As might be expected, the southeastern states in general possessed the lowest fiscal capacity, at 84 percent of the national average, compared to those to the far west, at 138 percent.[10] The issue of relative fiscal capacity was important because with program turnbacks the states would have been in quite different positions in their ability to assume the added fiscal responsibility. Since many of the federal grant-in-aid programs were designed with some measure of fiscal capacity affecting allocations among these states, state officials—particularly through the National Governors Association (NGA)—demanded that any transitional revenue transfer be allocated, in part, on an equalized basis. However, the dilemma still remained about how the less well-off states would be able to pick up the full program costs after the transitional period ended. These nagging practical concerns took some of the luster off the theoretical attractiveness of devolution.

The big swap and its associated package of program turnbacks never really got much beyond the preliminary discussion stage. Although in general agreement over the desirability of realignment, both the states and the Reagan administration were scared off by its fiscal implications. State policy makers were worried about the added fiscal burden that might be imposed, particularly in an environment in which the strength of well-entrenched interest groups would make it very difficult for the states to shed any of their inherited responsibilities. The Reagan administration, in light of the growing national deficit associated with the 1981–2 recession, appeared to develop serious second thoughts—not only about the fiscal viability of transitional revenue assistance but also about the extent to which the administration would make major budget cuts in the affected programs as another means of restraining domestic spending and balancing the federal budget. On the administration's side, faced with a worsening budget picture, Reagan became unwilling to make the fiscal concessions that appeared necessary to win gubernatorial backing for his initiative. The emphasis on improving U.S. military strength and the integrity of the president's fiscal policy proved to be higher priorities than his New Federalism initiative.

The George H. W. Bush Years: Continuity and Departure

In some ways President George H.W. Bush followed the lead of his predecessor. Like Reagan, he continued to seek consolidation of categorical grants into broader block grants. In his budget proposals for the 1992 fiscal year, President Bush offered Congress and the states a $20 billion list of categoricals from which Congress, after counsel from the states, could choose $15 billion worth for consolidation into a single new block grant. Under his proposal, the states would have lost an estimated $27.3 billion in federal funds over five years. The biggest prospective losers through consolidation would have included New York ($3 billion) and Texas and California ($1 billion each). The Bush administration suggested the categorical grants it preferred to see consolidated at reduced funding levels, but invited state policy makers to offer substitutions.

In response to that invitation, the NGA proposed that seven block grants be created from forty-two categorical grant programs, totaling $14.1 billion. The National Conference of State Legislatures (NCSL) upped the ante, calling for twelve block grants forged from eighty-five categoricals, to the tune of $21.3 billion. Unlike the Bush initiative, both proposals included provisions mandating stable funding for the new block grants, including a prospective adjustment for inflation.[11]

Local governments failed to share the NGA's or NCSL's enthusiasm for more block grants. They viewed it as further eroding their influence with the federal government and their already weakened discretion over the allocation of grant funds. They saw block grants as strengthening the hand of governors and state legislatures. Urban cities and counties questioned whether rural-dominated legislatures in many states would respond sympathetically to their needs.

The opposition of local governments, along with the budgetary implications of inflation-proof funding in an environment of growing national deficit, sealed the doom of further block grants. The prospects of increased federal administrative efficiencies and added state decision-making flexibility proved to be insufficiently attractive to mold executive–congressional agreement in the face of strong local opposition. In addition, the states would not lend their endorsement without a guarantee of stable and inflation-proof funding. At the same time, the demand for a guarantee precluded the administration's support, reinforcing the commonly held perception that the prospects for future shrinkage best explained the Bush administration's support of block grants.

Although President Bush, like President Reagan before him, continued to champion the elimination of ideologically objectionable programs such as those of the Economic Development Administration as well as operating subsidies for mass transit, overall federal aid to state and local governments fared far better under Bush than under Reagan. Caught up in the politics of a growing budget deficit with no end in sight, President Bush's sights became fixed on finding a macro-level solution to the pervasive budgetary gridlock.

Toward that end, the president and congressional leadership fashioned the comprehensive deficit-reduction package of October 1990 (known as the Budget Enforcement Act), which was discussed in depth in chapter 6. It established separate caps on defense, foreign aid, and discretionary domestic spending through the 1994 fiscal year. Yet it also added more than $20 billion in **budget authority** for domestic **discretionary spending** between the 1991 and 1993 fiscal years, and provided that the cap for domestic discretionary spending be adjusted annually for inflation.

These concessions gave President Bush and Congress additional fiscal room to do more for state and local governments. The tight constraints in place during the Reagan era had been loosened. State and local governments accordingly turned to the Bush administration and the Democrat-controlled Congress to make up for lost ground. Despite President Bush's conservative rhetoric, the data suggest that that is just what happened during the remaining years of his presidency. Instead of declining in constant dollars, as federal grants-in-aid had done during the Reagan years, they rose by nearly a quarter between the 1990 and 1992 fiscal years alone, as Figure 9.1 illustrates. Federal grants-in-aid also rose as a percentage of state and local spending, reversing a pattern of decline associated with the Reagan years. Increases in both discretionary and entitlement-driven aid, particularly Medicaid in the latter category, contributed to the remarkable turnaround in federal assistance. No longer did significant cuts in discretionary aid result in aggregate reductions in federal aid to state and local governments despite automatic increases in entitlement spending. The discretionary spending spigot had once again been turned on.

The Bill Clinton Years: Constrained Empathic Federalism

From the beginning of his campaign through the early years of his presidency, Bill Clinton expressed empathy toward state and local governments. As governor of Arkansas, he was on the receiving end of federal retrenchment during the Reagan administration and the first half of the Bush administration. Unlike his recent predecessors, President Clinton called for greater federal leadership to address many of the problems facing the urban areas of the United States. He also appreciated, however, that state and local governments were not likely to launch costly new programs without the availability of federal funding.

Clinton's empathy was constrained by the federal budget deficit he inherited from Republican President Bush and the Democrat-controlled Congress. Having campaigned on a pledge to reduce the deficit and put the brakes on future growth, Clinton found himself with little room to undertake new spending initiatives, a point about which Republicans were not shy in reminding the new president or the American public. Yet the Clinton administration needed no reminder that deficit reduction was its top priority, for it was Clinton himself who took the lead in fashioning deficit reduction legislation in 1993, his first year in office. It was also the president who cajoled recalcitrant Democrats into lending their support.

Not all Democrats eagerly jumped on the bandwagon. Some found the $241 billion tax increase (to be paid over four years) just too much to swallow, even though the legislation would also slow down spending by $255 billion over the same period. Others swallowed a little more easily, realizing that most of the income tax increase would come from upper-income taxpayers; but even with active presidential lobbying, the deficit-reduction package passed the U.S. House of Representatives by a mere two votes. Vice President Albert Gore had to break a deadlock in the U.S. Senate, giving the president a razor-thin one-vote margin in that chamber. Republicans, for their part, called for lower taxes and more spending cuts, as well as voicing their belief that the tax increase would dampen economic recovery, costing jobs rather than creating them.

Clinton also won enough support from the Democratic majority in Congress to gain passage of legislation aimed at helping local communities address the problems of their most depressed neighborhoods. Following the president's lead, Congress provided modest funding to support nine so-called empowerment zones, with six to be designated in urban cities and the other three in rural areas. Under the legislation, each city with designated empowerment zones received $100 million to be used to foster economic development and create jobs; each rural area received $40 million. As part of the application process for designation, local governments had to show how nonfederal resources would be packaged with federal funds to achieve the zone's objectives. Detroit's successful application included a commitment to create three thousand jobs within the zone, and a consortium of Detroit-based universities pledged to focus applied research and outreach efforts in the zone.[12]

The Democratic majority in Congress followed their president's call again the next year, passing an omnibus crime bill in the waning hours before the 1994 recess. With most Democrats championing the bill's passage, Republican minority leaders attempted to brand the measure as laden with pork barrel spending at the very time that more needed to be done to reduce the national budget deficit—a strategy that won over a number of fiscally conservative Democrats. Yet the defection of moderate Republicans and those who grew increasingly concerned about appearing obstructionist on legislation that the public favored added enough votes to a solid Democratic block to secure the bill's passage. President Clinton and the Democratic majority's support launched an unprecedented federal venture into fighting crime back home, a domain historically the province of state and local governments.

But state and local governments, on the whole, championed the federal government's initiative. State and local policy makers, along with law enforcement leaders, welcomed the sizable financial support. After all, a large share of the $30.2 billion crime bill went to state and local governments. The biggest slice, $8.8 billion, was intended for the addition of 100,000 police officers across the nation, an estimate considered highly inflated by the Republican leadership. Another $7.9 billion went to states in the form of construction grants for prisons and correctional "boot camps." The third-largest share, $6.9 billion, was to be distributed by formula to local communities in support of crime prevention programs. Smaller amounts also hit responsive chords with state and local leaders, including $1.8 billion to reimburse states for the costs of incarcerating illegal aliens convicted of felony offenses and $1.6 billion to finance the Local Partnership Act, a provision originally rejected by Congress as part of Clinton's economic stimulus package offered early in his administration.

The federal financial help was not without a catch, however. Congress, in writing the authorization, placed a five-year limit on funding, with a descending percentage of federal funds distributed over the period. That meant local governments had to absorb the difference, and ultimately the total loss of federal funds, to keep the newly initiated programs going.

The 1994 election brought an end to the Democrats' majority in Congress and put a damper on Congress's inclination to support presidential initiatives to aid state and local governments. A wave of Republican victories gave the GOP control of both congressional chambers and left Congress with a decidedly conservative cast. With such a dramatic changeover, it is not surprising that state and local leaders viewed 1994 as probably the last hurrah for new federal programs of targeted federal aid. The congressional Republican leaders, especially those in the House, seemed much more intent on devolving federal programs to the states than on adding new ones. In fact, the House GOP's "Contract with America" called for reforming welfare and ending its long-standing entitlement status (under which anyone meeting eligibility standards for welfare received benefits, regardless of the cost).

Welfare reform became a Republican-led initiative that finally prevailed in 1996, following two vetoes by President Clinton. The new program, entitled Temporary Assistance for Needy Families (TANF), lost the entitlement status accorded to the AFDC program it replaced and took the form of an appropriation-limited block grant to support state efforts aimed at moving participants from welfare dependence to work. Supporters hoped that state experimentation within the framework of federally imposed time limits on benefits would result in a continuation of declining caseloads.

The combination of President Clinton's own promise to eliminate the federal budget deficit and Republican pressure on him to follow through on that commitment took its toll on real-dollar federal aid to state and local governments. Whereas inflation-adjusted federal aid rose by a staggering 40 percent between the 1990 and 1994 fiscal years (disproportionately a product of the Bush administration/Democrat-controlled Congress), its rate of growth fell to only 8 percent between 1994 and 1998 (see Figure 9.1).

The political ingredients appeared right for Congress to continue its search for ways to devolve federal programs to the states while restraining new federal initiatives and the growth in federal aid. However, the transition from federal budget deficit to budget surplus at the end of the 1998 fiscal year gave Congress tempting fiscal flexibility to reverse its course of federal restraint. Reflecting the increasingly more rosy revenue picture, Congress raised its real-dollar federal aid spending by 11 percent in the two years preceding the 2000 election, nearly tripling the average inflation-adjusted growth rate of the prior two biennial periods.

George W. Bush and Recentralizing Federalism

After only a month in office, President George W. Bush committed his administration to a return to Reagan's New Federalism ideals. In late February 2001, Bush created a new Interagency Working Group on Federalism. He charged the group with identifying (1) federal endeavors that would be more appropriately carried out by state and local governments; (2) measures for improving federal responsiveness to state and local concerns; and (3) opportunities for flexible funding, waivers from regulatory requirements, and initiatives that promote state and local innovation and flexibility.[13]

Yet the policies his administration pursued suggested a return not to greater state discretion in federal–state relations but instead to a federal recentralization. Less than four months later, President Bush began his successful push for new federal legislation that required state education officials to test student proficiency statewide and make test results public. It also mandated that states allow students in failing schools to transfer to better performing schools. And while the No Child Left Behind legislation would increase federal aid to cover the costs of compliance, the legislation represented clear federal intervention in a traditional realm of state policy making.

The Bush administration's declared "war on terrorism" and the initiatives of the newly founded Department of Homeland Security reinforced state and local policy makers' concerns that practice might not square with the rhetoric of decentralization and local flexibility. The practical requirements of enhanced security called for increased federal leadership and coordination, especially in the areas of emergency preparedness and response, and protection of critical infrastructure. State and local officials worried that increased federal direction would come at the expense of lost state and local control, and that federal financial support would fail to compensate state and local governments for their added contribution to beefed-up homeland security.

Congress responded to the latter concern in May 2003 by appropriating $20 billion in one-time funds to the states, about half earmarked to assist states and local governments to cover costs associated with homeland defense, and the other half intended to help the states reduce their large budget deficits, occasioned significantly by rapidly rising Medicaid costs. Although President Bush originally opposed the additional federal assistance, he ultimately agreed to the increase as part of a compromise to win support for his successful tax cut legislation.

Although both the major national associations of governors and big-city mayors welcomed the federal aid for homeland security, they also noted the increased expense that states and cities have been forced to bear in improving security. The National Governors Association reports that states spent $6 billion of their own funds on homeland security in the twelve months following the September 11, 2001 terrorist attacks, and that they could be expected to bear a similar annual financial burden in the years to come. The U.S. Conference of Mayors put the cities' annual share of spending at $2.6 billion.[14]

Based on a new needs assessment conducted in 2005, the Department of Homeland Security reallocated funding among states and cities, while Congress reduced state and local grants by a modest $119 million for fiscal year 2006. Big losers under the reallocation included Washington, D.C. and New York City, the sites of the 2001 terrorist attacks, which saw their grant funding decline by 40 percent combined. Atlanta, Chicago, and Los Angeles, among other cities, experienced gains.[15]

As part of his budget recommendations for fiscal year 2009, President Bush proposed a large $1.9 billion cut (a 47 percent reduction) in federal first-responder grants to state and local governments for security, law enforcement, firefighters, and emergency medical teams responding to emergencies. Bush proposed that the savings be shifted to help fund expanded border security.[16]

The federal government's reach also extended to voting administration, a traditional prerogative of the states. Against the backdrop of controversy surrounding the administration of the 2000 presidential election, and with the support of President Bush, Congress passed the Help America Vote Act of 2002, a program that provided financial grants to the states to assist them in conforming to new federal standards governing voter registration and voting.

Yet despite these prominent examples of recentralization, Figure 9.1 illustrates that constant-dollar federal spending on grants-in-aid to state and local governments overall essentially flattened out during Bush's second term as president, after having risen substantially during his first term. In fact, you would have to go back to the Reagan years to find more restrictive federal aid.

Barack Obama and Fiscal Stimulus-Centered Federalism and Major Policy Initiative

Immediately following the 2008 presidential election, and facing the worst recession since the Great Depression, the Obama presidential transition team put together a legislative initiative intended to boost aggregate demand and, at the same time, assist states and local governments hard pressed by large and growing revenue shortfalls. That initiative, the American Recovery and Reinvestment Act—enacted in February 2009 without a single Republican vote in either congressional chamber—passed most of the $787 billion stimulus package through states and local governments between FY 2009 and FY 2011, including $87 billion earmarked for state Medicaid programs, $40 billion for local school districts and institutions of higher education, $28 billion for highways, $18 billion for mass transit and commuter rail, and $54 billion in a State Fiscal Stabilization Fund aimed at reducing the need for spending cuts and employee layoffs.[17]

Yet in spite of the transfusion of federal funding, most states still increased taxes and cut spending in their attempts to balance their budgets. Moreover, the increased federal aid represented a two-year stopgap measure, leaving state and local governments to cover shortfalls after the 2011 fiscal year. Fortunately, economic recovery helped them turn the fiscal corner, generating steady improvement in state finances. General fund spending increased by a solid 4 percent in FY 2013, and rose by 5 percent in FY 2014.[18]

In addition to stimulating demand through markedly increased federal spending destined for state and local governments to help them make fiscal ends meet in a time of lowered revenues and heightened pressure for increased spending to assist needy residents hardest hit by the Great Recession, the Obama administration advanced a major policy initiative to reform America's health care system—if its disparate parts can even be appropriately called a system. In the 2008 presidential campaign, candidate Obama laid out several principles he believed should guide health care reform. After nearly a year and a half of highly partisan debate, President Obama signed health care reform legislation into law on March 23, 2010, which passed both chambers without a single Republican vote.

The Patient Protection and Affordable Care Act (PPACA), commonly labeled Obamacare, included some highly significant departures from prior policy which largely incorporated incentives to elicit participation in the provision of health care. Prior to the passage of PPACA, participation in providing health care was largely voluntary. Employers were not required to offer health insurance to their employees; nor were individuals not covered by employer-funded health insurance or by any governmental program required to purchase health care in the private marketplace. Rather, federal policy relied on tax incentives for employers and employees to encourage them to provide and acquire health insurance. Moreover, no state is required to provide Medicaid coverage to its neediest residents, but the sheer magnitude of the burden on states to go it alone constitutes a compelling incentive to accept federal funding (which covers on average 57 percent of the costs of the Medicaid program), along with the regulatory strings that accompany it.[19]

The act adds mandates and sanctions alongside financial incentives. The legislation requires private employers with fifty or more employees to provide minimal essential coverage to their workers, or be subject to a financial penalty for noncompliance. For smaller employers it reverts to incentive over mandate, as it uses a tax credit of up to 50 percent of employee health insurance premiums to entice them to offer insurance for their employees. The legislation turns again to mandate, requiring states to uniformly expand Medicaid eligibility to households with incomes up to 133 percent of the federal poverty level or face losing Medicaid funds. This provision to broaden Medicaid coverage was subsequently struck down by the U.S. Supreme Court on June 28, 2012, in *National Federation of Independent Business v. Sebelius*.[20] Although mandated state expansion of Medicaid eligibility has been foreclosed by the Supreme Court, the PPACA still contains a financial carrot to elicit support by governors and state legislatures to expand eligibility to households with incomes up to 133 percent of the poverty levels, in the absence of a mandate. For states electing to expand coverage, the federal government will pay the full costs of that expanded coverage for three years; thereafter, the federal government's share will gradually decrease to 90 percent in 2020 and beyond. As of the end of August 2014, the legislatures in twenty-eight states had authorized expansion.

Switching back to mandate, the act requires individuals not covered by an employer or another governmental program such as Medicare or Veterans Administration care to purchase health insurance providing minimal essential coverage from private insurers, or face a financial penalty for not doing so. Low-income individuals can be eligible for financial assistance toward purchasing insurance, with funding coming from federal tax credits or vouchers financed by employers. The Supreme Court, in *National Federation of Independent Business v. Sebelius*, found the so-called individual mandate constitutional.

To facilitate individuals and employers to find suitable insurance coverage, the PPACA requires that health benefit exchanges be established to bring together insurers and individual and businesses seeking insurance coverage within the private sector, giving would-be purchasers cost and coverage options from which to choose. States have the option of creating the exchanges; if they elect not to do so, the act gives the federal government the authority to do it itself, but at state expense.

The Salience of State Aid to Local Units of Government in Intergovernmental Fiscal Relations

Local assistance consists of state payments to local units of government to meet costs that otherwise would have to be borne by the local jurisdictions. Such aid can take one of two general forms: unrestricted or restricted. Unrestricted aid can be used for any functional purpose, whereas restricted aid is provided for a specific purpose, such as education, highways, public welfare, or mass transit. On average about a third of all state expenditures go to local assistance, but there is considerable variation among the states, as Table 9.2 shows. At the high

Table 9.2   State Aid to Local Units of Government, Fiscal Year, 2008

State	State aid (in $ millions)	Percentage of state general expenditures
California	93,644	46.1
Nevada	3,860	41.4
New York	52,821	41.2
Michigan	19,513	39.2
Wyoming	1,769	38.8
Arizona	10,242	37.2
Minnesota	11,189	37.0
Wisconsin	10,088	36.0
Ohio	18,106	33.2
Colorado	6,228	32.3
North Carolina	13,196	31.6
Oregon	5,641	31.2
Kansas	4,214	30.9
Arkansas	4,392	30.6
Mississippi	5,112	30.5
Virginia	11,032	30.4
Alabama	6,721	30.3
New Mexico	4,348	30.2
Idaho	2,038	30.0
Pennsylvania	17,801	29.4
Georgia	10,415	28.8
Florida	19,703	28.5

(Continued)

Table 9.2 (Continued)

State	State aid (in $ millions)	Percentage of state general expenditures
Vermont	1,341	28.5
Texas	25,158	28.3
Indiana	7,969	28.0
Maryland	8,509	28.1
Iowa	4,143	27.9
Illinois	14,750	27.2
Washington	9,144	26.8
Tennessee	6,510	26.7
New Hampshire	1,452	25.6
Oklahoma	4,392	25.5
South Carolina	5,719	24.9
Nebraska	1,982	24.7
Montana	1,319	24.3
Missouri	5,639	23.9
Utah	3,050	23.5
New Jersey	10,928	23.3
Massachusetts	9,252	22.9
West Virginia	2,130	22.0
North Dakota	805	21.2
Connecticut	4,231	21.1
Kentucky	4,701	21.0
Louisiana	6,023	20.0
South Dakota	680	20.0
Maine	1,335	18.0
Delaware	1,172	17.9
Rhode Island	1,054	16.9
Alaska	1,488	16.3
Hawaii	138	1.4

Source: Bureau of the Census, Statistical Abstract of the United States: 2012, Table 454.

end of the scale are California (46.1 percent), Nevada (41.4 percent), New York (41.2 percent), Michigan (39.2 percent), and Wyoming (38.8 percent). At the bottom are Hawaii (1.4 percent), Alaska (16.3 percent), Rhode Island (16.9 percent), Delaware (17.9 percent), and Maine (18.0 percent). Overall, state aid funds about one-third of local government general expenditures, on average.

From their size alone, one would expect local assistance budget items to command notable attention in the state budgetary process, but even so their political significance frequently transcends their size. Local assistance budget items not only provide funds to support politically salient programs, but also provide property tax relief—a perennial plank in campaigns for governor and the legislature.

The local assistance portion of the budget is typically of particular interest to the legislature, since each legislator represents at least one municipality, one county, and one school district. Moreover, local assistance items, along with tax policy, tend to be the bread and butter of legislators' informed and politically active constituents. With today's computer modeling of local assistance formulas, legislators can readily discern how changes in local assistance policy and funding affect their districts. This "politics of printouts" can forge bipartisan coalitions of "winners" and "losers," brought together by the ways in which their districts fare.

Summary and Conclusions

State governments operate within a federal system. The U.S. Constitution allocates power between the federal government and the states, enumerating the expressed powers of each and providing a framework within which the national government and the states can exercise powers that are not expressly granted to them by the Constitution. That framework most importantly includes the Tenth Amendment to the Constitution, along with key provisions in Article 1. The Tenth Amendment provides that "any powers not explicitly delegated to the United States by the Constitution, nor prohibited by it to the states, are reserved to the states respectively." However, Article 1 gives Congress the authority to "make all laws which shall be necessary and proper for carrying into execution the foregoing (enumerated) powers," enabling the federal government to interpret what constitutes necessary and proper federal initiatives.

Article 1 further gives the federal government the authority to "provide for the common defense and general welfare," giving it an even broader legal basis for national policy leadership. This tension between the Tenth Amendment and the provisions in Article 1 has underlain a raft of litigation which has found its way to the U.S. Supreme Court for resolution. The Constitution makes no reference to local units of government. They are legal creatures of the states. State constitutions and statutory law govern their creation and operations, including their ability to levy taxes and receive financial assistance from the federal government and the states. This aid becomes an important element of public budgeting: not only augmenting state and local resources, but serving as a significant vehicle charting policy direction.

Federal–state relations have taken a number of turns since the Constitution's ratification in 1788, but the overall direction has been toward increased intervention by the federal partner in the affairs of the states. In recent history, it was the federal initiatives of President Lyndon Johnson's Great Society program that thrust the national government to the forefront of policy leadership. Newly created federal grants-in-aid articulated national policy goals and frequently used federal financial aid as a fiscal carrot to elicit state participation in, and matching state funds in support of, federal policy initiatives. During the Johnson administration alone, Congress created 209 new federal grants-in-aid, most notably including Medicaid, which provides health care insurance for the needy.

Presidential administrations and Congresses in the years following the Johnson administration continued support of the Great Society programs, and significantly increased their funding, as well. They also added 134 new grants-in-aid between 1969 and 1980, spanning the presidential administrations of Richard Nixon, Gerald Ford, and Jimmy Carter. As a result, federal grants-in-aid rose as a percentage of state and local expenditures, and state and local governments became even more financially dependent on the federal partner. But that would change with President Ronald Reagan's administration.

For President Reagan, the reach of the federal government via its many grants-in-aid had gotten out of hand. From Reagan's perspective, not only had the cost of federal aid grown inordinately high, but the federal government had initiated domestic programs that should best be left to the states. In response, the Reagan administration sought to cut funding to state and local governments and reduce the number of grants-in-aid, and it had success in both areas. In contrast to annual constant-dollar increases averaging over 8 percent between 1960 and 1980, federal aid decreased by 1.4 percent annually in constant dollars between 1980 and 1988, and by over 10 percent during the first two years of the Reagan presidency. That downward course was subsequently reversed during the presidency of George H.W. Bush, as federal aid once again rose as a percentage of state and local spending.

The near-$300 billion federal budget deficit inherited by the Clinton administration in 1993 greatly constrained its ability to continue increases in federal aid, even though, as a former governor, President Clinton was on the receiving end of federal retrenchment during the Reagan years and empathized with the plight of the states. Yet in spite of fiscal constraints, President Clinton led the Democrat-controlled Congress to pass an omnibus crime bill just prior to the 1994 elections, with most of the $30.2 billion package aiding state and local governments' crime-fighting efforts. Most politically popular in the election year was the president's assurance that the legislation would put another 100,000 police officers on the streets.

In the aftermath of the 9/11 terrorist attacks, President George W. Bush's federal aid policy centered on grants to state and local governments to support their efforts in the war on terror. Although Congress appropriated $10 billion of one-time funds in 2003 for state and local governments for improvements in homeland security, local government officials worried about how much enhanced protection would cost state and local treasuries.

Bush's successor, President Barack Obama, found the ante of federal aid raised to new heights. In the throes of the Great Recession, significantly increased federal aid assisted state and local governments facing both mounting claims for recession-sensitive services and spending cuts, while it also contributed to macroeconomic policy aimed at shoring up aggregate demand. Included in the American Recovery and Reinvestment Act, enacted in just the second month of the new Obama administration, was $87 billion for state Medicaid programs, $40 billion for local school districts and institutions of higher education, $28 billion for highways, and $18 billion for mass transit and commuter rail, as well as $54 billion in a Fiscal Stabilization Fund intended to minimize required budget cuts and resulting employee layoffs.

Beyond fighting the effects of the recession, the centerpiece of President Obama's domestic legislative agenda has been health care reform—reform that would have major implications for the states. Congress, without a single Republican vote, passed the Patient Protection and Affordable Care Act on March 23, 2010. Of great interest to state policy makers, the legislation required the states to expand Medicaid eligibility to households with incomes up to 133 percent of the federal poverty level, or face losing Medicaid funds. However, the U.S. Supreme Court subsequently struck down that mandate. Left in place was a substantial financial carrot for states to expand coverage in the absence of a federal mandate. For states electing to expand coverage, the federal government would pay the full costs of that expanded coverage for three years; thereafter, the federal share would gradually decrease to 90 percent in 2020 and beyond.

Just as the federal government financially aids the states, the states financially assist local units of government. The major areas of support include education, revenue sharing, highways, mass transit, and public welfare. On average, about one-third of state expenditures go to local assistance, though the percentage varies considerably among the states. At the high end can be found large states such as California (46.1 percent), New York (41.2 percent), and Michigan (39.2 percent). At the low end are Hawaii, with only 1.4 percent of its expenditures going to local units of government, followed by Alaska (16.3 percent), Rhode Island (16.9 percent), and Delaware (17.9 percent).

Local assistance budget items not only constitute a significant share of state spending; they tend to be among the most politically sensitive parts of state budgets. In providing property tax relief, they also affect programs closest to legislators' constituencies, the most important politically being the teachers whose salaries and benefits are funded in large part by state aid to local governments.

Notes

1 The term "cooperative federalism" was coined by Deil S. Wright in his 1974 article "Intergovernmental Relations: An Analytical Overview," which appeared in the Annals of the American Academy of Political and Social Science 416 (November 1974): 1–16. Thomas R. Dye used the term "centralized federalism" to describe the relationship between the federal government and the states that emerged from the Great Society years; see Dye, Politics in States and Communities, 8th ed. (Englewood Cliffs, N.J.: Prentice Hall, 1988), 70–2.
2 Jeffrey R. Henig, Public Policy and Federalism (New York: St. Martin's, 1985), 16.
3 Charles A. Bowsher, "Federal Cutbacks Strengthen State Role," State Government News, February 1986, 18.
4 Henig, Public Policy and Federalism, 16.
5 Bowsher, "Federal Cutbacks Strengthen State Role," 18.
6 Ronald Reagan, State of the Union Address, January 1982.

7 Significant Features of Fiscal Federalism, vol. 2 (Washington, D.C.: Advisory Council on Intergovernmental Relations, 1990), 42.
8 David B. Walker et al., "The First Ten Months: Grant-in-Aid, Regulatory, and Other Changes," Intergovernmental Perspective 8, no. 1 (winter 1982): 5.
9 George E. Peterson, "Federalism and the States: An Experiment in Decentralization," in Reagan Record, ed. John L. Palmer and Isabel V. Sawhill (Cambridge, M.A.: Ballinger, 1984), 224–6.
10 Carol E. Cohen, "1984 State Tax Wealth: Preview of the RTS Estimates," Intergovernmental Perspective 12, no. 3 (summer 1986): 25.
11 Bruce D. McDowell, "Grant Reform Reconsidered," Intergovernmental Perspective 17, no. 3 (summer 1991): 8–11.
12 David C. Saffell and Harry Basehart, Governing States and Cities (New York: McGraw-Hill, 1979), 46.
13 Ruben Barrales, "Federalism in the Bush Administration," Spectrum (summer 2001): 5–6.
14 The National Strategy for Homeland Security (Washington, D.C.: The White House, 2003), 64–5.
15 Dan Eggen and Mary Beth Sheridan, "Anti-Terror Funding Cut in D.C. and New York," The Washington Post, June 1, 2006, A1.
16 Spencer S. Hsu, "Local Security Grants Cut by Nearly Half," The Washington Post, February 5, 2008, A13.
17 Furhana Hossain et al., "The Stimulus Plan: How to Spend $787 Billion," New York Times, April 7, 2009, http://projects.nytimes.com/44th_president/stimulus
18 National Association of State Budget Officers, The fiscal Survey of States, Spring 2014 (Washington, D.C.: National Association of State Budget Officers).
19 See Donald F. Kettl, "Medicaid, Incentives and the Future of Federalism," Governing, February 2011, www.governing.com/templates/gov_print_article?id=114582659
20 National Federation of Independent Business v. Sebelius, 567 U.S. (2012), 132 S. Ct 2566.

Chapter 10

Budget Execution and Financial Management

Discussions of the routines and politics of the budgetary process are frequently restricted to budget making—the process whereby budget proposals are advanced, reviewed, and ultimately passed. The budgetary process and its politics, however, do not come to an end with legislative passage of the **budget bill** or bills. Budgetary politics simply move to a different arena—budget execution—and take on changed forms.

Even making the distinction between budget making and budget execution draws too specific a dividing line, for budgets can continue to be "made" during the post-appropriation phase of the process. The budget that has been executed at the end of a fiscal year is almost never identical to the plan enacted at the outset.

Several developments can alter the composition of a budget. During the course of the fiscal year, the legislative body (the U.S. Congress, a state legislature, a city council, or a county board, but referred to hereafter by the generic term "legislature") can pass legislation that supplements the budget, cuts it, or reallocates funds from one agency to another or from one program or account to another within the same agency. Similarly, the executive budget office can permit agencies to transfer funds under restrictions set by the legislature. In addition, under certain conditions, the chief executive or the top budget official (acting on the executive's behalf) can refuse to permit appropriated funds to be spent. Such a situation might occur, for example, when expenditures are expected to exceed appropriation levels for non-entitlement programs.

Midyear changes in the budget may be required when revenues fall short of projections or when expenditures rise at a faster rate than expected, necessitating expenditure cutbacks not anticipated at the time of budget approval. In a worst-case scenario, both can occur simultaneously. Unexpected downturns in the economy, such as those occasioned by recession, can push revenues well below projected levels while simultaneously increasing pressure on expenditures, creating greater demand for economically sensitive government services and financial assistance, most notably public assistance programs such as Temporary Assistance for Needy Families, food stamps, Medicaid, and general assistance. Heightened inflation can also drive the cost of government services and procurements upward. Other external forces (mandates levied by higher levels of government, court rulings, and wage settlements imposed by arbitration) may require governments to make budget adjustments.

Because the budget is subject to change throughout the course of the year, the process of budget execution must accommodate and keep track of changes; it also must ensure that the budget is executed in accordance with the legislature's intent in passing it in the first place. The budget originally passed is a plan of action, containing the authorization to spend public money in specified amounts for identified public purposes. Therefore, to permit that plan to be carved out as closely as intended, its implementation must be controlled and any departures must be explicitly approved.

Budget control becomes the task of those vested with the authority to oversee budget execution, who are charged with ensuring that spending does not exceed authorized levels, that it occurs for approved purposes, and that it remains consistent with legislative intent. Ultimately such authority resides with the legislature, but the legislature frequently delegates some of it to the executive branch.

Budgetary accounting provides the information necessary for the exercise of budget control. Accounting systems accumulate and organize data about revenues, obligations, and expenditures so that they can be used by agency officials, budget officers, legislative staffs, and others to monitor execution of the legislatively approved budget.

Periodic revenue and expenditure reports give agency administrators important information that they can use in making management decisions throughout the fiscal year. Similarly, these reports provide central budget officers and legislators and their staffs with the information they need to make judgments about requests for funding transfers and supplementary appropriations. In both cases, officials need to know how much has been committed from an appropriation for a given program within a specific organizational unit.

Ideally, government officials and budget participants are in the best position to make financial management decisions when they have both current revenue and expenditure information and comparable information for prior years. Comparable time-series information allows managers and reviewers to identify patterns and analyze trends, and that ability facilitates sound projections.

This chapter deals with the "how and why" of budget execution, highlighting similarities and differences among the various levels of government. It covers the institutional actors involved in budget execution—their respective roles, authority, and patterns of interaction; the tools they use to control budget execution; and the problems they characteristically face in the process.

Budgetary Control through the Appropriations and Allotment Processes

Appropriations and direct spending authorizations (the latter usually found in entitlement legislation) give government agencies the authority to spend funds up to prescribed levels. For most governments in the United States, with the exception of local governments with weak executives, those funds are not available for spending until they have been allotted. At the national level, the Office of Management and Budget (OMB) apportions appropriations, usually on a quarterly basis, to prevent agencies from spending at a rate that would exhaust their spending authority before the end of a fiscal year. It makes a single apportionment for each appropriation or fund account; it does not break out spending authority by program or organizational unit within an agency. That responsibility is delegated to the agency, which initiates **allotments** that divide spending authority among the agency's various programs and units, such as divisions, bureaus, and field units. As might be expected, the total amount allotted may not exceed the amount apportioned.

At the state level, instead of the executive budget office first apportioning appropriations and then delegating the initiation of allotments to the live agency, state budget offices initiate allotments directly. The allotments themselves apportion spending authority for agencies—by program and organizational unit. Allotments at the state level and in most local governments can cover an entire fiscal year or be broken down into quarters or even months. Allotments can cover initial apportionment, following passage of appropriations, or they can be adjusted during the course of the fiscal year as changed circumstances require reapportionment. Most states employ allotments; those that do not include Alaska, Delaware, Illinois, Kansas, North Dakota, South Dakota, Texas, Vermont, and Wyoming.[1]

The allotment process in the states is managed by the central budget agency in conformance with statutory law, administrative rules and regulations, and procedural instructions issued under legal authority. The central budget office organizes the process that governs allotment preparation, review, and approval. It prescribes the responsibilities of the agencies and the manner in which those responsibilities are to be exercised.

Through allotments, particularly quarterly or monthly allotments, central budget offices can control spending. Agencies are limited in how much they can spend within each allotment period. This restriction ensures not only that agencies do not spend more than their allotted authority by year's end, but also that they cannot spend funds freely during the last few months of the fiscal year in order to avoid the lapse of unspent funds back into the treasury. Subannual allotments, particularly monthly allotments, can also be used to slow down or speed up government spending. National government policy might call for slower spending when there is a growing revenue shortfall, whereas it might encourage accelerated spending as an instrument of fiscal policy in recessionary times.

Using Allotments to Impound Funding

The allotment process can be used to impound funding—to prevent appropriated funds from being spent. The central budget office, acting on behalf of the chief executive, can impound, in whole or in part, the funding for an appropriation, a single program financed by that appropriation, a particular object of expenditure, or any other level included in the approved budget. Impoundments are most commonly employed selectively to reduce the amount of funding available rather than to prevent it from being spent altogether. As an example of the former, a governor might insist that executive branch agencies reduce spending on supplies and travel by 20 percent in tough economic times. Reducing agency allotments for the supply and travel lines renders those funds unavailable for expenditures. If the economic situation facing the state improves in midyear, the state budget office can then supplement the allotments.

Funds can be impounded at any level of government where allotments are used, but impoundment is employed most often at the federal level, less at the state level, and seldom at the local level. Its use has been most controversial at the national level.

Although presidents since Thomas Jefferson have impounded funds, no president made more liberal use of impoundments than did Richard Nixon.[2] Not only did the Nixon administration impound funds broadly, but also it used the impoundment authority as a policy tool to shift congressional priorities. Congress believed that the Nixon administration was trying to "snatch victory from defeat" by using impoundment to starve programs approved by Congress that were opposed by the president during the budget-making process.

During 1973, the OMB impounded more than $18 billion in federal aid to state and local governments including appropriations slated for water pollution control, public transportation, housing, education, rural development, and other domestic programs, to lever Congress into approving special revenue-sharing and block grants.[3] In response, state and local governments initiated more than a hundred lawsuits in federal courts challenging the legality of the impoundments. Some sixty cases were decided, and a sizable majority of them went against the Nixon administration.[4]

This liberal use of impoundments was based on the authority given the president in the Employment Act of 1946 and the Anti-Deficiency Act of 1950. The former gave the president responsibility for economic policy, and the Nixon administration argued that this responsibility included the authority to limit expenditures in a manner consistent with national economic objectives. The latter allowed the president to establish agency reserve accounts by using the allotment process.[5]

In response to Nixon's use of impoundments, as well as his use of reprogramming (discussed later in this chapter), Congress acted in 1974 to restrict the president's use of impoundment. Under the Congressional Budget and Impoundment and Control Act of 1974, the president, or the OMB staff acting as his agent, cannot refuse to release appropriated funds unless Congress approves the proposed **rescission** within forty-five working days. In addition, the legislation prohibited the president or the OMB from deferring spending from one fiscal year to the next if either chamber of Congress objected by passing a resolution.

In 1987, the U.S. Court of Appeals for the District of Columbia ruled against the continued use of deferrals. The court reasoned that since an earlier Supreme Court decision (*Chadha*, 1983) barred the use of the legislative veto, wherein either the U.S. House of Representatives or the U.S. Senate could nullify regulations, contracts, grants, and other executive proposals without passing legislation subject to the presidential veto, similar logic applied to deferrals. The court reasoned that Congress would not have given the president deferral power without itself having the ability to retain legislative veto power.[6] Subsequently, the comptroller general of the United States advised Congress that twenty-five "policy deferrals" submitted by President Ronald Reagan were illegal. The Reagan administration chose not to appeal the decision to the U.S. Supreme Court. Now all deferrals, like decisions, must be submitted to Congress for approval.

Of recent presidents, Reagan made the most use of rescission authority (see Table 10.1). During his two terms he proposed 602 separate rescissions, amounting to $43.4 billion. Congress approved 214 rescissions, totaling $15.7 billion. Interestingly, Congress approved nearly $10.9 billion worth of rescissions during Reagan's first year as president, reflecting the "honeymoon" atmosphere pervading presidential–congressional relations following his landslide electoral victory. During Reagan's second term, however, Congress approved only five of 162 requests, totaling just $181 million. Reagan's successor, President George H. W. Bush, fared somewhat better than Reagan did in his second term; yet Congress approved only 20 percent of his 169 proposals, cutting anticipated spending by $2.4 billion.

President Bill Clinton, a Democrat, had greater success in getting his proposals approved by Congress than did his Republican predecessors. During his first twenty-one months in office, working with a Democrat majority in Congress, he proposed seventy-five rescissions, totaling $3.5 billion. Congress approved nearly two-thirds of them, amounting to almost $1.5 billion. President Clinton then faced a Republican-controlled Congress during most of the following fiscal year, 1994–95. Working in an environment shaped by the congressional Republicans' calls for budget cuts, consistent with the House GOP's "Contract with America," President Clinton's proposed rescissions experienced an even higher success rate. Of the twenty-eight proposed rescissions in fiscal year 1995, Congress approved twenty-four of them (86 percent), cutting spending by $846 million—a reduced amount, however, from the preceding fiscal year. The Republican majority in Congress was busy preparing to launch its own budget-cutting initiative, as it worked to develop its deficit-reducing budget resolution for the coming 1995–6 fiscal year. The rescissions considered for 1994–5 were dwarfed in comparison to the magnitude of budget cuts offered by Congress for 1995–6.

Table 10.1   Rescissions Proposed and Enacted, by President, Fiscal Years, 1974–2008

President	Year	Proposed rescissions	Proposed ($millions)	Approved by Congress	Rescinded ($millions)
Ford	1974	2	496	0	0
	1975	87	2,722	38	386
	1976	50	3,582	7	148
	1977	13	1,135	7	718
Carter	1977	7	792	2	96
	1978	12	1,290	5	519
	1979	11	909	9	724
	1980	59	1,618	34	77
	1981*	33	1,142	0	0
Reagan	1981	133	15,362	101	10,881
	1982	32	7,907	5	4,365
	1983	21	1,569	0	0
	1984	9	636	3	55
	1985	245	1,856	98	174
	1986	83	10,127	4	143
	1987	73	5,836	2	36
	1988	0	0	0	0
	1989	6	143	1	
Bush	1989	0	0	0	0
	1990	11	554	0	0
	1991	30	4,859	8	286
	1992	128	7,880	26	2,068
	1993	0	0	0	0
Clinton	1993	7	356	4	206
	1994	65	3,172	45	1,278
	1995	28	1,200	24	846
	1996	24	1,426	8	963
	1997	10	407	7	347
	1998	25	25	21	17
	1999	3	35	2	17
	2000	3	128	0	0
Bush	2001–2008	0	0	0	0

Note: *The 33 rescissions proposed by President Carter for fiscal year 1981, which were converted by the Reagan administration.

Sources: Allen Schick, The Federal Budget: Politics, Policy, Process (Washington, D.C.: Brookings Institution Press, 1995), 178; data for 1994–2008 provided by the Office of Management and Budget.

The transition from budget deficit to budget surplus provided a changed environment that dampened enthusiasm for rescissions. President Clinton proposed thirty-one rescissions, totaling only $188 million, during his last three years in office. Congress approved twenty-three of them. President George W. Bush sent no revisions to Congress during his two terms of office.

Governors can also impound approved spending, but most states restrict a governor's ability to withhold funds after the budget has been signed into law.

Twelve states place no restrictions on the governor's authority to cut spending during the fiscal year; ten states require that the governor reduce spending across the board rather than on the basis of selective gubernatorial priorities; seven states place limits on the percentage by which an appropriation of funds can be reduced by gubernatorial action; twelve states require the governor to consult with the legislature before apportioning allotment reductions; and the remainder require the legislature to approve any midyear spending reductions.[7] In all cases, upon approval of cuts to the enacted budget, the state budget office processes revised allotments that reflect the lower levels of spending authority. The principal tool for executive budget reductions, however, is not impoundment but the gubernatorial item-veto, which is exercised before the budget becomes law.

The central budget office can also use the allotment process to set funds aside for contingencies and emergencies, a practice often followed in making subagency allotments. Contingency accounts can be open-ended or earmarked. As an illustration of the latter, funds required to match a federal grant may be placed in unallotted reserve pending its receipt. If the grant materializes, the matching funds can be released; if it does not, the funds remain unallotted, and the state or local agency is unable to spend them for any other purpose.

Midyear Adjustments

After initial allotments are approved and agencies begin executing their spending plans, they may want to alter those plans in response to changing circumstances. Several factors can prompt agencies to seek adjustments. They may reach midyear faced with imbalances between available funding and need. For instance, the projected level of client growth in one program area may not materialize, while in another it exceeds expected levels. The agency accordingly may project that the former program area is unlikely to use its allotted funding while the latter is likely to exhaust its authority. Faced with these developments, agency officials may request that expenditure authority be shifted from the former program area to the latter.

In another instance, the prices of supplies and capital may increase greatly because of unexpectedly high inflation, rendering the allotted amounts for those categories insufficient to meet costs. In response, agencies might delay filling positions vacated through normal turnover and use the resulting salary savings to cover the higher costs of supplies and capital. In both instances, however, agencies typically lack the authority to take action on their own; external approval is required.

Depending on the jurisdiction involved, that approval can come from within the executive branch or the legislative. Where the executive is empowered to approve funding shifts, the central budget office acts as its agent. Where legislative action is required, some jurisdictions require that the full legislature approve the change; in others, that authority can be delegated to the appropriations or budget committee.

At the national level, the OMB has great flexibility to approve the movement of funds between objects of expenditure (such as salaries, travel, supplies, contracts, and capital) or between activities within the same program in an agency's budget (for example between special operations forces and airlift and sealift within the Department of Defense). Other requests that involve shifts of funds between programs within the same appropriation or between appropriations require congressional concurrence.

Reprogramming is the term used to describe the shifting of funds between programs within the same appropriation or fund account. **Budget transfers** refer to shifts of funds from one appropriation or fund account to another. Both require congressional approval if the requested shift exceeds thresholds specified in enabling legislation or the appropriations acts themselves. If the amounts requested for reprogramming or transfer do not reach the thresholds, the requested actions can be approved by the OMB through the allotment process. For transfers, however, agencies usually seek the prior approval of the appropriations subcommittee having oversight over them before allotment adjustments are sent to the OMB.[8]

When thresholds would be exceeded by a requested transfer, or when no threshold provision is included in enabling legislation or the appropriations act, agencies must obtain the approval of the appropriations subcommittee. Requests are usually made in writing, and the subcommittee responds in writing as well. Staff members handle the correspondence, review the requests, take action on behalf of the subcommittee on routine requests, and recommend action to the chair on matters of greater significance. Congressional approval triggers the agency to initiate allotment adjustments, which the OMB then processes as a matter of course.

At the state level, the authority of central budget offices to approve budget transfers after budget passage varies among the states, but several patterns emerge. Fourteen states restrict to the legislature the authority to approve transfers of appropriations between state agencies; eighteen states do not allow these midyear transfers at all; thirteen states allow the governor or the state budget office, acting on the governor's behalf, to make them; and the remaining states require the joint approval of the governor (or executive budget agency as a proxy for the governor) and legislature. State budget offices are given greater freedom to approve transfers of funds from one program or unit to another within the same agency, and they possess that authority in twenty-six states.[9]

When the focus turns to midyear transfers between objects of expenditure (for example from salaries to supplies), limitations are less pronounced. Thirty-two states allow agencies to make such transfers at their own discretion. Another ten require the state budget office's approval. The other states require either the governor's or the legislature's approval.[10]

With the exception of transfers between object classes, mayors and county executives have much less flexibility than governors to transfer funds after the budget has been enacted. They can recommend that their legislative bodies tap carry-forward balances when revenues fall short of expenditures, or they can recommend supplemental appropriations when revenues appear adequate to finance the increased spending. They can also delay capital projects or equipment purchases when revenue shortfalls appear imminent. A state's fiscal environment can deteriorate to the point that budget transfers become inadequate to bring the budget into balance. A deep recession can reduce revenues well below projected levels, as well as push up recession-sensitive spending. The resulting expected gap between revenues and expenditures might then only be closed by the infusion of new revenues from tax or fee increases and/or by major cuts in authorized spending. Legislatures called into special session can enact changes to the approved budget, including revenue increases.

Budget implementation is not only affected by midyear budget adjustments, but also can be shaped by conditions placed on budget execution that are written into the appropriations acts themselves. Legislatures at all levels of government can set standards and conditions on the use of appropriated funds, proscribing their use for specified purposes; they can require prior legislative approval before funds can be shifted; and they can order that certain information be provided to the legislative branch before funding can continue.

Legislative intent is established clearly when it is spelled out in the statutes or in an appropriations bill or accompanying statements. Its status can be less clear when it takes other forms. When the chairperson of an appropriations committee or subcommittee expresses strong sentiments that funds be used in a certain way, even though such an expression fails to make it into the appropriations bill or a record of the committee's official action, the question of intent can become murky. Agency heads know that they must treat such counsel seriously because it is most likely that the agency will come before the same chairperson during the next budget cycle, and its fortunes could be jeopardized if its officials cannot show that they have honored the chair's wishes.

The following hypothetical case illustrates the political sensitivity involved in making decisions based on interpretations of legislative intent. Assume that during annual budget deliberations the legislature reduced the governor's recommendation for corrections and specified that all reductions should come out of the adult institutions program (a subprogram that shares the general program operations appropriation for all of corrections, along with the other subprograms, including juvenile institutions, parole supervision, and general administration). In addition, documents prepared by the legislative staff noted that the assembly speaker strongly urged that no funds for parole supervision be cut, a position supported by the assembly and later concurred with by the senate. Halfway through the fiscal year, agency administrators project that funds for adult institutions will be inadequate during the last two months of the fiscal year because an unexpected increase in prisoners necessitated scheduling considerable overtime to provide adequate supervision. At the same time, they disclose that an amount of funding roughly corresponding to what they need is likely to become available from funds for parole supervision because fewer inmates than expected have received parole, increasing the average length of stay and swelling the inmate population. Except for parole supervision, expenditures for all other correctional services programs are in line with the original budget plans. The agency is thus faced with the decision whether to request that funds be transferred from parole supervision or to ask for a supplemental appropriation (assuming that corrections officials are unwilling to accept a reduced standard of prison security).

If it selects the former alternative, the state budget office can legally approve the requested allotment adjustment, but in so doing it will almost certainly incur the wrath of the legislature—especially that of the speaker. Moreover, if the budget or appropriations committee has the discretion to review executive-approved reallocations in this state, the committee may reverse the action. Conversely, the committee could approve the transfer, and thereby modify the intent expressed by the full legislature—an action that could rankle legislative leaders and challenge internal protocols. Thus, before acting, the committee chairperson would probably want to consult key legislative leaders.

This example shows that legislative intent is subject to interpretation, and that interpretation is often grounded in politics.

Post-Allotment Budgetary Control and Financial Management

After the central budget office issues the initial allotments, agency managers can then commit the approved funding for allowable purposes, but they still cannot do so without controls. If agencies can overspend appropriations and move funding among budget categories at will, the chief executive and the legislature would have no assurance that the budget would be implemented as approved. Therefore, in addition to controls placed on budget adjustments made during the fiscal year, other controls are designed to ensure that the actual expenditure of funds is consistent with the approved budget and accompanying allotments. These controls are exercised both before and after budgeted funds have been spent.

Preaudit Controls

Even after agencies have received their approved allotments, their spending choices are subject to scrutiny. Proposed expenditures are compared to appropriation authority and to the amounts allotted to ensure that funds are committed for authorized purposes and that sufficient amounts are available to cover them. If the proposed expenditures meet these tests, checks are issued or funds are transferred, and encumbrances are entered into the agency's books to reflect the lower amounts available for subsequent commitment.

Supervision of the preaudit function is normally a responsibility of the executive branch, but it usually resides outside the central budget office. Although that office develops the executive budget and approves certain types of allotment adjustments, the preaudit function is usually carried out by the agencies themselves or by a central accounting office.

At the federal level, agencies exercise the preaudit function under guidelines promulgated by the OMB, and the OMB judges whether these **preaudit controls** comply with those guidelines. At the state and local level, supervision of the preaudit function is usually exercised by a bureau or office of financial operations, often attached to an executive department of administration (which may also house the state budget office when it is not located within the governor's office).

In a few states, elected comptrollers or auditors have responsibility for preaudit, alone or as an independent check on the administration. The rationale underlying the latter arrangement is that electoral independence might better situate the auditor to protect the public purse, free from the direct authority of the governor or a gubernatorial appointee.

In practice, however, a state or larger local government typically delegates the preaudit function to the larger and administratively sophisticated line agencies. The central audit authority then conducts selective reviews of how that authority has been used, and, if deficiencies are found, it can revoke the delegation.

Postaudit Controls

After the close of the fiscal year, another set of financial audits is conducted. This time the view taken is retrospective, as auditors try to assess the extent to which budgeted funds were committed in a manner consistent with appropriations authority and legislative intent and to ensure that the associated transactions were reflected fully and accurately in the accounting system. This focus requires a review of the financial transactions completed in the past fiscal year. Since an audit of all transactions would be impossible for an average-size audit operation to conduct, postauditors rely on samples. Auditors select their samples on the basis of a number of factors, including a program's cost, proportional relationships that appear out of line, "red flags" identified by computerized reviews, and allegations of impropriety.

The administrative responsibility for **postaudits** at the federal level resides with the Government Accountability Office (GAO), an arm of Congress. At the state level, postaudits can be the responsibility of either the executive branch or the legislative. Legislative auditors conduct over half of the postaudits done in the states.[11] For local governments, postaudits are commonly conducted by executive branch personnel, whether they are organizationally located in the chief executive's office or in a separate department responsible to the chief executive.

In addition to traditional financial auditing, audit shops at all levels of government have increasingly turned to so-called **performance auditing**. Instead of focusing on actual expenditures and the adequacy of financial control procedures, performance auditing looks at how well government programs are accomplishing their goals and objectives. It attempts to answer such questions as the following: Are programs accomplishing what agency representatives claimed they would? Are they being implemented and operated efficiently? Is the legislature that appropriated the funding getting its money's worth?

Following this line of inquiry, performance auditing has largely become the domain of the legislative branch. Of the thirty-one offices conducting performance audits in the states, twenty-six (84 percent) are attached to state legislatures.[12] At the national level, performance auditing has grown to rival financial auditing as the mainstay of GAO activities.[13]

Performance auditing has become still another tool of the legislature in its competition with the executive over state policy making. Although the executive branch disproportionately shapes budget execution during the fiscal year, the legislative branch increasingly assesses whether the promised "goods" have been delivered, and with what degree of efficiency. The results of performance audits are made available to agency officials, chief executives, legislative leaders, and staffs, at which point they can influence budgetary choices in the next budget-making cycle. With the completion of postaudits, a given budget cycle is brought to a close.

Cash Management

Revenue collections and expenditures do not coincide during the course of the fiscal year. In managing fiscal resources, financial administrators of the executive branch must ensure that cash is available to pay government bills when they come due. At the same time, they do not want to have more cash on hand than they need to meet known obligations, because cash accounts yield lower rates of return than do less liquid investments. Occasionally the dates for major expenditures are known in advance and government finance managers can plan for them accordingly, moving funds out of higher-yield accounts and into cash accounts for payment. This is most common among the states, where the statutes frequently specify payment dates for state aid to local units of government. The goal of a state, city, or county investment manager is then to increase yields to the maximum extent possible, at minimum risk, while ensuring that enough cash is readily available to meet obligations. In contrast, the choice is easier at the national level: federal law requires that receipts be invested in U.S. Treasury securities.

Pursuing the flexibility they have, state and local government financial officers invest their funds in a range of instruments, including federal securities, private corporate stocks and bonds, money market accounts, fixed-term savings certificates, and regular savings accounts. Smaller local governments tend to be fairly conservative in their investment strategies, often depositing their funds in savings certificates and on-demand savings accounts in their community banks. States and the larger local governments are generally more diversified, including stocks and bonds in their portfolios. Yet as states and local governments search for greater diversification and higher yields, some observers worry that investment officials will assume undue risks.

Orange County, California provides a case of one large local government that went after yield over security with disastrous results. Using borrowed money to invest in high-yielding but low-rated bonds and derivatives—instruments that are essentially bets on what future interest rates will be—the Orange County Treasurer lost a staggering $1.7 billion during a short period of time in 1994. The loss not only caused Orange County to declare bankruptcy and default on its bonds, but also hit hard the 187 localities and government agencies that were part of the Orange County-managed consolidated investment pool.

The Orange County debacle caught the attention of local government officials throughout the nation. They were quick to reassess the soundness of their own governments' investment policies and practices. As a result, they are likely to tip the balance between risk and security a little more in favor of secure investments.

In addition to making sound investments, yield can be increased by speeding up the collection and depositing of tax and other revenues while slowing down cash outflows. If government payments are too slow in coming, however, private vendors, clients, individual recipients, and other units of government can be quick to voice their displeasure in the political arena. In response to mounting pressure, both Congress and several state legislatures have passed laws requiring that government agencies pay penalties to private enterprises if payments are not received after a specified number of days.

Yields can also be increased by pooling investment resources. Many states and some counties (such as the Orange County case cited) manage investment pools that allow local governments to combine their resources to obtain higher interest rates. In the words of one close observer, investment pools have become the "public sector version of money market funds."[14] Their growing popularity, while having increased the rate of return for government, has diverted funds that otherwise might have been deposited in local banks or used to purchase federal securities.

Besides securing high yields consistent with safety and adequate liquidity, financial managers also want to ensure that payments are deposited as quickly as possible, maximizing interest earned. Toward that end, the federal government, most states, and an increasing number of local governments have turned to the use of lockbox deposits. Using this mechanism, those who owe the government money remit their payments not to a government office but directly to the government's bank account. There, bank employees, for a negotiated fee, open the envelopes, deposit the enclosed checks, and enter the payment data.

Only after the funds have been deposited do bank employees send the encoded records to the appropriate government agencies for posting. This method eliminates the time traditionally required for agencies to handle records and forward remittances to the central finance office, and for that office in turn to transmit the checks to the government's bank account.

Capital Finance and Debt Management

Unlike the states and most local governments, the federal government has no separate capital budget. Congress finances capital expenditures by current revenues through annual appropriations. Federal borrowing, for the most part, is unrelated to capital spending. Borrowing provides resources necessary to finance the national deficit.

States and most local governments do not rely on current revenues to pay for their capital projects. Such projects—for example the construction of public university and school buildings, prisons, or mental health institutes—are usually financed from bond revenues. Bond purchasers, in effect, lend states and local governments the funds necessary to finance construction. Governments, in turn, pledge to pay the bondholders the principal of the loan plus a stipulated rate of return.

State and local governments commonly offer two kinds of bonds: **general obligation bonds** and **revenue bonds**. General obligation bonds have the "full faith and credit" of the general treasury behind the promise that bondholders will be repaid. Not only do the issuers of these bonds commit general-purpose revenues to retire their indebtedness, but they also promise that bondholders will have "first claim" to available revenues. Because of the high degree of security that this commitment affords, bond purchasers are willing to accept lower rates of return than they could get from less secure investments. However, Orange County's bankruptcy and default show that even general obligation bonds carry investor risk in a deep financial emergency. Faced with bankruptcy, Orange County used funds set aside for debt repayments to keep county government running—failing to honor the traditional "first claim on resources" pledge to bondholders. Unlike private businesses declaring bankruptcy, governments cannot liquidate their assets and go out of business. They must continue to provide their residents with necessary services. Orange County found itself forced to cut its budget and personnel, temporarily divert revenue from the transportation fund, and issue a new wave of bonds carrying higher interest rates. Fortunately for Orange County, its bankruptcy did not follow the traditional model of urban decline, population and tax base loss, and challenging future economic prospects.[15]

State and local governments also issue what are called revenue bonds, for which governments pledge specified revenues, to the extent that they are expected to be available, as the source of repayment. Unlike general obligation bonds, revenue bonds do not have the resources of the general treasury behind them. For example, a state may sell revenue bonds to finance major highway projects, but, rather than paying back the bondholders with general revenues, the state pledges motor fuel tax revenues generated by highway users. No other revenue source is available as a backup if motor fuel taxes fall significantly short of projections. To attract investors, the state must make a convincing case that its revenue forecasts are so sound that prospective investors have little to worry about. Because of the higher relative risk, however, revenue bonds carry higher rates of return than general obligation bonds issued by the same entity, thus costing that government more in interest. State and local governments can enhance the perceived security of revenue bonds by pledging other revenues as a secondary source of repayment. In the highway example, the state could commit revenues from vehicle registration fees. Bondholders would then have the added assurance that if motor fuel tax revenues were to drop off precipitously (as might occur if there were an oil shortage), the more stable vehicle registration revenues would be in reserve. That additional element of security would reduce the interest rate on these bonds and the corresponding costs to the state.

The interest rates that state and local governments must pay in the bond market are greatly influenced by ratings made by two major private Wall Street corporations: Moody's Investors Services and Standard and Poor's Corporation. Their judgments about the bonds' relative security form the basis for their ratings. For general obligation bonds, the raters look at a state or local government's overall financial condition, together with the relative quality of its financial management. For revenue bonds, they evaluate the likelihood that adequate revenues will be generated to repay the bondholders on schedule.

Ratings range from AAA for the most secure bonds to C for the most risky. Bonds receiving an AAA rating pay the lowest interest rates but are still best able to attract the greatest investor interest nationally because of the security they offer. As a rule of thumb, general obligation bonds win higher ratings than revenue bonds, but very strong revenue bonds can carry higher ratings than general obligation bonds offered by a government in financial trouble.

The actual interest rates that bonds carry are determined by public sale or by negotiation. At public sales, potential buyers submit sealed bids, and the state or local government selects what it judges to be the best offer. Negotiated sales begin with a government establishing the rate it is willing to pay, then negotiating with one or more prospective buyers who purchase in large quantities. These big buyers typically acquire the bonds to resell them to smaller investors at a slightly lower rate of interest, thus capturing the difference.[16]

According to the established principles of public finance, long-term debt (debt lasting ten to twenty years) is appropriately employed as an instrument to finance the acquisition of fixed assets with useful lives extending well beyond a current budgetary period. As the theory goes, future generations who will benefit from a capital project should help to retire its debt. A new community college will benefit its students and the community for many years; therefore, in financing its construction with long-term obligation bonds, residents—current and future—will help to pay for it through their taxes.

Legislative bodies at both the state and local government levels must approve bond issues. In addition, state law characteristically requires that local governments receive approval from the electorate (through referenda) of the sale of fully guaranteed bonds that incur long-term debt (also the practice in twelve states).[17] This requirement applies to municipalities, counties, and school districts alike.

State and local governments use the regular budgetary process to appropriate funds for debt service to pay bondholders back. Hence budgeters must be alert to the added annual costs associated with capital projects. At the same time, capital budget planners need to keep abreast of policy and programmatic changes that are being considered in the budgetary process. For example, if a governor recommends substantial changes in parole eligibility, such changes could markedly affect future prison populations and therefore become an important element in the decision whether to build a new prison.

In addition to incurring long-term bonded indebtedness, governments may take on short-term debt, usually for one year or less. Financial managers typically resort to short-term borrowing to cover emergencies or temporary inability to meet statutorily required payments because of cash flow problems. It is considered bad practice for government managers to need to turn regularly to short-term borrowing to balance operating budgets—a lesson well illustrated by New York City's checkered fiscal history: Nassau County, New York, one of the wealthiest counties in the nation, faced a bond crisis in 1999 as a result of a $200 million budget deficit and over-reliance on short-term borrowing. Credit rating agencies lowered its bond rating to just above "junk-bond" status.[18]

Debt has grown dramatically at all levels of government. The greatest growth occurred at the federal level, as debt held by the public increased by a whopping 1,423 percent between 1980 and 2011, reflecting the expansive debt fueled by deficit spending associated with the Great Recession.[19] State debt rose

Table 10.2 State and Local Debt, Fiscal Years, 1980 and 2011 Compared

	Amount FY 1980 (in $ millions)	Amount FY 2011 (in $ millions) change	Percentage
States			
Total debt	121,958	1,232,814	911
Long-term debt	119,821	1,127,498	841
Short-term debt	2,137	5,316	149
Local Governments			
Total debt	213,645	1,774,941	731
Long-term debt	202,635	1,745,519	761
Short-term debt	11,010	29,422,167	167

Source: Bureau of the Census, U.S. Department of Commerce.

by 911 percent during the period, followed by local government debt at 731 percent. Long-term obligations account for the vast majority of dollar-value growth in both state and local debt (see Table 10.2). Most of the new long-term debt incurred by both state and local governments has not been backed by the full faith and credit of the borrower.

Two factors account for this development. First, in many states the constitution or the statutes limit the amount of full-faith-and-credit debt that can be incurred. However, revenue bonds or bonds issued by special authorities are not usually covered by these limits. Second, constitutional or statutory requirements for voter approval of bond issues apply only to those carrying the full-faith-and-credit guarantee. Thus politicians can bypass a potential stumbling block by taking on debt that does not require approval.

Municipalities and townships account for the largest share of local debt, about 38 percent. Special districts, such as sewer and water, account for another 24 percent, followed by counties (20 percent) and school districts (18 percent).[20] No widely accepted standards exist for what constitutes prudent or excessive debt. Defaults at the state or local level remain rare, and the interest paid on debt is still comparatively small, at only 3 percent of expenditures. The bond market itself exerts a practical constraint on borrowing. Too much "bond paper" offered by the same state or local government (or collection of overlapping local governments that draw their tax resources from the same residents) in the same year (or over a few years) may prompt rating firms and investors to worry about those jurisdictions' ability to manage their debt service requirements.

Executive–Legislative Balance in Budget Execution

Since the 1970s, Congress has girded itself to compete more effectively with the president and the OMB in budget execution. As noted earlier in this chapter, Congress acted in 1974 to restrict the president's ability to impound appropriated funds. Congress also greatly increased its use of the so-called legislative veto: Of approximately five hundred veto provisions approved from the 1930s to 1983, over three-quarters were initiated after 1970.[21] As mentioned at the beginning of the chapter, the *Chadha* decision of 1983 put a damper on single-chamber legislative vetoes. Thereafter, administrative acts could be vetoed only through joint resolutions or bills subject to presidential veto.

Even with that restriction, Congress, through its appropriations committees, continues to exercise considerable power over budget implementation by the executive branch. Shifts of funds across appropriations accounts or between agencies require committee approval, and even in those cases where approval is not legally required (for example, when a budget transfer falls under the legal threshold requiring congressional approval of midyear budget transfers), federal agencies often seek committee approval before initiating their request to

OMB. In addition, agencies alter their implementation of programs on the basis of performance audits conducted by the GAO. Agency managers do so because they know that members of Congress and their staff assistants receive copies of the audit reports and that they will be expected to explain why they have not acted to improve program or administrative performance.

Nevertheless, the OMB still manages the allotment process and administers sequestration (discussed in chapter 6), initiates rescissions and deferrals, oversees productivity improvements and information collection in the executive branch, controls the use of consulting services, and reviews agency plans for promulgating regulations—all of which are directly or indirectly related to budget implementation. This ubiquitous presence of the OMB gives the executive the clear edge in federal budget execution.

The ascendancy of state legislatures in matters of budget execution is even more apparent than that of Congress. State legislatures today are challenging governors in areas of traditional executive prerogative. As noted earlier, they have increasingly restricted the executive authority to impound or transfer funds after the budget has been signed into law. They have also become more involved in reviewing and acting upon the receipt of federal funds. Under the separation-of-powers doctrine, because the governor is chief executive officer, the receipt and use of federal funds have traditionally been viewed as matters of executive discretion. As recently as 1979, most state legislatures did not include federal funds in their appropriations. Instead, the schedule of appropriations contained estimates of federally funded expenditures rather than of binding (sum-certain) appropriations with specific amounts. Where estimates were used, the actual receipt and expenditure of federal funds could legally be greater than the estimates.

By the mid-1980s, the picture had changed dramatically. In the 1981 legislative session alone, almost half the state legislatures passed laws increasing their oversight of federal funds and placing controls on the receipt and expenditure of federal funds.[22] By 2012, thirty-four state legislatures had given themselves the authority to make sum-certain appropriations of federal funds through their normal appropriations process while another eleven required approval, but that approval could come outside of the normal appropriations process.[23]

But how are unanticipated federal funds handled during the course of the year when the legislature is not in session? State legislatures have tended to give the governor authority to receive and spend unanticipated federal funds—authority that the state budget office typically exercises on the governor's behalf. In fourteen states the governor and legislature share that authority, and in eleven others the legislature retains that authority exclusively. Yet when the legislature is not in session, it generally delegates the exercise of its authority to its budget or fiscal committee(s).[24]

Another area of legislative incursion can be found in the traditionally executive area of administrative rule making. After the budget is approved, agencies often adopt administrative rules (similar to federal regulations), which have the force of law, to guide program implementation. Although state agencies have the authority to adopt such rules, following a statutorily prescribed process that requires public notice and hearings, in most states the rule-making process also provides for legislative review. In this connection, state legislatures have given themselves varying degrees of authority.

While forty-six state legislatures have adopted some form of oversight, twenty-four have assumed the authority to veto, suspend, or modify agency rules. Sixteen delegate that authority to standing committees.[25]

The legislative veto has been a subject of controversy and litigation at the state level just as it has at the national level. The dispute at the state level has concerned the authority of a legislative committee to suspend or repeal administrative rules outside the normal legislative process because this practice denies the governor an opportunity to veto the legislature's action. State courts in Alaska, Connecticut, Montana, New Hampshire, New Jersey, and West Virginia have ruled that the delegated legislative veto violates the state constitution.[26]

Finally, state legislatures have expanded their own postaudit capacities. They began to assume authority for postauditing in the 1960s, removing it from the executive branch.[27] Today the legislature appoints postauditors in most states, although voters directly elect them in twenty states. The executive branch retains sole authority for postauditing in only five.[28]

Increasingly, the activities of legislative auditors have turned from the traditional financial audit to the performance audit, evaluating the extent to which legislatively approved programs have been achieving their stated objectives and are operating efficiently.

Legislative auditors do not function autonomously. Legislative committees approve the audit agenda, accept or reject audit reports, and at times propose legislation that takes corrective action. Although a committee may decide which audits should be conducted, the legislative auditor can greatly influence the audit agenda, having important input about audit scope and recommendations.

An eight-year study of legislative performance audits, involving nearly five hundred reports from thirty-one states, reviewed their recommendations. Almost one-half proposed statutory changes as remedies and about one-quarter suggested budgetary action, providing a significant source of legislative initiatives.[29]

Summary and Conclusions

The budget, as passed by the legislature, is a fiscal plan of action for the coming year, authorizing government agencies to spend money for specified public purposes. For that plan to be carved out as intended, its execution must be controlled; any departures must be approved. If controls did not exist, government agencies could use resources as they wished, ignoring the intent of the elected officials who appropriated them. Thus budget controls exist to ensure that spending does not exceed authorized levels, that funds are used for approved purposes, and that the process is consistent with legislative intent.

The allotment process serves as a key means of controlling budget execution. Allotments, which are approved by the central budget office of the executive branch, release appropriated funds to be spent up to a certain limit in designated categories and within a specified period of time. Hence, they can be used to control spending.

One form of spending control is impoundment, or refusal to release funds for expenditure. The central budget office, acting on behalf of the chief executive, can impound funds for an entire appropriation, for a single program financed by that appropriation, or for any other expenditure category included in the allotment. Although funds can be impounded at any level of government where allotments are used, impoundment is employed most often at the federal level. It is used less frequently within the states and only minimally at the local level.

In reaction to what it regarded as misuse of impoundment by President Nixon, Congress acted in 1974 to restrict the president's impoundment authority. Those restrictions, modified somewhat by court rulings in recent years, still limit the president's ability to prevent funds from being spent for congressionally approved purposes. Similarly, states commonly restrict the governor's ability to withhold funds after the budget has been signed into law. The real tool for executive budget reduction within the states is the gubernatorial **item-veto**, which is exercised before the budget becomes law.

Agency spending is not only restricted by the amounts allotted, but also is limited by conditions the legislature places on the use of appropriated funds, whether they appear in the appropriations language itself, in an accompanying footnote, in a committee report, or in a letter of intent directed to agency officials.

Adjustments to the budget can become necessary during the course of the fiscal year. They can take the form of reductions, supplements, deferrals, and transfers.

Even after the budget has been approved, allotments issued, and authorized adjustments made, controls continue to be placed on agency spending. This is done to ensure that agencies are making discrete spending choices within available appropriations authority and for allowable purposes. These controls are exercised both before and after funds have been spent. Controls exercised before funds are spent are called preaudit controls. Those exercised after funds have been spent are called postaudit controls. The latter include both financial audits and performance audits. Performance audits have grown at all levels of government over the past two decades, as policy makers have increasingly asked how well government programs are accomplishing their objectives.

In addition to controlling budget execution, government officials and their staffs manage the day-to-day financial affairs of government. In managing the receipts that flow into government, fiscal officers strive to obtain the highest available rate of return commensurate with acceptable levels of safety, while retaining sufficient cash to pay the government's bills when they fall due. Fiscal officers also manage their government's debt. The states and most local units of government sell bonds to finance their major capital projects, such as the construction of university and school buildings, prisons, and new highways. The federal government, in contrast, uses debt to finance the national deficit. The federal government has no capital budget, and it pays for its capital expenses with current revenues.

Notes

1 National Association of State Budget Officers, Budget Processes in the States (Washington, D.C.: National Association of State Budget Officers, Summer 2008), 98.
2 Louis Fisher, "The Politics of Impounded Funds," Administrative Science Quarterly 15 (September 1970): 361–7.
3 Allen Schick, Congress and Money: Budgeting, Spending and Taxing (Washington, D.C.: Urban Institute, 1980), 44–8; Robert D. Lee Jr. and Ronald W. Johnson, Public Budgeting Systems, 4th ed. (Rockville, M.D.: Aspen, 1989), 185.
4 Louis Fisher, Court Cases on Impoundment of Appropriated Funds: A Public Policy Analysis (Washington, D.C.: Congressional Research Service, 1974).
5 Lee and Johnson, Public Budgeting Systems, 165.
6 City of New Haven, Connecticut v. United States of America, slip opinion 86–5319, DC Circuit (1987).
7 National Conference of State Legislatures, Legislative Authority to Cut the Enacted Budget (Denver, CO: National Conference of State Legislatures, March 25, 1999).
8 Allen Schick, The Federal Budget: Politics, Policy, Process (Washington, D.C.: Brookings Institution, 1995), 168–73.
9 National Association of State Budget Officers, Budget Processes in the States, 100.
10 Ibid.
11 National Association of State Auditors, Comptrollers, and Treasurers, Auditing and the States (Lexington, K.Y.: National Association of State Auditors, Comptrollers, and Treasurers, 1992), 25.
12 Ibid.
13 Frederick C. Mosher, A Tale of Two Agencies: A Comparative Analysis of the General Accounting Office and Office of Management and Budget (Baton Rouge: Louisiana State University Press, 1984), 136–63.
14 David E. Maynard and Priscilla M. Wheatley, "At the Crossroads: Private Sector Perspectives on Public Sector Investing," Government Finance Review 2 (February 1986): 17.
15 Public Policy Institute of California, "Why Government Fails: The Orange County Bankruptcy," March 18, 1998; John E. Petersen, "Municipal Bond Market: The Post-Orange County Era," Governing 9 (November 1995): 77–87.
16 Lee and Johnson, Public Budgeting Systems, 271–2.
17 Robert Axelrod, Budgeting for Modern Government (New York: St. Martin's Press, 1988), 124.
18 Sue Schultz, "A Wealthy New York County Struggles to Stay Solvent," Governing 12 (September 1999): 58.

19 Office of Management and Budget, Budget of the United States Government, FY 2015, Historical Tables, Table 7.1.
20 U.S. Bureau of the Census, 2001 Census of Government (Washington, D.C.: Bureau of the Census, U.S. Department of Commerce, December 2003), tables 1–3.
21 Donald Axelrod, A Budget Quartet: Critical Policy and Management Issues (New York: St. Martin's Press, 1989), 66.
22 William Pound, "The State Legislatures," in The Book of the States, 1982–83 (Lexington, K.Y.: Council of State Governments, 1982), 184.
23 National Conference of State Legislatures, Legislative Oversight of Federal Funds, NCSL Webinar, 2013 www.ncsl.org/legislators-staff/legislative-staff/legal-services/webinar-legislative-oversight-of-federal-funds.aspx
24 Ibid.
25 Council of State Governments, The Book of the States, 2010 (Lexington, K.Y.: Council of State Governments, 2010), Table 3.26.
26 Alan Rosenthal, "Legislative Oversight and the Balance of Power in State Government," State Government 56 (fall 1983): 94.
27 Karen Schuele Walton and Richard E. Brown, "State Legislators and State Auditors," Public Budgeting and Finance 10 (spring 1990): 4.
28 Information provided by the State Auditor Training Program, Council of State Governments, Lexington, Kentucky, October 1986.
29 Alan Rosenthal, Legislative Life (New York: HarperCollins, 1981), 326–8.

About the Author

James J. Gosling is Professor of Political Science at the University of Utah. His research interests include politics and public policy, political economy, budgetary politics, and state and local politics. His recent books include *Politics and Policy in American States and Communities*, 8th edition (2013, with Dennis L. Dresang); *Economics, Politics, and American Public Policy*, 2nd edition (2013, with Marc Allen Eisner); and *Understanding, Informing, and Appraising Public Policy* (2004). Professor Gosling has held a number of top administrative positions in government, having served as Secretary and Deputy Secretary of the Wisconsin Department of Industry, Labor, and Human Relations, and as Deputy Secretary of the Wisconsin Department of Transportation.

Glossary

Allotments Usually approved by the central executive budget office, allotments give government agencies the authority to commit appropriated funds up to a stipulated amount, in designated budget categories, and within a specified period of time. They can cover initial apportionment, or they can be adjusted during the course of a fiscal year as changed circumstances require.

Appropriation The authority to spend or obligate public funds.

Authorization A legislative act that provides authority for the establishment or continuation of a governmental program. A program or agency must be authorized before funds can be appropriated in its support or obligations can be incurred.

Backdoor spending Spending based on budget authority included in authorization acts, which does not have to be appropriated separately.

Balanced budget A budget in which revenues equal or exceed expenditures.

Baseline A projection of future revenues, expenditures, and debt under current laws and assumed economic conditions.

Biennial budget A budget covering two years.

Budget authority The legal authority to commit or spend public funds, whether in the form of an appropriation or the authority to borrow or enter into contractual obligations.

Budget bill(s) One or more legislative bills that at the very least contain appropriations to finance governmental activities during a given period of time. In some jurisdictions, budget bills can also include statutory modifications, limitations on the use of funds, and expressions of legislative intent.

Budget deficit A condition in which spending exceeds revenues for a given budgetary period.

Budget surplus A condition in which revenues exceed spending for a given budgetary period.

Budget transfer A shift of funds from one appropriation or fund account to another.

Capital budget A budget for capital investment. State and local governments use the capital budget to segregate capital investments from operating expenditures. The federal government has no separate capital budget.

Cash management Ensuring that sufficient cash is available to pay a government's bills when they fall due while realizing the highest possible yield consistent with acceptable risk of capital.

Concurrent budget resolution An act of Congress not requiring presidential approval that establishes aggregate binding ceilings for revenues, budget authority, and outlays, yielding a projected surplus or deficit. It also includes estimates of budget authority and outlays for each budget function comprising the federal budget.

Constant dollars Dollars converted to the monetary value of a reference year, adjusted to the purchasing power of the dollar in that year.

Continuing appropriations resolution A legislative act that continues current-year spending at last year's levels, although those levels can be selectively adjusted in the resolution.

Current dollars The current-year value of the dollar, unadjusted for changes in the dollar's purchasing power over time.

Deferral As employed at the federal level, an action of the president that delays the obligation or expenditure of appropriated funds for a duration not to exceed the end of the fiscal year. Deferrals must be approved by both chambers of Congress.

Discretionary spending Spending over which budget makers have discretion, within limits set by law.

Enhanced rescission Enhanced rescissionary authority given the president to cancel discretionary spending, new entitlement authority, and tax provisions that benefit special interests at the expense of the public interest. Congress can block presidential cancellations only by passing legislation that would overturn them—an act that itself would be subject to presidential veto. The enabling legislation, passed by Congress in March, 1996, took effect on January 1, 1997. See Line-item veto.

Entitlement A requirement in federal law, applied to certain programs, that individuals who meet eligibility requirements for federal assistance have a legal right to that assistance, regardless of the amounts appropriated in support of the program.

Equalization The concept of distributing financial assistance on the basis of need rather than population or a proportional return to the contributing source.

Executive budget The chief executive's budget recommendations for a government jurisdiction, usually described in a volume called the executive budget book.

Federal Funds Rate (FFR) The rate of interest, set by the Federal Reserve through its open market transactions, that lending institutions charge one another for overnight loans.

Federal grants-in-aid Federal financial assistance to state or local governments in support of federal programs.

Fiscal policy Economic policy that incorporates taxing and spending decisions to expand or contract economic demand.

General obligation bonds Debt instruments pledging the "full faith and credit" of a government's general treasury to repay bondholders.

Gross Domestic Product (GDP) The aggregate value of goods and services produced within a country.

Horizontal tax equity Presumes equal treatment of taxpayers who have an equal capacity to pay taxes.

Impoundment Executive action to prevent appropriated funds from being obligated or spent. The central budget office, acting on behalf of the chief executive, can impound, in whole or in part, the funding for an appropriation, a single program financed by that appropriation, a particular object of expenditure, or any other level included in the approved budget.

Inflation A rise in the overall price structure.

Line-item veto The authority of a chief executive to veto part of an appropriations act, along with, in some jurisdictions, the ability to disapprove accompanying statutory provisions or expressions of legislative intent. See Enhanced rescission.

Local assistance State financial aid to local units of government.

Misery index The combined rate of unemployment and inflation.

Monetary policy Economic policy that deals with the availability and cost of loanable funds. Unlike fiscal policy, the authority for monetary policy has been vested in an independent government agency, the Federal Reserve.

Outlays Actual expenditures in a given fiscal year, which can include payment of obligations incurred in a prior year as well as the current year.

Own-source revenue Revenue collected from a government jurisdiction's own revenue-raising instruments, in contrast to revenues provided by another government jurisdiction.

Performance auditing An approach to auditing that looks at how well government programs are accomplishing their goals and objectives instead of focusing on actual expenditures and the adequacy of financial control procedures.

Postaudit controls After-the-fact review to assess the extent to which budgeted funds were committed in a manner consistent with appropriation authority and legislative intent and to ensure that the associated transactions were reflected fully and accurately in the accounting system.

Preaudit controls Administrative actions to ensure that proposed expenditures or obligations are consistent with appropriation authority and allotments.

Program budgeting In the pure sense, budgets structured along programmatic lines instead of organizational lines. Programs can cut across organizational boundaries, grouping like activities together and relating them to a common purpose or goal.

Progressive tax A tax that increases as ability to pay rises. Most typically associated with the income tax, where rates increase as income rises.

Proportional tax A tax that applies the same rate to all levels of income.

Recession A condition in which the real (inflation-adjusted) gross domestic product declines for at least two consecutive quarters.

Reconciliation The process by which Congress modifies authorizations or appropriations to comply with the limits included in the concurrent budget resolution. Where necessary, the budget committees issue instructions to committees directing them to report out legislation to bring the budget into compliance with the resolution. If any committee fails to act in accordance with the instructions, the budget committees are empowered to initiate the required legislation themselves.

Regressive tax A tax carrying a burden that is inversely related to ability to pay.

Reprogramming Shifting funds between programs within the same appropriation or fund account.

Rescission As employed at the federal level, an action of the president that indefinitely prevents appropriated funds from being obligated or spent. For a proposed rescission to take effect, both chambers of Congress must approve it within forty-five days. If the rescission is not approved, the impounded funds must be released for obligation. See Enhanced rescission.

Revenue bonds Debt instruments pledging specified earmarked revenues—not the "full faith and credit" of a government's treasury—as the source of repayment to bond holders.

Securitization The process of pooling liquid assets (e.g., home mortgages) to create securities that can be sold to investors.

Sequestration A presidential order to withhold federal budget authority in excess of the deficit level permitted by the act for a given year. Any withholding is to be apportioned in uniform percentages across defense and domestic discretionary spending.

Sum-certain appropriation An appropriation that restricts spending to the amounts in the schedule. They cannot be exceeded by law.

Sum-sufficient appropriation An appropriation in which the amounts in the schedule represent estimated outlays, but the actual draw on the treasury is a product of the costs of providing financial assistance or services to all those who meet statutorily prescribed eligibility requirements. A term typically used at the state level, comparable to entitlement at the federal level.

Tax capacity The amount of tax revenue a governmental jurisdiction would raise if it applied a national average set of tax rates to commonly used tax bases.

Tax effort The ratio of a governmental jurisdiction's actual tax collections to its capacity to generate tax revenue.

Tax expenditures Forgone revenues that would otherwise have been collected had special provisions not been included in federal, state, or local income tax codes.

User fees Fees charged in return for service. With user fees, only those who receive the service bear the cost of its provision.

Vertical tax equity Concerns the appropriate relationship between the relative taxes to be paid by persons with different abilities to pay. The comparison is of unequals, and the focus is the extent to which their tax obligations should differ.

Zero-base budgeting A budgetary system that identifies decision packages to show how the composition of the budget would change at alternative levels of funding. Despite its name, zero-base budgeting does not force all budgets to be examined and re-justified from "scratch."

Index